W9-CUA-070

CONTENTS

vii

PART I
THE STRUGGLE FOR SURVIVAL

HISTORY OF TRADE UNIONISM IN THE U. S.

CHAPTER 1

LABOR MOVEMENTS BEFORE THE CIVIL WAR

(1) *Early Beginnings, to 1827*

23607

The customary chronology records the first American labor strike in 1741. In that year the New York bakers went out on strike. A closer analysis discloses, however, that this outbreak was a protest of master bakers against a municipal regulation of the price of bread, not a wage earners' strike against employers. The earliest genuine labor strike in America occurred, as far as known, in 1786, when the Philadelphia printers "turned out" for a minimum wage of six dollars a week. The second strike on record was in 1791 by Philadelphia house carpenters for the ten-hour day. The Baltimore sailors were successful in advancing their wages through strikes in the years 1795, 1805, and 1807, but their endeavors were recurrent, not permanent. Even more ephemeral were several riotous sailors' strikes as well as a ship builders' strike in 1817 at Medford, Massachusetts. Doubt[...] many other such outbreaks occurred during the pe[...] to 1820, but left no record of their existence.

A strike undoubtedly is a symptom of discon[...]

However, one can hardly speak of a beginning of trade unionism until such discontent has become expressed in an organization that keeps alive after a strike, or between strikes. Such permanent organizations existed prior to the twenties only in two trades, namely, shoemaking and printing.

The first continuous organization of wage earners was that of the Philadelphia shoemakers, organized in 1792. This society, however, existed for less than a year and did not even leave us its name. The shoemakers of Philadelphia again organized in 1794 under the name of the Federal Society of Journeymen Cordwainers and maintained their existence as such at least until 1806. In 1799 the society conducted the first organized strike, which lasted nine or ten weeks. Prior to 1799, the only recorded strikes of any workmen were "unorganized" and, indeed, such were the majority of the strikes that occurred prior to the decade of the thirties in the nineteenth century.

The printers organized their first society in 1794 in New York under the name of The Typographical Society and it continued in existence for ten years and six months. The printers of Philadelphia, who had struck in 1786, neglected to keep up an organization after winning their demands. Between the years 1800 and 1805, the shoemakers and the printers had continuous organizations in Philadelphia, New York, and Baltimore. In 1809 the shoemakers of Pittsburgh and the Boston printers were added to the list, and somewhat later the Albany ⸻ Washington printers. In 1810 the printers organized ⸻ New Orleans.

⸻ he separation of the jorneymen from the masters, first ⸻ n in the formation of these organizations, was emphasized in the attitude toward employer members. The question arose over the continuation in membership of those who became employers. The shoemakers excluded such members from the organization. The printers, on the other hand, were more liberal. But in 1817 the New York society put them out on the ground that "the interests of the journeymen are *separate* and in some respects *opposite* to those of the employers."

The strike was the chief weapon of these early societies. Generally a committee was chosen by the society to present a price list or scale of wages to the masters individually. The first complete wage scale presented in this country was drawn up by the organized printers of New York in 1800. The strikes were mainly over wages and were generally conducted in an orderly and comparatively peaceful manner. In only one instance, that of the Philadelphia shoemakers of 1806, is there evidence of violence and intimidation. In that case "scabs" were beaten and employers intimidated by demonstrations in front of the shop or by breaking shop windows. During a strike the duties of "picketing" were discharged by tramping committees. The Philadelphia shoemakers, however, as early as 1799, employed for this purpose a paid officer. This strike was for higher wages for workers on boots. Although those who worked on shoes made no demands of their own, they were obliged to strike, much against their will. We thus meet with the first sympathetic strike on record. In 1809 the New York shoemakers, starting with a strike against one firm, ordered a general strike when they discovered that that firm was getting its work done in other shops. The payment of strike benefits dates from the first authenticated strike, namely in 1786. The method of payment varied from society to society, but the constitution of the New York shoemakers, as early as 1805, provided for a permanent strike fund.

The aggressive trade unionism of these early trade societies forced the masters to combine against them. Associations of masters in their capacity as merchants had usually preceded the journeymen's societies. Their function was to counteract destructive competition from "advertisers" and sellers in the "public market" at low prices. As soon, however, as the wage question became serious, the masters' associations proceeded to take on the function of dealing with labor—mostly aiming to break up the trade societies. Generally they sought to create an available force of non-union labor by means of advertising, but often they turned to the courts and brought action against the journeymen's societies on the ground of conspiracy.

The bitterness of the masters' associations against the the journeymen's societies perhaps was caused not so much by their resistance to reductions in wages as by their imposition of working rules, such as the limitation of the number of apprentices, the minimum wage, and what we would now call the "closed shop." The conspiracy trials largely turned upon the "closed shop" and in these the shoemakers figured exclusively.[1]

Altogether six criminal conspiracy cases are recorded against the shoemakers from 1806 to 1815. One occurred in Philadelphia in 1806; one in New York in 1809; two in Baltimore in 1809; and two in Pittsburgh, the first in 1814 and the other in 1815. Each case was tried before a jury which was judge both of law and fact. Four of the cases were decided against the journeymen.

[1] See below, 147-148.

In one of the Baltimore cases judgment was rendered in favor of the journeymen. The Pittsburgh case of 1815 was compromised, the shoemakers paying the costs and returning to work at the old wages. The outcome in the other cases is not definitely known. It was brought out in the testimony that the masters financed, in part at least, the New York and Pittsburgh prosecutions.

Effective as the convictions in court for conspiracy may have been in checking the early trade societies, of much greater consequence was the industrial depression which set in after the conclusion of the Napoleonic Wars. The lifting of the Embargo enabled the foreign traders and manufacturers to dump their products upon the American market. The incipient American industries were in no position to withstand this destructive competition. Conditions were made worse by past over investment and by the collapse of currency inflation.

Trade unionism for the time being had to come to an end. The effect on the journeymen's societies was paralyzing. Only those survived which turned to mutual insurance. Several of the printers' societies had already instituted benefit features, and these now helped them considerably to maintain their organization. The shoemakers' societies on the other hand had remained to the end purely trade-regulating organizations and went to the wall.

Depression reached its ebb in 1820. Thereafter conditions improved, giving rise to aggressive organizations of wage earners in several industries. We find strikes and permanent organizations among hatters, tailors, weavers, nailers, and cabinet makers. And for the first time we meet with organizations of factory workers—female workers.

Beginning with 1824 and running through 1825, the year which saw the culmination of a period of high prices, a number of strikes occurred in the important industrial centers. The majority were called to enforce higher wages. In Philadelphia, 2900 weavers out of about 4500 in the city were on strike. But the strike that attracted the most public attention was that of the Boston house carpenters for the ten-hour day in 1825.

The Boston journeymen carpenters chose the most strategic time for their strike. They called it in the spring of the year when there was a great demand for carpenters owing to a recent fire. Close to six hundred journeymen were involved in this struggle. The journeymen's demand for the ten-hour day drew a characteristic reply from the "gentlemen engaged in building," the customers of the master builders. They condemned the journeymen on the moral ground that an agitation for a shorter day would open "a wide door for idleness and vice"; hinted broadly at the foreign origin of the agitation; declared that all combinations intending to regulate the value of labor by abridging the working day were in a high degree unjust and injurious to the other classes in the community; announced their resolution to support the masters at the sacrifice of suspending building altogether; and bound themselves not to employ any journeyman or master who might enforce the ten-hour day. The strike failed.

The renewed trade-union activities brought forth a fresh crop of trials for conspiracy.[1] One case involved Philadelphia master shoemakers who combined to reduce wages, two were against journeymen tailors in Philadelphia and Buffalo and the fourth was a hatters' case in

[1] See below, 148-149.

New York. The masters were acquitted and the hatters were found guilty of combining to deprive a non-union man of his livelihood. In the Philadelphia tailors' case, the journeymen were convicted on the charge of intimidation. Of the Buffalo tailors' case it is only known that it ended in the conviction of the journeymen.

(2) *Equal Citizenship, 1827-1832*

So far we have dealt only with trade societies but not yet with a labor movement. A labor movement presupposes a feeling of solidarity which goes beyond the boundaries of a single trade and extends to other wage earners. The American labor movement began in 1827, when the several trades in Philadelphia organized the Mechanics' Union of Trade Associations, which was, so far as now known, the first city central organization of trades in the world. This Union, originally intended as an economic organization, changed to a political one the following year and initiated what was probably the most interesting and most typically American labor movement—a struggle for "equality of citizenship." It was brought to a head by the severe industrial depression of the time. But the decisive impulse came from the nation-wide democratic upheaval led by Andrew Jackson, for which the poorer classes in the cities displayed no less enthusism than the agricultural West. To the wage earner this outburst of democratic fervor offered an opportunity to try out his recently acquired franchise. Of the then industrial States, Massachusetts granted suffrage to the workingmen in 1820 and New York in 1822. In Pennsylvania the constitution of 1790 had extended the right of suffrage to those who paid any kind of a state or county tax, however small.

The wage earners' Jacksonianism struck a note all its own. If the farmer and country merchant, who had passed through the abstract stage of political aspiration with the Jeffersonian democratic movement, were now, with Jackson, reaching out for the material advantages which political power might yield, the wage earners, being as yet novices in politics, naturally were more strongly impressed with that aspect of the democratic upheaval which emphasized the rights of man in general and social equality in particular. If the middle class Jacksonian was probably thinking first of reducing the debt on his farm or perchance of getting a political office, and only as an after-thought proceeding to look for a justification in the Declaration of Independence, as yet the wage earner was starting with the abstract notion of equal citizenship as contained in the Declaration, and only then proceeding to search for the remedies which would square reality with the idea. Hence it was that the aspiration toward equal citizenship became the keynote of labor's earliest political movement. The issue was drawn primarily between the rich and the poor, not between the functional classes, employers and employes. While the workmen took good care to exclude from their ranks "persons not living by some useful occupation, such as bankers, brokers, rich men, etc.," they did not draw the line on employers as such, master workmen and independent "producers."

The workingmen's bill of complaints, as set forth in the Philadelphia *Mechanic's Free Press* and other labor papers, clearly marks off the movement as a rebellion by the class of newly enfranchised wage earners against conditions which made them feel degraded in their own eyes as full fledged citizens of the commonwealth.

The complaints were of different sorts but revolved around the charge of the usurpation of government by an "aristocracy." Incontrovertible proof of this charge was found in special legislation chartering banks and other corporations. The banks were indicted upon two counts. First, the unstable bank paper money defrauded the wage earner of a considerable portion of the purchasing power of his wages. Second, banks restricted competition and shut off avenues for the "man on the make." The latter accusation may be understood only if we keep in mind that this was a period when bank credits began to play an essential part in the conduct of industry; that with the extension of the market into the States and territories South and West, with the resulting delay in collections, business could be carried on only by those who enjoyed credit facilities at the banks. Now, as credit generally follows access to the market, it was inevitable that the beneficiary of the banking system should not be the master or journeyman but the merchant for whom both worked.[1] To the uninitiated, however, this arrangement could only appear in the light of a huge conspiracy entered into by the chartered monopolies, the banks, and the unchartered monopolist, the merchant, to shut out the possible competition by the master and journeyman. The grievance appeared all the more serious since all banks were chartered by special enactments of the legislature, which thus appeared as an accomplice in the conspiracy.

In addition to giving active help to the rich, the workingmen argued, the government was too callous to the suffering of the poor and pointed to the practice of imprisonment for debt. The Boston Prison Discipline So-

[1] See below, 270-272.

ciety, a philanthropic organization, estimated in 1829 that about 75,000 persons were annually imprisoned for debt in the United States. Many of these were imprisoned for very small debts. In one Massachusetts prison, for example, out of 37 cases, 20 were for less than $20. The Philadelphia printer and philanthropist, Mathew Carey, father of the economist Henry C. Carey, cited a contemporary Boston case of a blind man with a family dependent on him imprisoned for a debt of six dollars. A labor paper reported an astounding case of a widow in Providence, Rhode Island, whose husband had lost his life in a fire while attempting to save the property of the man who later caused her imprisonment for a debt of 68 cents. The physical conditions in debtors' jails were appalling, according to unimpeachable contemporary reports. Little did such treatment of the poor accord with their newly acquired dignity as citizens.

Another grievance, particularly exasperating because the government was responsible, grew in Pennsylvania out of the administration of the compulsory militia system. Service was obligatory upon all male citizens and non-attendance was punished by fine or imprisonment. The rich delinquent did not mind, but the poor delinquent when unable to pay was given a jail sentence.

Other complaints by workingmen went back to the failure of government to protect the poorer citizen's right to "life, liberty, and the pursuit of happiness." The lack of a mechanic's lien law, which would protect his wages in the case of his employer's bankruptcy, was keenly felt by the workingmen. A labor paper estimated in 1829 that, owing to the lack of a lien law on buildings, not less than three or four hundred thousand dollars in wages were annually lost.

But the most distinctive demands of the workingmen went much further. This was an age of egalitarianism. The Western frontiersmen demanded equality with the wealthy Eastern merchant and banker, and found in Andrew Jackson an ideal spokesman. For a brief moment it seemed that by equality the workingmen meant an equal division of all property. That was the program which received temporary endorsement at the first workingmen's meeting in New York in April 1829. "Equal division" was advocated by a self-taught mechanic by the name of Thomas Skidmore, who elaborated his ideas in a book bearing the self-revealing title of *"The Rights of Man to Property: being a Proposition to make it Equal among the Adults of the Present Generation: and to Provide for its Equal Transmission to Every Individual of Each Succeeding Generation, on Arriving at the Age of Maturity,"* published in 1829. This Skidmorian program was better known as "agrarianism," probably from the title of a book by Thomas Paine, *Agrarian Justice, as Opposed to Agrarian Law and to Agrarian Monopoly,* published in 1797 in London, which advocated equal division by means of an inheritance tax. Its adoption by the New York workingmen was little more than a stratagem, for their intention was to forestall any attempts by employers to lengthen the working day to eleven hours by raising the question of "the nature of the tenure by which all men hold title to their property." Apparently the stratagem worked, for the employers immediately dropped the eleven-hour issue. But, although the workingmen quickly thereafter repudiated agrarianism, they succeeded only too well in affixing to their movement the mark of the beast in the eyes of their opponents and the general public.

Except during the brief but damaging "agrarian" episode, the demand for free public education or "Republican" education occupied the foreground. We, who live in an age when free education at the expense of the community is considered practically an inalienable right of every child, find it extremely difficult to understand the vehemence of the opposition which the demand aroused on the part of the press and the "conservative" classes, when first brought up by the workingmen. The explanation lies partly in the political situation, partly in the moral character of the "intellectual" spokesmen for the workingmen, and partly in the inborn conservatism of the tax-paying classes upon whom the financial burden would fall. That the educational situation was deplorable much proof is unnecessary. Pennsylvania had some public schools, but parents had to declare themselves too poor to send their children to a private school before they were allowed the privilege of sending them there. In fact so much odium attached to these schools that they were practically useless and the State became distinguished for the number of children not attending school. As late as 1837 a labor paper estimated that 250,000 out of 400,000 children in Pennsylvania of school age were not in any school. The Public School Society of New York estimated in a report for 1829 that in New York City alone there were 24,200 children between the ages of five and fifteen years not attending any school whatever.

To meet these conditions the workingmen outlined a comprehensive educational program. It was not merely a literary education that the workingmen desired. The idea of industrial education, or training for a vocation, which is even now young in this country, was undoubtedly first introduced by the leaders of this early labor movement. They demanded a system of public education which would "combine a knowledge of the practical arts with that of the useful sciences."   The idea of industrial education appears to have originated in a group of which two "intellectuals," Robert Dale Owen and Frances Wright, were the leading spirits.

Robert Dale Owen was the eldest son of Robert Owen, the famous English manufacturer-philanthropist, who originated the system of socialism known as "Owenism." Born in Scotland, he was educated at Hofwyl, Switzerland, in a school conducted by Emmanuel von Fellenberg, the associate of the famous Pestalozzi, as a self-governing children's republic on the manner of the present "Junior Republics."   Owen himself said that he owed his abiding faith in human virtue and social progress to his years at Hofwyl.   In 1825 Robert Dale left England to join his father in a communistic experiment at New Harmony, Indiana, and together they lived through the vicissitudes which attended that experiment.   There he met Frances Wright, America's first suffragist, with whom he formed an intimate friendship lasting through many years.   The failure at New Harmony convinced him that his father had overlooked the importance of the anti-social habits which the members had formed before they joined; and he concluded that those could be prevented only by applying a rational system of education to the young.   These conclusions, together with the recollections of his experience at Hofwyl, led him to advocate a new system of education, which came to be called "state guardianship."

State guardianship was a demand for the establishment by the state of boarding schools where children should receive, not only equal instruction, general as well as industrial, but equal food and equal clothing at the public expense. Under this system, it was asserted, public schools would become "not schools of charity, but schools of the nation, to the support of which all would contribute; and instead of being almost a disgrace, it would become an honor to have been educated there." It was urged as an especial advantage that, as children would be clothed and cared for at all times, the fact that poor parents could not afford to dress their children "as decently as their neighbors" would not prevent their attendance.

State guardianship became the battle cry of an important faction in the Workingmen's party in New York. Elsewhere a less radical program was advocated. In Philadelphia the workingmen demanded only that high schools be on the Hofwyl model, whereas in the smaller cities and towns in both Pennsylvania and New York the demand was for "literary" day schools. Yet the underlying principle was the same everywhere. A labor candidate for Congress in the First Congressional District of Philadelphia in 1830 expressed it succinctly during his campaign. He made his plea on the ground that "he is the friend and indefatigable defender of a system of general education, which will place the citizens of this extensive Republic on an equality; a system that will fit the children of the poor, as well as the rich, to become our future legislators; a system that will bring the children of the poor and the rich to mix together as a band of Republican brethren."

In New England the workingmen's movement for equal citizenship was simultaneously a reaction against the factory system. To the cry for a Republican system of education was added an anti-child labor crusade. One who did more than any other to call attention to the evils of the factory system of that day was a lawyer by the name of Seth Luther, who, according to his own account, had "for years lived among cotton mills, worked in them, travelled among them." His *"Address to the Working Men of New England on the State of Education, and on the Condition of the Producing Classes in Europe and America, with Particular Reference to the Effect of Manufacturing (as now conducted) on the Health and Happiness of the Poor, and on the Safety of our Republic"* was delivered widely and undoubtedly had considerable influence over the labor movement of the period. The average working day in the best factories at that time was nearly thirteen hours. For the children who were sent into the factories at an early age these hours precluded, of course, any possibility of obtaining even the most rudimentary education.

The New England movement was an effort to unite producers of all kinds, including not only farmers but factory workers with mechanics and city workingmen. In many parts of the State of New York the workingmen's parties included the three classes—"farmers, mechanics, and working men,"—but New England added a fourth class, the factory operatives. It was early found, however, that the movement could expect little or no help from the factory operatives, who were for the most part women and children.

The years 1828, 1829, and 1830 were years of political labor movements and labor parties. Philadelphia originated the first workingmen's party, then came New York and Boston, and finally state-wide movements and political organizations in each of the three States. In New York the workingmen scored their most striking single success, when in 1829 they cast 6000 votes out of a total of 21,000. In Philadelphia the labor ticket polled 2400 in 1828 and the labor party gained the balance of power in the city. But the inexperience of the labor politicians coupled with machinations on the part of "designing men" of both older parties soon lost the labor parties their advantage. In New York Tammany made the demand for a mechanics' lien law its own and later saw that it became enacted into law. In New York, also, the situation became complicated by factional strife between the Skidmorian "agrarians," the Owenite state guardianship faction, and a third faction which eschewed either "panacea." Then, too, the opposition parties and press seized upon agrarianism and Owen's alleged atheism to brand the whole labor movement. The labor party was decidedly unfortunate in its choice of intellectuals and "ideologists."

It would be, however, a mistake to conclude that the Philadelphia, New York, or New England political movements were totally without results. Though unsuccessful in electing their candidates to office, they did succeed in placing their demands to advantage before the public. Humanitarians, like Horace Mann, took up independently the fight for free public education and carried it to success. In Pennsylvania, public schools, free from the taint of charity, date since 1836. In New York City the public school system was established in 1832. The same is true of the demand for a mechanics' lien law, of the abolition of imprisonment for debt, and of others.

(3) *The Period of the "Wild-cat" Prosperity, 1833-1837*

With the break-up of the workingmen's parties, labor's newly acquired sense of solidarity was temporarily lost, leaving only the restricted solidarity of the isolated trade society. Within that limit, however, important progress began to be made. In 1833, there were in New York twenty-nine organized trades; in Philadelphia, twenty-one; and in Baltimore, seventeen. Among those organized in Philadelphia were hand-loom weavers, plasterers, bricklayers, black and white smiths, cigar makers, plumbers, and women workers including tailoresses, seamstresses, binders, folders, milliners, corset makers, and mantua workers. Several trades, such as the printers and tailors in New York and the Philadelphia carpenters, which formerly were organized upon the benevolent basis, were now reorganized as trade societies. The benevolent New York Typographical Society was reduced to secondary importance by the appearance in 1831 of the New York Typographical Association.

But the factor that compelled labor to organize on a much larger scale was the remarkable rise in prices from 1835 to 1837. This rise in prices was coincident with the "wild-cat" prosperity, which followed a rapid multiplication of state banks with the right of issue of paper currency—largely irredeemable "wild-cat" currency. Cost of living having doubled, the subject of wages became a burning issue. At the same time the general business prosperity rendered demands for higher wages easily attainable. The outcome was a luxuriant growth of trade unionism.

In 1836 there were in Philadelphia fifty-eight trade unions; in Newark, New Jersey, sixteen; in New York, fifty-two; in Pittsburgh, thirteen; in Cincinnati, fourteen; and in Louisville, seven. In Buffalo the journeymen builders' association included all the building trades. The tailors of Louisville, Cincinnati, and St. Louis made a concentrated effort against their employers in these three cities.

The wave of organization reached at last the women workers. In 1830 the well-known Philadelphia philanthropist, Mathew Carey, asserted that there were in the cities of New York, Boston, Philadelphia, and Baltimore about 20,000 women who could not by constant employment for sixteen hours out of twenty-four earn more than $1.25 a week. These were mostly seamstresses and tailoresses, umbrella makers, shoe binders, cigar makers, and book binders. In New York there was in 1835 a Female Union Association, in Baltimore a United Seamstresses' Society, and in Philadelphia probably the first federation of women workers in this country. In Lynn, Massachusetts, a "Female Society of Lynn and Vicinity for the Protection and Promotion of Female Industry" operated during 1833 and 1834 among the shoe binders and had at one time 1000 members, who, like the seamstresses, were home workers and earned scanty wages.

Where nearly every trade was in motion, it did not take long to discover a common direction and a common purpose. This was expressed in city "trades' unions," or federations of all organized trades in a city, and in its ascendency over the individual trade societies.

The first trades' union was organized August 14, 1833, in New York. Baltimore followed in September, Philadelphia in November, and Boston in March 1834. New York after 1820 was the metropolis of the country and also the largest industrial and commercial center. There the house carpenters had struck for higher wages in the latter part of May 1833, and fifteen other trades met and pledged their support. Out of this grew the New York Trades' Union. It had an official organ in a weekly, the *National Trades' Union,* published from 1834 to 1836, and a daily, *The Union,* issued in 1836. Ely Moore, a printer, was made president. Moore was elected a few months later as the first representative of labor in Congress.

In addition, trades' unions were organized in Washington; in New Brunswick and Newark, New Jersey; in Albany, Troy, and Schenectady, New York; and in the "Far West"—Pittsburgh, Cincinnati, and Louisville.

Except in Boston, the trades' unions felt anxious to draw the line between themselves and the political labor organizations of the preceding years. In Philadelphia, where as we have seen, the formation of an analogous organization, the Mechanics' Union of Trade Associations of 1828, had served as a preliminary for a political movement, the General Trades' Union took especial precaution and provided in the constitution that "no party, political or religious questions shall at any time be agitated in or acted upon in the Union." Its official organ, the *National Laborer,* declared that "*the Trades' Union never will be political* because its members have learned from experience that the introduction of politics into their societies has thwarted every effort to ameliorate their conditions."

The repudiation of active politics did not carry with it a condemnation of legislative action or "lobbying." On the contrary, these years witnessed the first sustained legislative campaign that was ever conducted by a labor organization, namely the campaign by the New York Trades' Union for the suppression of the competition from prison-made goods. Under the pressure of the New York Union the State Legislature created in 1834 a special commission on prison labor with its president,

Ely Moore, as one of the three commissioners. On this question of prison labor the trade unionists clashed with the humanitarian prison reformers, who regarded productive labor by prisoners as a necessary means of their reform to an honest mode of living; and the humanitarian won. After several months' work the commission submitted what was to the Union an entirely unsatisfactory report. It approved the prison-labor system as a whole and recommended only minor changes. Ely Moore signed the report, but a public meeting of workingmen condemned it.

The rediscovered solidarity between the several trades now embodied in the city trades' unions found its first expression on a large scale in a ten-hour movement.

The first concerted demand for the ten-hour day was made by the workingmen of Baltimore in August 1833, and extended over seventeen trades. But the mechanics' aspiration for a ten-hour day—perhaps the strongest spiritual inheritance from the preceding movement for equal citizenship,[1] had to await a change in the general condition of industry to render trade union effort effective before it could turn into a well sustained movement. That change finally came with the prosperous year of 1835.

The movement was precipitated in Boston. There, as we saw, the carpenters had been defeated in an effort to establish a ten-hour day in 1825,[2] but made another attempt in the spring of 1835. This time, however, they did not stand alone but were joined by the masons and stone-cutters. As before, the principal attack was di-

---

[1] The workingmen felt that they required leisure to be able to exercise their rights of citizens.

[2] The ship carpenters had been similarly defeated in 1832.

rected against the "capitalists," that is, the owners of the buildings and the real estate speculators. The employer or small contractor was viewed sympathetically. "We would not be too severe on our employers," said the strikers' circular, which was sent out broadcast over the country, "they are slaves to the capitalists, as we are to them."

The strike was protracted. The details of it are not known, but we know that it won sympathy throughout the country. A committee visited in July the different cities on the Atlantic coast to solicit aid for the strikers. In Philadelphia, when the committee arrived in company with delegates from New York, Newark, and Paterson, the Trades' Union held a special meeting and resolved to stand by the "Boston House Wrights" who, "in imitation of the noble and decided stand taken by their Revolutionary Fathers, have determined to throw off the shackles of more mercenary tyrants than theirs." Many societies voted varying sums of money in aid of the strikers.

The Boston strike was lost, but the sympathy which it evoked among mechanics in various cities was quickly turned to account. Wherever the Boston circular reached, it acted like a spark upon powder. In Philadelphia the ten-hour movement took on the aspect of a crusade. Not only the building trades, as in Boston, but most of the mechanical branches were involved. Street parades and mass meetings were held. The public press, both friendly and hostile, discussed it at length. Work was suspended and after but a brief "standout" the whole ended in a complete victory for the workingmen. Unskilled laborers, too, struck for the ten-hour day and, in the attempt to prevent others from taking their jobs, riotous scenes occurred which attracted considerable attention. The movement proved so irresistible that the Common Council announced a ten-hour day for public servants. Lawyers, physicians, merchants, and politicians took up the cause of the workingmen. On June 8 the master carpenters granted the ten-hour day and by June 22 the victory was complete.

The victory in Philadelphia was so overwhelming and was given so much publicity that its influence extended to many smaller towns. In fact, the ten-hour system, which remained in vogue in this country in the skilled trades until the nineties, dates largely from this movement in the middle of the thirties.

The great advance in the cost of living during 1835 and 1836 compelled an extensive movement for higher wages. Prices had in some instances more than doubled. Most of these strikes were hastily undertaken. Prices, of course, were rising rapidly but the societies were new and lacked balance. A strike in one trade was an example to others to strike. In a few instances, however, there was considerable planning and reserve.

The strike epidemic affected even the girls who worked in the textile factories. The first strike of factory girls on record had occurred in Dover, New Hampshire, in 1828. A factory strike in Paterson, New Jersey, which occurred in the same year, occasioned the first recorded calling out of militia to quell labor disturbances. There the strikers were, however, for the most part men. But the factory strike which attracted the greatest public attention was the Lowell strike in February, 1834, against a 15 per cent. reduction in wages. The strike was short and unsuccessful, notwithstanding that 800 striking girls at first exhibited a determination to carry their struggle to the end. It appears that public opinion in New England was disagreeably impressed by this early manifestation of feminism. Another notable factory strike was one in Paterson in July 1835. Unlike similar strikes, it had been preceded by an organization. The chief demand was the eleven-hour day. The strike involved twenty mills and 2000 persons. Two weeks later the employers reduced hours from thirteen and a half to twelve hours for five days and to nine hours on Saturday. This broke the strike. The character of the agitation among the factory workers stamps it as ephemeral. Even more ephemeral was the agitation among immigrant laborers, mostly Irish, on canals and roads, which usually took the form of riots.

As in the preceding period, the aggressiveness of the trade societies eventually gave rise to combative masters' associations. These, goaded by restrictive union practices, notably the closed shop, appealed to the courts for relief. By 1836 employers' associations appeared in nearly every trade in which labor was aggressive; in New York there were at least eight and in Philadelphia seven. In Philadelphia, at the initiative of the master carpenters and cordwainers, there came to exist an informal federation of the masters' associations in the several trades.

From 1829 to 1842 there were eight recorded prosecutions of labor organizations for conspiracy. The workingmen were convicted in two cases; in two other cases the courts sustained demurrers to the indictments; in three cases the defendants were acquitted after jury trials; and the outcome of one case is unknown. Finally, in 1842, long after the offending societies had gone out of existence under the stress of unemployment and depressions, the Supreme Judicial Court of Massachusetts handed down a decision, which for forty years laid to rest the doctrine of conspiracy as applied to labor unions.[1]

The unity of action of the several trades displayed in the city trades' unions engendered before long a still wider solidarity in the form of a National Trades' Union. It came together in August 1834, in New York City upon the invitation of the General Trades' Union of New York. The delegates were from the trades' unions of New York, Philadelphia, Boston, Brooklyn, Poughkeepsie, and Newark. Ely Moore, then labor candidate for Congress, was elected president. An attempt by the only "intellectual" present, a Doctor Charles Douglass, representing the Boston Trades' Union, to strike a political note was immediately squelched. A second convention was held in 1835 and a third one in 1837.

The National Trades' Union played a conspicuous part in securing the ten-hour day for government employes. The victory of the ten-hour principle in private employment in 1835 generally led to its adoption by states and municipalities. However, the Federal government was slow to follow the example, since Federal officials were immune from the direct political pressure which the workingmen were able to use with advantage upon locally elected office holders.

In October 1835, the mechanics employed in the New York and Brooklyn Navy Yards petitioned the Secretary of the Navy for a reduction of the hours of labor to ten. The latter referred the petition to the Board of Navy Commissioners, who returned the petition with the opinion that it would be detrimental to the government to accede to their request. This forced the matter into the atten-

---

[1] For a detailed discussion of these trials see below, 149-152.

tion of the National Trades' Union. At its second convention in 1835 it decided to petition Congress for a ten-hour day for employes on government works. The petition was introduced by the labor Congressman from New York, Ely Moore. Congress curtly replied, however, that it was not a matter for legislation but "that the persons employed should redress their own grievances." With Congress in such a mood, the hopes of the workingmen turned to the President.

A first step was made in the summer of 1836, when the workers in the Navy Yard at Philadelphia struck for a ten-hour day and appealed to President Jackson for relief. They would have nothing further to do with Congress. They had supported President Jackson in his fight against the United States Bank and now sought a return favor. At a town meeting of "citizens, mechanics, and working men," a committee was appointed to lay the issue before him. He proved indeed more responsive than Congress and ordered the ten-hour system established.

But the order applied only to the localities where the strike occurred. The agitation had been chiefly local. Besides Philadelphia and New York the mechanics secured the ten-hour day in Baltimore and Annapolis, but in the District of Columbia and elsewhere they were still working twelve or fourteen hours. In other words, the ten-hour day was secured only where trade societies existed.

But the organized labor movement did not rest with a partial success. The campaign of pressure on the President went on. Finally, although somewhat belatedly, President Van Buren issued on March 31, 1840, the famous executive order establishing the ten-hour day on government work without a reduction in wages.

The victory came after the National Trades' Union had gone out of existence and should be, more correctly, correlated with a labor political movement. Early in 1837 came a financial panic. The industrial depression wiped out in a short time every form of labor organization from the trade societies to the National Trades' Union. Labor stood defenseless against the economic storm. In this emergency it turned to politics as a measure of despair.

The political dissatisfaction assumed the form of hostility towards banks and corporations in general. The workingmen held the banks responsible for the existing anarchy in currency, from which they suffered both as consumers and producers. Moreover, they felt that there was something uncanny and threatening about corporations with their continuous existence and limited liability. Even while their attention had been engrossed by trade unionism, the workingmen were awake to the issue of monopoly. Together with their employers they had therefore supported Jackson in his assault upon the largest "monster" of them all—the Bank of the United States. The local organizations of the Democratic party, however, did not always remain true to faith. In such circumstances the workingmen, again acting in conjunction with their masters, frequently extended their support to the "insurgent" anti-monopoly candidates in the Democratic party conventions. Such a revolt took place in Philadelphia in 1835; and in New York, although Tammany had elected Ely Moore, the President of the General Trades' Union of New York, to Congress in 1834, a similar revolt occurred. The upshot was a triumphant return of the rebels into the fold of Tammany in 1837. During the next twenty years, Tammany came nearer

Emerson, had much in common with the present-day efficiency engineers. This "old" efficiency of theirs, like the new one, was chiefly concerned with increasing the production of wealth through the application of the "natural" laws of human nature. With the enormous increase in production to be brought about by "Fourierism" and "Association," the question of justice in distribution was relegated to a secondary place. Where they differed from the new efficiency was in method, for they believed efficiency would be attained if only the human instincts or "passions" were given free play, while the efficiency engineers of today trust less to unguided instinct and more to "scientific management" of human "passions."

Midway between trade unionism and the simon-pure, idealistic reform philosophies stood producers' and consumers' coöperation. It had the merit of being a practical program most suitable to a time of depression, while on its spiritual side it did not fail to satisfy the loftiest intellectual. It was the resultant of the two most potent forces which acted upon the movement of the forties, the pressure of an inadequate income of the wage earner and the influence of the intellectuals. During no other period has there been, relatively speaking, so much effort along that line.

Although, as we shall see, the eighties were properly the era of producers' coöperation on a large scale, the self-governing workshop had always been familiar to the American labor movement. The earliest attempt, as far as we have knowledge, occurred in Philadelphia in 1791, when the house carpenters out on strike offered by way of retaliation against their employers to undertake contracts at 25 per cent. less than the price charged by the

to being a workingmen's organization than at any
time in its career.

(4) *The Long Depression, 1837-1862*

The twenty-five years which elapsed from 1837 to 1
form a period of business depression and industrial
organization only briefly interrupted during 1850-18
by the gold discoveries in California. The aggressi
unions of the thirties practically disappeared. With i
dustry disorganized, trade unionism, or the effort to pr
tect the standard of living by means of strikes, was out of
question. As the prospect for immediate amelioration became dimmed by circumstances, an opportunity arrived
for theories and philosophies of radical social reform.
Once the sun with its life-giving heat has set, one begins
to see the cold and distant stars.

The uniqueness of the period of the forties in the labor
movement proceeds not only from the large volume of star-
gazing, but also from the accompanying fact that, for
the first and only time in American history, the labor
movement was dominated by men and women from the
educated class, the "intellectuals," who thus served in
the capacity of expert astrologers.

And there was no lack of stars in the heaven of social
reform to occupy both intellectual and wage earner. First,
there was the efficiency scheme of the followers of Charles
Fourier, the French socialist, or, as they preferred to
call themselves, the Associationists. Theirs was a proposal aiming directly to meet the issue of the prevailing
industrial disorganization and wasteful competition. Albert Brisbane, Horace Greeley, and the Brook Farm
enthusiasts and "Associationists" of the forties, made famous by their intimate association with Ralph Waldo

masters. Fourteen years later, in 1806, the journeymen cordwainers of the same city, following their conviction in court on the charge of conspiracy brought in by their masters, opened up a coöperative shoe warehouse and store. As a rule the workingmen took up productive coöperation when they had failed in strikes.

In 1836 many of the trade societies began to lose their strikes and turned to coöperation. The cordwainers working on ladies' shoes entered upon a strike for higher wages in March 1836, and opened three months later a "manufactory" or a warehouse of their own. The hand-loom weavers in two of the suburbs of Philadelphia started coöperative associations at the same time. At the end of 1836 the hand-loom weavers of Philadelphia proper had two coöperative shops and were planning to open a third. In New Brunswick, New Jersey, the journeymen cordwainers opened a shop after an unsuccessful strike early in 1836; likewise the tailors of Cincinnati, St. Louis, and Louisville. In New York the carpenters had done so already in 1833, and the painters of New York and Brooklyn opened their shops in 1837.

Before long the spirit became so contagious that the Trades' Union of Philadelphia, the city federation of trade societies, was obliged to take notice. Early in 1837 a conference of about 200 delegates requested each trade society to submit estimates for a shop to employ ten members. However, further steps were prevented by the financial panic and business depression.

The forties witnessed several similar attempts. When the iron molders of Cincinnati failed to win a strike in the autumn of 1847, a few of their number collected what funds they could and organized a sort of joint-stock company which they called "The Journeymen Molders' Union

Foundry." Two local philanthropists erected their buildings. In Pittsburgh a group of puddlers tried to raise money by selling stock to anyone who wished to take an interest in their coöperative venture.

The coöperative ventures multiplied in 1850 and 1851, following a widespread failure of strikes and were entered upon with particular readiness by the German immigrants. Among the Germans was an attitude towards producers' coöperation, based more nearly on general principles ~~in~~ the practical exigencies of a strike. Fresh from the ~~scenes~~ of revolutions in Europe, they were more given to ~~dreams~~ about reconstructing society and more trustful ~~in~~ the honesty and integrity of their leaders. The coöperative movement among the Germans was identified with the name of Wilhelm Weitling, the well-known German communist, who settled in America about 1850. This movement centered in and around New York. The coöperative principle met with success among the English-speaking people only outside the larger cities. In Buffalo, after an unsuccessful strike, the tailors formed an association with a membership of 108 and in October 1850, were able to give employment to 80 of that number.

Again, following an unsuccessful Pittsburgh strike of iron founders in 1849, about a dozen of the strikers went to Wheeling, Virginia, each investing $3000, and opened a coöperative foundry shop. Two other foundries were opened on a similar basis in Stetsonville, Ohio, and Sharon, Pennsylvania. These associations of iron founders, however, might better be called association of small capitalists or master-workmen.

During the forties, consumers' or distributive coöperation was also given a trial. The early history of consumers' coöperation is but fragmentary and, so far as we know, the first coöperative attempt which had for its exclusive aim "competence to purchaser" was made in Philadelphia early in 1829. A store was established on North Fifth Street, which sold goods at wholesale prices to members, who paid twenty cents a month for its privileges.

In 1831 distributive coöperation was much discussed in Boston by a "New England Association of Farmers, Mechanics, and Other Working Men." A half dozen coöperative attempts are mentioned in the *Coöperator*, published in Utica in 1832, but only in the case of the journeymen cordwainers of Lynn do we discover an undertaking which can with certainty be considered as an effort to achieve distributive coöperation. Several germs of coöperative effort are found between 1833 and 1845, but all that is known about them is that their promoters sought to effect a saving by the purchase of goods in large quantities which were then broken up and distributed at a slight advance above original cost in order to meet expenses. The managers were unpaid, the members' interest in the business was not maintained, and the stores soon failed, or passed into the possession of private owners.

It was the depression of 1846–1849 which supplied the movement for distributive coöperation with the needed stimulus, especially in New England. Although the matter was discussed in New York, New Jersey, Pennsylvania, Maryland, and even as far west as Ohio and Illinois, yet in none of the industrial centers of these States, except perhaps in New York, was it put into successful operation.

In New England, however, the conditions were exceptionally favorable. A strike movement for higher wages during a partial industrial revival of 1843–1844 had failed completely. This failure, added to the fact that women and girls were employed under very unsatisfactory conditions, strengthened the interest of humanitarians in the laboring people and especially in coöperation as a possible means of alleviating their distress.

Under the stimulus of these agitations, the New England Protective Union was formed in 1845. Until 1849, however, it bore the name of the Working Men's Protective Union. As often happens, prosperity brought disunion and, in 1853, a schism occurred in the organization due to personal differences. The seceders formed a separate organization known as the American Protective Union.

The Working Men's Protective Union embodied a larger conception of the coöperative idea than had been expressed before. The important thought was that an economy of a few dollars a year in the purchase of commodities was a poor way out of labor difficulties, but was valuable only as a preparation for something better.

Though the resources of these laborers were small, they began the work with great hopes. This business, starting so unpretentiously, assumed larger and increasing proportions until in October, 1852, the Union embraced 403 divisions of which 167 reported a capital of $241,712 and 165 of these announced annual sales amounting to $1,-696,825. Though the schism of 1853, mentioned above, weakened the body, the agent of the American Protective Union claimed for the divisions comprising it sales aggregating in value over nine and one-fourth millions dollars in the seven years ending in 1859.

It is not possible to tell what might have been the outcome of this coöperative movement had the peaceful development of the country remained uninterrupted. As it happened, the disturbed era of the Civil War witnessed the near annihilation of all workingmen's coöperation. It is not difficult to see the causes which led to the destruction of the still tender plant. Men left their homes for the battle field, foreigners poured into New England towns and replaced the Americans in the shops, while share-holders frequently became frightened at the state of trade and gladly saw the entire coöperative enterprise pass into the hands of the storekeeper.

This first American coöperative movement on a large scale resembled the British movement in many respects, namely open membership, equal voting by members irrespective of number of shares, cash sales and federation of societies for wholesale purchases, but differed in that goods were sold to members nearly at cost rather than at the market price. Dr. James Ford in his *Coöperation in New England, Urban and Rural*,[1] describes two survivals from this period, the Central Union Association of New Bedford, Massachusetts, founded in 1848, and the Acushnet Coöperative Association, also of New Bedford, which began business in 1849.

But the most characteristic labor movement of the forties was a resurgence of the old Agrarianism of the twenties.

Skidmore's "equal division" of all property appealed to the workingmen of New York because it seemed to be based on equality of opportunity. One of Skidmore's temporary associates, a Welshman by the name of George Henry Evans, drew from him an inspiration for a new kind of agrarianism to which few could object.

[1] Published in 1916 by the Russell Sage Foundation, pp. 16-18.

This new doctrine was a true Agrarianism, since it followed in the steps of the original "Agrarians," the brothers Gracchi in ancient Rome. Like the Gracchi, Evans centered his plan around the "ager publicum"—the vast American public domain. Evans began his agitation about 1844.

Man's right to life, according to Evans, logically implied his right to use the materials of nature necessary for being. For practical reasons he would not interfere with natural resources which have already passed under private ownership. Evans proposed instead that Congress give each would-be settler land for a homestead free of charge.

As late as 1852 debaters in Congress pointed out that in the preceding sixty years only 100,000,000 acres of the public lands had been sold and that 1,400,000,000 acres still remained at the disposal of the government. Estimates of the required time to dispose of this residuum at the same rate of sale varied from 400 or 500 to 900 years. With the exaggerated views prevalent, it is no wonder that Evans believed that the right of the individual to as much land as his right to live calls for would remain a living right for as long a period in the future as a practical statesman may be required to take into account.

The consequences of free homesteads were not hard to picture. The landless wage earners could be furnished transportation and an outfit, for the money spent for poor relief would be more profitably expended in sending the poor to the land. Private societies and trade unions, when laborers were too numerous, could aid in transporting the surplus to the waiting homesteads and towns that would grow up. With the immobility of labor thus offering no serious obstacle to the execution of the plan, the wage earners of the East would have the option of continuing to work for wages or of taking up their share of the vacant lands. Moreover, mechanics could set up as independent producers in the new settlements. Enough at least would go West to force employers to offer better wages and shorter hours. Those unable to meet the expenses of moving would profit by higher wages at home. An equal opportunity to go on land would benefit both pioneer and stay-at-home.

But Evans would go still further in assuring equality of opportunity. He would make the individual's right to the resources of nature safe against the creditors through a law exempting homesteads from attachment for debts and even against himself by making the homestead inalienable. Moreover to assure that right to the American people *in perpetuo* he would prohibit future disposal of the public land in large blocks to moneyed purchasers as practiced by the government heretofore. Thus the program of the new agrarianism: free homesteads, homestead exemption, and land limitation.

Evans had a plan of political action, which was as unique as his economic program. His previous political experiences with the New York Workingmen's party had taught him that a minority party could not hope to win by its own votes and that the politicans cared more for offices than for measures. They would endorse any measure which was supported by voters who held the balance of power. His plan of action was, therefore, to ask all candidates to pledge their support to his measures. In exchange for such a pledge, the candidates would receive the votes of the workingmen. In case neither candidate would sign the pledge, it might be necessary to nominate an independent as a warning to future candidates; but not as an indication of a new party organization.

Evans' ideas quickly won the adherence of the few labor papers then existing.   Horace Greeley's New York *Tribune* endorsed the homestead movement as early as 1845.   The next five years witnessed a remarkable spread of the ideas of the free homestead movement in the press of the country.   It was estimated in 1845 that 2000 papers were published in the United States and that in 1850, 600 of these supported land reform.

Petitions and memorials having proved of little avail, the land reformers tried Evans' pet plan of bargaining votes for the support of their principles.   Tammany was quick to start the bidding.   In May, 1851, a mass-meeting was held at Tammany Hall "of all those in favor of land and other industrial reform, to be made elements in the Presidential contest of 1852."   A platform was adopted which proclaimed man's right to the soil and urged that freedom of the public lands be endorsed by the Democratic party.   Senator Isaac A. Walker of Wisconsin was nominated as the candidate of the party for President.

For a while the professional politician triumphed over the too trusting workingman reformer.   But the cause found strong allies in the other classes of the American community.   From the poor whites of the upland region of the South came a similar demand formulated by the Tennessee tailor, Andrew Johnson, later President of the United States, who introduced his first homestead bill in 1845.   From the Western pioneers and settlers came the demand for increased population and development of resources, leading both to homesteads for settlers and land grants for railways.   The opposition came from manufacturers and landowners of the East and from the Southern slave owners. The West and East finally combined and the policy of the West prevailed, but not before the South had seceded from the Union.

Not the entire reform was accepted. The Western spirit dominated. The homestead law, as finally adopted in 1862, granted one hundred and sixty acres as a free gift to every settler. But the same Congress launched upon a policy of extensive land grants to railways. The homestead legislation doubtless prevented great estates similar to those which sprang of a different policy of the Australian colonies, but did not carry out the broad principles of inalienability and land limitation of the original Agrarians.

Their principle of homestead exemption, however, is now almost universally adopted. Thus the homestead agitation begun by Evans and a group of wage earners and farmers in 1844 was carried to victory, though to an incomplete victory. It contained a fruitful lesson to labor in politics. The vested interests in the East were seen ultimately to capitulate before a popular movement which at no time aspired toward political power and office, but, concentrating on one issue, endeavored instead to permeate with its ideas the public opinion of the country at large.

Of all the "isms" so prevalent during the forties, "Agrarianism" alone came close to modern socialism, as it alone advocated class struggle and carried it into the political field, although, owing to the peculiarity of the American party structure, it urged a policy of "reward your friends, and punish your enemies" rather than an out and out labor party. It is noteworthy that of all social reform movements of the forties Agrarianism alone was not initiated by the intellectuals. On the other hand, another movement for legislative reform, namely the shorter-hour movement for women and children working in the mills and factories, was entirely managed by humanitarians. Its philosophy was the furthest removed from the class struggle idea.

For only a short year or two did prosperity show itself from behind the clouds to cause a mushroom growth of trade unions, once in 1850-1851 and again in 1853–1854, following the gold discoveries in California. During these few years unionism disentangled itself from humanitarianism and coöperationism and came out in its wholly modern form of restrictive craft unionism, only to be again suppressed by the business depressions that preceded and followed the panic of 1857. Considered as a whole, however, the period of the forties and fifties was the zenith in American history of theories of social reform, of "panaceas," of humanitarianism.

The trade union wave of the fifties was so short lived and the trade unionists were so preoccupied with the pressing need of advancing their wages to keep pace with the soaring prices caused by the influx of California gold, that we miss the tendency which was so strong in the thirties to reach out for a wider basis of labor organization in city trades' unions, and ultimately in a National Trades' Union. On the other hand, the fifties foreshadowed a new form of expansion of labor organization—the joining together in a nation-wide organization of all local unions of one trade. The printers [1] organized na-

---

[1] The printers had organized nationally for the first time in 1836, but the organization lasted less than two years; likewise the cordwainers or shoemakers. But we must keep in mind that what constituted national organization in the thirties would pass only for regional or sectional organization in later years.

tionally in 1850, the locomotive engineers and the hat-finishers in 1854; and the iron molders, and the machinists and blacksmiths in 1859; in addition there were at least a half dozen less successful attempts in other trades.

CHAPTER 2

THE "GREENBACK" PERIOD, 1862-1879

The few national trade unions which were formed at the close of the fifties did not constitute by themselves a labor movement. It needed the industrial prosperity caused by the price inflation of the Civil War time to bring forth again a mass movement of labor.

We shall say little of labor's attitude towards the question of war and peace before the War had started. Like many other citizens of the North and the Border States the handful of organized workers favored a compromise. They held a labor convention in Philadelphia, in which a great labor leader of the sixties, William H. Sylvis, President of the International Molders' Union, took a prominent part and pronounced in favor of the compromise solution advanced by Congressman Critten-den of Kentucky. But no sooner had Fort Sumter been fired upon by the secessionists than labor rallied to the support of the Federal Union. Entire local unions enlisted at the call of President Lincoln, and Sylvis himself assisted in recruiting a company composed of molders.

The first effect of the War was a paralysis of business and an increase of unemployment. The existing labor organizations nearly all went to the wall. The period of industrial stagnation, however, lasted only until the middle of 1862.

The legal tender acts of 1862 and 1863 authorized the issue of paper currency of "greenbacks" to the amount of $1,050,000,000, and immediately prices began to soar. For the next sixteen years, namely until 1879, when the government resumed the redemption of greenbacks in gold, prices of commodities and labor expressed in terms of paper money showed varying degrees of inflation; hence the term "greenback" period. During the War the advance in prices was due in part to the extraordinary demand by the government for the supply of the army and, of course, to speculation.

In July 1863, retail prices were 43 per cent. above those of 1860 and wages only 12 per cent. above; in July 1864, retail prices rose to 70 per cent. and wages to 30 per cent. above 1860; and in July 1865, prices rose to 76 per cent. and wages only to 50 per cent. above the level of 1860. The unequal pace of the price movement drove labor to organize along trade-union lines.

The order observed in the thirties was again followed out. First came a flock of local trade unions; these soon combined in city centrals—or as they came to be called, trades' assemblies—paralleling the trades' union of the thirties; and lastly, came an attempt to federate the several trades' assemblies into an International Industrial Assembly of North America. Local trade unions were organized literally in every trade beginning in the second half of 1862. The first trades' assembly was formed in Rochester, New York, in March 1863; and before long there was one in every town of importance. The International Industrial Assembly was attempted in 1864, but failed to live up to the expectations: The time had passed for a national federation of city centrals. As in the thirties the spread of unionism over the breadth of the land called out as a counterpart a widespread movement of employers' associations. The latter differed, however, from their predecessors in the thirties in that they made little use of the courts in their fight against the unions.

The growth of the national trade unions was a true index of the condition of business. Four were organized in 1864 as compared to two organized in 1863, none in 1862, and one in 1861. During 1865, which marked the height of the intense business activity, six more national unions were organized. In 1866 industry entered upon a period of depression, which reached its lowest depth in 1867 and continued until 1869. Accordingly, not a single national union was organized in 1866 and only one in 1867. In 1868 two new national labor unions were organized. In 1869 two more unions were formed—a total of seven for the four depressed years, compared with ten in the preceding two prosperous years. In the summer of 1870 business became good and remained good for approximately three years. Nine new national unions appeared in these three years. These same years are marked also by a growth of the unions previously organized. For instance, the machinists and blacksmiths, with only 1500 members in 1870, had 18,000 in 1873. Other unions showed similar gains.

An estimate of the total trade union membership at any one time (in view of the total lack of reliable statistics) would be extremely hazardous. The New York *Herald* estimated it in August 1869, to be about 170,000. A labor leader claimed at the same time that the total was as high as 600,000. Probably 300,000 would be a conservative estimate for the time immediately preceding the panic of 1873.

Although the strength of labor was really the strength of the national trade unions, especially during the depression of the later sixties, far greater attention was at-

tracted outside as well as inside the labor movement by
the National Labor Union, a loosely built federation of
national trade unions, city trades' assemblies, local trade
unions, and reform organizations of various descriptions,
from philosophical anarchists to socialists and woman
suffragists. The National Labor Union did not excel in
practical activity, but it formed an accurate mirror of
the aspirations and ideals of the American mechanics of
the time of the Civil War and after. During its six years'
existence it ran the gamut of all important issues which
agitated the labor movement of the time.

The National Labor Union came together in its first
convention in 1866. The most pressing problem of the
day was unemployment due to the return of the demob-
ilized soldiers and the shutting down of war industries.
The convention centered on the demand to reduce the
working day to eight hours. But eight hours had by that
time come to signify more than a means to increase employment. The eight-hour movement drew its inspiration from an economic theory advanced by a self-taught
Boston machinist, Ira Steward. And so naturally did
this theory flow from the usual premises in the thinking
of the American workman that once formulated by Steward it may be said to have become an official theory of the
labor movement.

Steward's doctrine is well expressed by a couplet which
was very popular with the eight-hour speakers of that
period: "Whether you work by the piece or work by the
day, decreasing the hours increases the pay." Steward
believed that the amount of wages is determined by no
other factor than the worker's standard of living. He
held that wages cannot fall below the standard of living
not because, as the classical economists said, it would

cause late marriages and a reduction in the supply of labor, but solely because the wage earner will refuse to work for less than enough to maintain his standard of living. Steward possessed such abundant faith in this purely psychological check on the employer that he made it the cornerstone of his theory of social progress. Raise the worker's standard of living, he said, and the employer will be immediately forced to raise wages; no more can wages fall below the level of the worker's standard of living than New England can be ruled against her will. The lever for raising the standard of living was the eight-hour day. Increase the worker's leisure and you will increase his wants; increase his wants and you will immediately raise his wages. Although he occasionally tried to soften his doctrine by the argument that a shorter work-day not only does not decrease but may actually increase output, his was a distinctly revolutionary doctrine; he aimed at the total abolition of profits through their absorption into wages. But the instrument was nothing more radical than a progressive universal shortening the hours.

So much for the general policy. To bring it to pass two alternatives were possible: trade unionism or legislation. Steward chose the latter as the more hopeful and speedy one. Steward knew that appeals to the humanity of the employers had largely failed; efforts to secure the reform by coöperation had failed; the early trade unions had failed; and there seemed to be no recourse left now but to accomplish the reduction of hours by legislative enactment.

In 1866 Steward organized the Grand Eight-Hour League of Massachusetts as a special propagandist organization of the eight-hour philosophy. The League

was a secret organization with pass words and obligations, intended as the central organization of a chain of
subordinate leagues in the State, afterwards to be created.
Of a total of about eighty local leagues in existence from
1865 to 1877, about twenty were in Massachusetts, eight
elsewhere in New England, at least twenty-five in Michigan, four or five in Pennsylvania, about seven in Illinois,
as many in Wisconsin, and smaller numbers in Missouri,
Iowa, Indiana, and California.   Michigan, Illinois, Iowa,
and Pennsylvania had each a Grand Eight-Hour League.
Practically all of these organizations disappeared soon
after the panic of 1873.

The National Labor Union centered on the passage of
an eight-hour law for employes of the Federal government. It was believed, perhaps not without some justice,
that the effect of such law would eventually lead to the
introduction of the same standard in private employment
—not indeed through the operation of the law of supply
and demand, for it was realized that this would be practically negligible, but rather through its contagious effect
on the minds of employes and even employers. It will be
recalled that, at the time of the ten-hour agitation of
the thirties, the Federal government had lagged about
five years behind private employers in granting the demanded concession. That in the sixties the workingmen
chose government employment as the entering wedge
shows a measure of political self-confidence which the
preceding generation of workingmen lacked.

The first bill in Congress was introduced by Senator
Gratz Brown of Missouri in March 1866.   In the summer
a delegation from the National Labor Union was received
by President Andrew Johnson. The President pointed to
his past record favorable to the workingmen but refrained

from any definite promises. Finally, an eight-hour bill for government employes was passed by the House in March 1867, and by the Senate in June 1868. On June 29, 1868, President Johnson signed it and it went into effect immediately.

The result of the eight-hour law was not all that the friends of the bill hoped. The various officials in charge of government work put their own interpretations upon it and there resulted much diversity in its observance, and consequently great dissatisfaction. There seemed to be no clear understanding as to the intent of Congress in enacting the law. Some held that the reduction in working hours must of necessity bring with it a corresponding reduction in wages. The officials' view of the situation was given by Secretary Gideon Wells. He pointed out that Congress, by reducing the hours of labor in government work, had forced upon the department of the Navy the employment of a larger number of men in order to accomplish the necessary work; and that at the same time Congress had reduced the appropriation for that department. This had rendered unavoidable a twenty per cent. reduction in wages paid employes in the Navy Yard. Such a state of uncertainty continued four years longer. At last on May 13, 1872, President Grant prohibited by proclamation any wage reductions in the execution of the law. On May 18, 1872, Congress passed a law for the restitution of back pay.

The expectations of the workingmen that the Federal law would blaze the way for the eight-hour system in private employment failed to materialize. The depression during the seventies took up all the impetus in that direction which the law may have generated. Even as far as government work is concerned forty years had to elapse before its application could be rounded out by extending it to contract work done for the government by private employers.

We have dealt at length with this subject because it marked an important landmark. It demonstrated to the wage earners that, provided they concentrated on a modest object and kept up a steady pressure, their prospects for success were not entirely hopeless, hard as the road may seem to travel. The other and far more ambitious object of the workingman of the sixties, that of enacting general eight-hour laws in the several States, at first appeared to be within easy reach—so yielding political parties and State legislatures seemed to be to the demands of the organized workmen. Yet before long these successes proved to be entirely illusory.

The year 1867 was the banner year for such State legislation. Eight-hour laws were passed in Illinois, Wisconsin, Connecticut, Missouri, and New York. California passed such a law in 1868. In Pennsylvania, Michigan, Maryland, and Minnesota bills were introduced but were defeated. Two common features characterized these laws, whether enacted or merely proposed to the legislatures. There were none which did not permit of longer hours than those named in the law, provided they were so specified in the contract. A contract requiring ten or more hours a day was perfectly legal. The eight-hour day was the legal day only "when the contract was silent on the subject or where there is no express contract to the contrary," as stated in the Wisconsin law. But the greatest weakness was a lack of a provision for enforcement. New York's experience is typical and characteristic. When the workingmen appealed to Governor Fenton to enforce the law, he replied that the act had received his official signature and he felt that it "would be an unwarrantable assumption" on his part to take any step requiring its enforcement. "Every law," he said, "was obligatory by its own nature, and could derive no additional force from any further act of his."

In Massachusetts, however, the workingmen succeeded after hard and protracted labor in obtaining an enforceable ten-hour law for women—the first effective law of its kind passed in any American State. This law, which was passed in 1874, provides that "no minor under the age of eighteen years, and no woman over that age" shall be employed more than ten hours in one day or sixty hours in any one week in any manufacturing establishment in the State. The penalty for each violation was fixed at fifty dollars.

The repeated disappointments with politics and legislation led in the early seventies to a revival of faith in trade unionism. Even in the early sixties we find not a few unions, national and local, limiting their hours by agreement with employers. The national unions, however, for the most part left the matter to the local unions for settlement as their strength or local conditions might dictate. In some cases the local unions were advised to accept a reduction of wages in order to secure the system, showing faith in Steward's theory that such reduction could not be permanent.

The movement to establish the eight-hour day through trade unionism reached its climax in the summer of 1872, when business prosperity was at its height. This year witnessed in New York City a general eight-hour strike. However, it succeeded in only a few trades, and even there the gain was only temporary, since it was lost during the years of depression which followed the financial panic of 1873.

To come back to the National Labor Union. At the second convention in 1867 the enthusiasm was transferred from eight-hour laws to the bizarre social reform philosophy known as "greenbackism."

"Greenbackism" was, in substance, a plan to give the man without capital an equal opportunity in business with his rich competitor. It meant taking away from bankers and middlemen their control over credit and thereby furnishing credit and capital through the aid of the government to the producers of physical products. On its face greenbackism was a program of currency reform and derived its name from the so-called "greenback," the paper money issued during the Civil War. But it was more than currency reform—it was industrial democracy.

"Greenbackism" was the American counterpart of the contemporary radicalism of Europe. Its program had much in common with that of Lassalle in Germany who would have the state lend its credit to coöperative associations of workingmen in the confident expectation that with such backing they would drive private capitalism out of existence by the competitive route. But greenbackism differed from the scheme of Lassalle in that it would utilize the government's enormous Civil War debt, instead of its taxing power, as a means of furnishing capital to labor. This was to be done by reducing the rate of interest on the government bonds to three per cent. and by making them convertible into legal tender currency and convertible back into bonds, at the will of the holder of either. In other words, the greenback currency, instead of being, as it was at the time, an irredeemable promise to pay in specie, would be redeemable in government bonds. On the other hand, if a government bondholder could secure slightly more than three per cent. by lending to a private borrower, he would return his bonds to the government, take out the corresponding amount in greenbacks and lend it to the producer on his private note or mortgage. This would involve, of course, the possible inflation of legal tender currency to the amount of outstanding bonds. But inflation was immaterial, since all prices would be affected alike and meanwhile the farmers, the workingmen, and their coöperative establishments would be able to secure capital at slightly more than three per cent. instead of the nine or twelve per cent. which they were compelled to pay at the bank. Thereby they would be placed on a competitive level with the middleman, and the wage earner would be assisted to escape the wage system into self-employment.

Such was the curious doctrine which captured the leaders of the organized wage earners in 1867. The way had indeed been prepared for it in 1866, when the wage earners espoused producers' coöperation as the only solution. But, in the following year, 1867, they concluded that no system of combination or coöperation could secure to labor its natural rights as long as the credit system enabled non-producers to accumulate wealth faster than labor was able to add to the national wealth. Coöperation would follow "as a natural consequence," if producers could secure through legislation credit at a low rate of interest. The government was to extend to the producer "free capital" in addition to free land which he received with the Homestead Act.

The producers' coöperation, which offered the occasion for the espousal of greenbackism, was itself preceded by a movement for consumers' coöperation. Following the upward sweep of prices, workmen had begun toward the end of 1862 to make definite preparations for distributive coöperation. They endeavored to cut off the profits of the middleman by establishing coöperative grocery stores, meat markets, and coal yards. The first substantial effort of this kind to attract wide attention was the formation in December 1862, of the Union Coöperative Association of Philadelphia, which opened a store. The prime mover and the financial secretary of this organization was Thomas Phillips, a shoemaker who came from England in 1852, fired with the principles of the Rochdale pioneers, that is, cash sales, dividends on purchases rather than on stock, and "one man, one vote." By 1866 the movement had extended until practically every important industrial town between Boston and San Francisco had some form of distributive coöperation. This was the high tide of the movement. Unfortunately, the condition of the country was unfavorable to these enterprises and they were destined to early collapse. The year 1865 witnessed disastrous business failures. The country was in an uncertain condition and at the end of the sixties the entire movement had died out.

From 1866 to 1869 experiments in productive coöperation were made by practically all leading trades including the bakers, coach makers, collar makers, coal miners, shipwrights, machinists and blacksmiths, foundry workers, nailers, ship carpenters, and calkers, glass blowers, hatters, boiler makers, plumbers, iron rollers, tailors, printers, needle women, and molders. A large proportion of these attempts grew out of unsuccessful strikes. The most important undertakings were among the workers in iron, undoubtedly due in large measure to the inde-

fatigable efforts of William H. Sylvis, the founder of the
Iron Molders' International Union.

At the close of 1869 members of the Iron Molders'
International Union owned and operated many coöperative foundries chiefly in New York and Pennsylvania.
The first of the foundries established at Troy in the early
summer of 1866 was followed quickly by one in Albany
and then during the next eighteen months by ten more—
one each in Rochester, Chicago, Quincy, Louisville, Som-
erset, Pittsburgh, and two each in Troy and Cleveland.
The original foundry at Troy was an immediate financial
success and was hailed with joy by those who believed
that under the name of coöperationists the baffled trade
unionists might yet conquer. The New York *Sun* con-
gratulated the iron molders of Troy and declared that
Sylvis had checkmated the association of stove manufacturers and, by the establishment of this coöperative
foundry, had made the greatest contribution of the year
to the labor cause.

But the results of the Troy experiment, typical of the
others, show how far from a successful solution of the
labor problem is productive coöperation. Although this
"Troy Coöperative Iron Founders' Association" was
planned with great deliberation and launched at a time
when the regular stove manufacturers were embarrassed
by strikes, and although it was regularly incorporated
with a provision that each member was entitled to but
one vote whether he held one share at $100, or the maxi-
mum privilege of fifty in the total of two thousand
shares, it failed as did the others in furnishing permanent relief to the workers as a class. At the end of the
third year of this enterprise, the *American Workman*
published a sympathetic account of its progress uncon-

sciously disclosing its fatal weakness, namely, the inevitable tendency of coöperators to adopt the capitalistic view. The writer of this account quotes from these coöperators to show that "the fewer the stockholders in the company the greater its success."

A similar instance is furnished by the Coöperative Foundry Company of Rochester. This venture has also been a financial success, though a partial failure as a coöperative enterprise. When it was established in 1867 all employes were stockholders and profits were divided as follows: Twelve per cent. on capital and the balance in proportion to the earnings of the men. But the capitalist was stronger than the coöperative brother. Dividends on capital were advanced in a few years to seventeen and one-half per cent., then to twenty-five, and finally the distribution of any part of the profits in proportion to wages was discontinued. Money was made every year and dividends paid, which in 1884 amounted to forty per cent. on the capital. At that time about one-fifth of the employes were stockholders. Also in this case coöperation did not prevent the usual conflict between employer and employe, as is shown in a strike of three and a half months' duration. It is interesting to notice that one of the strikers, a member of the Molders' Union, owned stock to the amount of $7000.

The machinists, too, throughout this period took an active interest in coöperation. Their convention which met in October, 1865, appointed a committee to report on a plan of action to establish a coöperative shop under the auspices of the International Union. The plan failed of adoption, but of machinists' shops on the joint-stock plan there were a good many. Two other trades noted for their enthusiasm for coöperation at this time were

the shoemakers and the coopers. The former, organized
in the Order of St. Crispin, then the largest trade union
in the country, advocated coöperation even when their
success in strikes was at its height. "The present demand
of the Crispin is steady employment and fair wages, but
his future is self-employment" was one of their mottoes.
During the seventies they repeatedly attempted to carry
this motto into effect. The seventies also saw the beginning of the most successful single venture in productive
coöperation ever undertaken in this country, namely, the
eight coöperative cooperage shops in Minneapolis, which
were established at varying intervals from 1874 to 1886.
The coopers took care to enforce true coöperation by
providing for equal holding of stock and for a division
of ordinary profits and losses in proportion to wages.
The cooper shops prospered, but already ten years later
four out of the eight existing in 1886 had passed into
private hands.

In 1866 when the eight-hour demand was as yet upper-
most, the National Labor Union resolved for an independent labor party. The espousal of greenbackism in
1867 only reënforced that resolution. The leaders realized only too well that neither the Republican nor Democratic party would voluntarily make an issue of a scheme
purporting to assist the wage earner to become an independent producer. Accordingly, the history of the National Labor Union became largely the history of labor's
first attempt to play a lone political hand on a national
scale.

Each annual session of the National Labor Union
faithfully reaffirmed the decision to "cut loose" from the
old parties. But such a vast undertaking demanded time.
It was not until 1872 that the National Labor Union met

as a political convention to nominate a national ticket. From the first the stars were inauspicuous. Charges were made that political aspirants sought to control the convention in order to influence nominations by the Republican and Democratic parties. A "greenback" platform was adopted as a matter of course and the new party was christened the National Labor and Reform Party. On the first formal ballot for nomination for President, Judge David Davis of Illinois, a personal friend of Abraham Lincoln, received 88 votes, Wendell Phillips, the abolitionist, 52, and the remainder scattered. On the third ballot Davis was nominated. Governor J. Parker of New Jersey was nominated for Vice-President. At first Judge Davis accepted the nomination, but resigned after the Democrats had nominated Horace Greeley. The loss of the candidate spelled the death of the party. The National Labor Union itself had been only an empty shell since 1870, when the national trade unions, disaffected with the turn towards politics, withdrew. Now, its pet project a failure, it, too, broke up.

In 1873, on the eve of the financial panic, the national trade unions attempted to reconstruct a national labor federation on a purely trade-union basis in the form of a National Industrial Congress. But the economic disaster of the panic nipped it in the bud just as it cut off the life of the overwhelming majority of the existing labor organizations. Another attempt to get together on a national basis was made in the National Labor Congress at Pittsburgh in 1876. But those who responded were not interested in trade unionism and, mirroring the prevailing labor sentiment during the long years of depressions, had only politics on their mind, greenback or socialist. As neither greenbacker nor socialist would meet the other half-way, the attempt naturally came to naught.

Greenbackism was popular with the working people during the depressed seventies because it now meant to them primarily currency inflation and a rise of prices and, consequently, industrial prosperity—not the phantastic scheme of the National Labor Union. Yet in the Presidential election of 1876 the Greenback party candidate, Peter Cooper, the well known manufacturer and philanthropist, drew only a poor 100,000, which came practically from the rural districts only. It was not until the great strikes of 1877 had brought in their train a political labor upheaval that the greenback movement assumed a formidable form.

The strikes of 1877, which on account of the wide area affected, the degree of violence displayed, and the amount of life and property lost, impressed contemporaries as being nothing short of social revolution, were precipitated by a general ten per cent. reduction in wages on the three trunk lines running West, the Pennsylvania, the Baltimore & Ohio, and the New York Central, in June and July 1877. This reduction came on top of an earlier ten per cent. reduction after the panic. The railway men were practically unorganized so that the steadying influence of previous organization was totally lacking in the critical situation of unrest which the newly announced wage reduction created. One must take also into account that in the four terrible years which elapsed since the panic, America had developed a new type of a man—the tramp—who naturally gravitated towards places where trouble was expected.

The first outbreak occurred at Martinsburg, West Virginia, on July 17, the day after the ten per cent. re-

duction had gone into effect. The strike spread like
wildfire over the adjacent sections of the Baltimore &
Ohio road, the strikers assuming absolute control at
many points. The militia was either unwilling or powerless to cope with the violence. In Baltimore, where in the
interest of public safety all the freight trains had stopped
running, two companies of militia were beleaguered by a
mob to prevent their being dispatched to Cumberland,
where the strikers were in control. Order was restored
only when Federal troops arrived.

But these occurrences fade into insignificance when
compared with the destructive effects of the strike on the
Pennsylvania in and around Pittsburgh. The situation
there was aggravated by a hatred of the Pennsylvania
railway corporation shared by nearly all residents on
the ground of an alleged rate discrimination against the
city. The Pittsburgh militia fraternized with the strikers, and when 600 troops which arrived from Philadelphia
attempted to restore order and killed about twenty riot-
ers, they were besieged in a roundhouse by a furious mob.
In the battle the railway yards were set on fire. Damages
amounting to about $5,000,000 were caused. The be-
sieged militia men finally gained egress and retreated
fighting rear-guard actions. At last order was restored
by patrols of citizens. The strike spread also to the Erie
railway and caused disturbances in several places, but not
nearly of the same serious nature as on the Baltimore
& Ohio and the Pennsylvania. The other places to which
the strike spread were Toledo, Louisville, Chicago, St.
Louis, and San Francisco.

The strikes failed in every case but their moral effect
was enormous. The general public still retained a fresh
memory of the Commune of Paris of 1871 and feared for

the foundations of the established order. The wage earners, on the other hand, felt that the strikers had not been fairly dealt with. It was on this intense labor discontent that the greenback agitation fed and grew.

Whereas in 1876 the greenback labor vote was negligible, notwithstanding the exhortations by many of the former trade union leaders who turned greenback agitators, now, following the great strikes, greenbackism became primarily a labor movement. Local Greenback-Labor parties were being organized everywhere and a national Greenback-Labor party was not far behind in forming. The continued industrial depression was a decisive factor, the winter of 1877–1878 marking perhaps the point of its greatest intensity. Naturally the greenback movement was growing apace. One of the notable successes in the spring of 1878 was the election of Terence V. Powderly, later Grand Master Workman of the Knights of Labor, as mayor of Scranton, Pennsylvania.

The Congressional election in the autumn of 1878 marked the zenith of the movement. The aggregate greenback vote cast in the election exceeded a million, and fourteen Representatives were sent to Congress. In New England the movement was strong enough to poll almost a third of the total vote in Maine, over 8 per cent. of the total vote in both Connecticut and New Hampshire, and from 4 to 6 per cent. in the other States. In Maine the greenbackers elected 32 members of the upper house and 151 members of the lower house and one Congressman, Thompson Murch of Rochland, who was secretary of the National Granite Cutters' Union. However, the bulk of the vote in that State was obviously agricultural. In Massachusetts, the situation was dominated by General Benjamin F. Butler, lifelong Republican politician, who had succeeded in getting the Democratic nomination for governor and was endorsed by the Greenback convention. He received a large vote but was defeated for office.

But just as the Greenback-Labor movement was assuming promising proportions a change for the better in the industrial situation cut under the very roots of its existence. In addition, one month after the election of 1878, its principal issue disappeared. January 1, 1879, was the date fixed by the act for resumption of redemption of greenbacks in gold and on December 17, 1878, the premium on gold disappeared. From that day on, the greenback became a dead issue.

Another factor of great importance was the large increase in the volume of the currency. In 1881 the currency, which had averaged about $725,000,000 for the years 1876–1878, reached over $1,111,000,000. Under these conditions, all that remained available to the platform-makers and propagandists of the party was their opposition to the so-called "monopolistic" national banks with their control over currency and to the refunding of the bonded debt of the government.

The disappearance of the financial issue snapped the threads which had held together the farmer and the wage-worker. So long as depression continued, the issue was financial and the two had, as they thought, a common enemy—the banker. The financial issue once settled, or at least suspended, the object of the attack by labor became the employer, and that of the attack by the farmer—the railway corporation and the warehouse man. Prosperity had mitigated the grievances of both classes, but while the farmer still had a great deal to expect from politics in the form of state regulation of railway rates, the wage earners' struggle now turned entirely economic and not political.

In California, as in the Eastern industrial States, the railway strikes of 1877 precipitated a political movement. California had retained gold as currency throughout the entire period of paper money, and the labor movement at no time had accepted the greenback platform. The political issue after 1877 was racial, not financial, and the weapon was not merely the ballot, but also "direct action"—violence. The anti-Chinese agitation in California, culminating as it did in the Exclusion Law passed by Congress in 1882, was doubtless the most important single factor in the history of American labor, for without it the entire country might have been overrun by Mongolian labor and the labor movement might have become a conflict of races instead of one of classes.[1]

The seventies witnessed another of those recurring attempts of consumers' coöperation already noticed in the forties and sixties. This time the movement was organized by the "Sovereigns of Industry," a secret order, founded at Worcester, Massachusetts, in 1874 by one William H. Earle. The spirit of the Order was entirely peaceful and unobtrusive as expressed in the first paragraph of the Declaration of Purposes which reads as follows:

"The Order of the Sovereigns of Industry is an association of the industrial or laboring classes, without regard to race, sex, color, nationality, or occupation; not founded for the purpose of waging any war of aggression upon any other class, or for fostering any antagonism

[1] The National Labor Union came out against Chinese immigration in 1869, when the issue was brought home to the Eastern wage earners following the importation by a shoe manufacturer in North Adams, Massachusetts, of Chinese strike breakers.

of labor against capital, or of arraying the poor against the rich; but for mutual assistance in self-improvement and self-protection."

The scheme of organization called for a local council including members from the town or district, a state council, comprising representatives from the local councils and a National Council in which the States were represented. The president of the National Council was the founder of the Order, William H. Earle.

Success accompanied the efforts of the promoters of the Sovereigns of Industry for a few years. The total membership in 1875–1876 was 40,000, of whom seventy-five per cent. were in New England and forty-three per cent. in Massachusetts. Though the Order extended into other States and even reached the territories, its chief strength always remained in New England and the Middle States. During the last period of its existence a national organ was published at Washington, but the Order does not appear to have gained a foothold in any of the more Southern sections of the country.

In 1875, 101 local councils reported as having some method of supplying members with goods, 46 of whom operated stores. The largest store belonged to the council at Springfield, Massachusetts, which in 1875 built the "Sovereign Block" at a cost of $35,500. In his address at the fourth annual session in Washington, President Earle stated that the store in Springfield led all the others with sales amounting to $119,000 for the preceding year. About one-half of the councils failed to report, but at the Congress of 1876 President Earle estimated the annual trade at $3,000,000.

Much enthusiasm accompanied the progress of the movement. The hall in "Sovereign Block" at Springfield was dedicated amid such jubilation as marks an event thought to be the forerunner of a new era. There is indeed a certain pathos in the high hopes expressed in the Address of Dedication by President Earle, for, though the Order continued to thrive until 1878, shortly after a decline began, and dissolution was its fate in 1880.

The failure of the Sovereigns marked the latest attempt on a large scale [1] to innoculate the American workingmen with the sort of coöperative spirit which proved so successful in England.[2]

[1] There were many coöperative stores in the eighties and a concerted effort to duplicate the venture of the Sovereigns was attempted as late as 1919 under the pressure of the soaring cost of living.

[2] Where Consumers' Coöperation has worked under most favorable conditions as in England, its achievements have been all that its most ardent champions could have desired. Such is the picture presented by Mr. and Mrs. Sidney Webb in the following glowing terms:

"The organization of industry by Associations of Consumers offers, as far as it goes, a genuine alternative to capitalist ownership, because it supersedes the capitalist power, whether individual or joint-stock, alike in the control of the instruments of production by which the community lives, and in the absorption of the profits, which otherwise support a capitalist class. The ownership and control are vested in, and the profits are distributed among, the whole community of consumers, irrespective of their industrial wealth. Through the device of dividend on purchases the Coöperative Movement maintains an open democracy, through the control of this democracy of consumers it has directly or indirectly kept down prices, and protected the wage-earning class from exploitation by the Credit System and from the extortions of monopolist traders and speculators. By this same device on purchases, and the automatic accumulation of part of the profit in the capital of each society and in that of the Wholesales, it has demonstratedly added to the personal wealth of the manual working class, and has, alike in Great Britain, and in other countries, afforded both a valuable financial reserve to the wage-earners against all emergencies and an instrument for their elevation from the penury to which competition is always depressing them. By making possible the upgrowth of great business enterprises in working class hands, the Coöperative Movement has, without divorcing them from their fellows, given to thousands of the manual workers both administrative experience and a well-grounded confidence; and has thus enabled them to take a fuller part in political and social life than would otherwise have been probable."—*New Statesman,* May 30, 1916. "Special Supplement on the Coöperative Movement."

Indeed the success of the consumer's coöperative movement in European countries has been marvellous, even measured by bare

This failure of distributive coöperation to gain the strong and lasting foothold in this country that it has abroad has been accounted for in various ways by different writers. Great emphasis has been laid upon the lack of capital, the lack of suitable legislation on the subject of coöperation, the mutual isolation of the educated and wage-earning classes, the lack of business ability among wage earners, and the altogether too frequent venality and corruption among coöperators.

Probably the lack of adequate leadership has played as important a part as any. It is peculiar to America that the wage earner of exceptional ability can easily find a way for escaping into the class of independent producers or even employers of labor. The American trade union movement has suffered much less from this difficulty. The trade unions are fighting organizations; they demand the sort of leader who is of a combative spirit, who possesses the organizing ability and the "personal magnetism" to keep his men in line; and for this kind of ability the business world offers no particular demand. On the other hand, the qualifications which go to make a successful manager of a coöperative store, namely, steadiness, conservatism of judgment, attention to detail and business punctuality always will be in great demand in the business world. Hence, when no barrier is interposed in the form of preëmpted opportunities or class bias, the exceptional workingman who possesses these qualifications will likely desert his class and set up in business for him-

figures. In all Europe in 1914, there were about 9,000,000 coöperators of whom one-third lived in Great Britain and not less than two and a half millions in Germany. In England and Scotland alone, the 1400 stores and two Wholesale Coöperative Societies controlled in 1914 about 420 million dollars of retail distributive trade and employed nearly 50,000 operatives in processes of production in their own workshops and factories.

self.   In England, fortunately for the coöperative movement, such an escape is very difficult.

The failure of consumers' coöperation in America was
helped also by two other peculiarly American conditions.
European economists, when speaking of the working class,
assume generally that it is fixed in residence and contrast
it with capital, which they say is fluid as between city
and city and even between country and country.   American labor, however, native as well as immigrant, is probably more mobile than capital; for, tradition and habit
which keep the great majority of European wage earners
in the place where their fathers and forefathers had lived
before them are generally absent in this country, except
perhaps in parts of New England and the South.   It is
therefore natural that the coöperative spirit, which after
all is but an enlarged and more generalized form of the old
spirit of neighborliness and mutual trust, should have
failed to develop to its full strength in America.

Another condition fatal to the development of the co-
operative spirit is the racial heterogeneity of the American wage-earning class, which separates it into mutually
isolated groups even as the social classes of England
and Scotland are separated by class spirit.   As a result,
we find a want of mutual trust which depends so much on
"consciousness of kind."   This is further aggravated by
competition and a continuous displacement in industry
of nationalities of a high standard of living by those of a
lower one.   This conflict of nationalities, which lies also
at the root of the closed shop policy of many of the
American trade unions, is probably the most effective
barrier that there is to a widespread growth of the
coöperative spirit among American wage earners.   This
is further hindered by other national characteristics

which more or less pervade all classes of society, namely, the traditional individualism—the heritage of puritanism and the pioneer days, and the emphasis upon earning capacity with a corresponding aversion to thrift.

CHAPTER 3

THE BEGINNING OF THE KNIGHTS OF LABOR
AND OF THE AMERICAN FEDERATION
OF LABOR

With the practical disintegration of the organized labor movement in the seventies, two nuclei held together and showed promise of future growth. One was the "Noble Order of the Knights of Labor" and the other a small trade union movement grouped around the International Cigar Makers' Union.

The "Noble Order of the Knights of Labor," while it first became important in the labor movement after 1873, was founded in 1869 by Uriah Smith Stephens, a tailor who had been educated for the ministry, as a secret organization. Secrecy was adopted as a protection against persecutions by employers.

The principles of the Order were set forth by Stephens in the secret ritual. "Open and public association having failed after a struggle of centuries to protect or advance the interest of labor, we have lawfully constituted this Assembly," and "in using this power of organized effort and coöperation, we but imitate the example of capital heretofore set in numberless instances;" for, "in all the multifarious branches of trade, capital has its combinations, and, whether intended or not, it crushes the manly hopes of labor and tramples poor humanity into the dust." However, "we mean no conflict with legitimate enterprise, no antagonism to necessary capital." The remedy consists first in work of education: "We mean to create a healthy public opinion on the subject of labor (the only creator of values or capital) and the justice of its receiving a full, just share of the values or capital it has created." The next remedy was legislation: "We shall, with all our strength, support laws made to harmonize the interests of labor and capital, for labor alone gives life and value to capital, and also those laws which tend to lighten the exhaustiveness of toil." Next in order were mutual benefits. "We shall use every lawful and honorable means to procure and retain employ for one another, coupled with a just and fair remuneration, and, should accident or misfortune befall one of our number, render such aid as lies within our power to give, without inquiring his country or his creed."

For nine years the Order remained a secret organization and showed but a slow growth. In 1878 it was forced to abolish secrecy. The public mind was rendered uneasy by the revolutionary uprising of workingmen of Paris who set up the famous "Commune of Paris" of 1871, by the destructive great railway strikes in this country in 1877 and, lastly, by a wave of criminal disorders in the anthracite coal mining region in Eastern Pennsylvania,[1] and became only too prone to attribute revolutionary and criminal intents to any labor organization that cloaked itself in secrecy. Simultaneously with coming out into the open, the Knights adopted a new program, called the Preamble of the Knights of Labor, in place of

[1] After the defeat of a strong anthracite miners' union in 1869, which was an open organization, the fight against the employers was carried on by a secret organization known as the Molly Maguires, which used the method of terrorism and assassination. It was later exposed and many were sentenced and executed.

the vague Secret Ritual which hitherto served as the authoritative expression of aims.

This Preamble recites how "wealth," with its development, has become so aggressive that "unless checked" it "will inevitably lead to the pauperisation and hopeless degradation of the toiling masses." Hence, if the toilers are "to enjoy the blessings of life," they must organize "every department of productive industry" in order to "check" the power of wealth and to put a stop to "unjust accumulation." The battle cry in this fight must be "moral worth not wealth, the true standard of individual and national greatness." As the "action" of the toilers ought to be guided by "knowledge," it is necessary to know "the true condition of the producing masses"; therefore, the Order demands "from the various governments the establishment of bureaus of labor statistics." Next in order comes the "establishment of coöperative institutions productive and distributive." Union of all trades, "education," and producers' coöperation remained forever after the cardinal points in the Knights of Labor philosophy and were steadily referred to as "First Principles," namely principles bequeathed to the Order by Uriah Stephens and the other "Founders."[1]

[1] The Preamble further provides that the Order will stand for the reservation of all lands for actual settlers; the "abrogation of all laws that do not bear equally upon capital and labor, the removal of unjust technicalities, delays, and discriminations in the administration of justice, and the adopting of measures providing for the health and safety of those engaged in mining, manufacturing, or building pursuits"; the enactment of a weekly pay law, a mechanics' lien law, and a law prohibiting child labor under fourteen years of age; the abolition of the contract system on national, state, and municipal work, and of the system of leasing out convicts; equal pay for equal work for both sexes; reduction of hours of labor to eight per day; "the substitution of arbitration for strikes, whenever and wherever employers and employees are willing to meet on equitable grounds"; the establishment of "a purely national circulating medium based upon the faith and resources of the nation, issued

These idealistic "First Principles" found an ardent champion in Terence V. Powderly, a machinist by trade and twice mayor of Scranton, Pennsylvania, on a labor ticket, who succeeded Stephens in 1878 to the headship of the Order. Powderly bore unmistakably the stamp of this sort of idealism throughout all the time when he was the foremost labor leader in the country. Unlike Samuel Gompers, who came to supplant him about 1890, he was foreign to that spirit of combative unionism which accepts the wage system but concentrates on a struggle to wrest concessions from the employers. Even when circumstances which were largely beyond his control made Powderly a strike leader on a huge scale, his heart lay elsewhere—in circumventing the wage system by opening to the worker an escape into self-employment through coöperation.

Producers' coöperation, then, was the ambitious program by which the Order of the Knights of Labor expected to lead the American wage-earning class out of the bondage of the wage system into the Canaan of self-employment. Thus the Order was the true successor of the coöperative movement in the forties and sixties. Its motto was "Coöperation of the Order, by the Order, and for the Order." Not scattered local initiative, but the Order as a whole was to carry on the work. The plan resembled the Rochdale system of England in that it proposed to start with an organization of consumers—the large and ever-growing membership of the Order. But it departed radically from the English prototype in that instead of setting out to save money for the consumer,

directly to the people, without the intervention of any system of banking corporations, which money shall be a legal tender in payment of all debts, public or private".

it primarily aimed to create a market for the productive establishments which were to follow. Consumers' coöperation was to be but a stepping stone to producers' self-employment. Eventually when the Order had grown to include nearly all useful members of society—so the plan contemplated—it would control practically the whole market and coöperative production would become the rule rather than the exception. So far, therefore, as "First Principles" went, the Order was not an instrument of the "class struggle," but an association of idealistic coöperators. It was this pure idealism which drew to the Order of the Knights of Labor the sympathetic interest of writers on social subjects and university teachers, then unfortunately too few in number, like Dr. Richard T. Ely [1] and President John Bascom of Wisconsin.

The other survival in the seventies of the labor movement of the sixties, which has already been mentioned, namely the trade union movement grouped around the Cigar Makers' Union, was neither so purely American in its origin as the Knights of Labor nor so persistently idealistic. On the contrary, its first membership was foreign and its program, as we shall see, became before long primarily opportunist and "pragmatic." The training school for this opportunistic trade unionism was the socialist movement during the sixties and seventies, particularly the American branch of the International Workingmen's Association, the "First *Internationale*," which was founded by Karl Marx in London in 1864. The conception of *economic* labor organization which was ad-

[1] Dr. Ely in his pioneer work, *The Labor Movement in America*, published in 1886, showed a most genuine sympathy for the idealistic strivings and gropings of labor for a better social order. He even advised some of his pupils at the Johns Hopkins University to join the Knights of Labor in order to gain a better understanding of the labor movement.

vanced by the *Internationale* in a socialistic formulation
underwent in the course of years a process of change:
On the one hand, through constant conflict with the rival
conception of *political* labor organization urged by
American followers of the German socialist, Ferdinand
Lassalle, and on the other hand, through contact with
American reality. Out of that double contact emerged
the trade unionism of the American Federation of Labor.

The *Internationale* is generally reputed to have been
organized by Karl Marx for the propaganda of international socialism. As a matter of fact, its starting point
was the practical effort of British trade union leaders to
organize the workingmen of the Continent and to prevent the importation of Continental strike-breakers.
That Karl Marx wrote its *Inaugural Address* was merely
incidental. It chanced that what he wrote was acceptable
to the British unionists rather than the draft of an address representing the views of Giuseppe Mazzini, the
leader of the "New Italy" and the "New Europe," which
was submitted to them at the same time and advocated
elaborate plans of coöperation. Marx emphasized the
class solidarity of labor against Mazzini's harmony of
capital and labor. He did this by reciting what British
labor had done through the Rochdale system of coöperation without the help of capitalists and what the British
Parliament had done in enacting the ten-hour law of 1847
against the protest of capitalists. Now that British trade
unionists in 1864 were demanding the right of suffrage
and laws to protect their unions, it followed that Marx
merely stated their demands when he affirmed the independent economic and political organization of labor in
all lands. His *Inaugural Address* was a trade union
document, not a *Communist Manifesto*. Indeed not until

Bakunin and his following of anarchists had nearly captured the organization in the years 1869 to 1872 did the program of socialism become the leading issue.

The philosophy of the *Internationale* at the period of its ascendency was based on the economic organization of the working class in trade unions. These must precede the political seizure of the government by labor. Then, when the workingmen's party should achieve control, it would be able to build up successively the socialist state on the foundation of a sufficient number of existing trade unions.

This conception differed widely from the teaching of Ferdinand Lassalle. Lassallean socialism was born in 1862 with Lassalle's *Open Letter* to a workingmen's committee in Leipzig. It sprang from his antagonism to Schultze-Delizsch's [1] system of voluntary coöperation. In Lassalle's eagerness to condemn the idea of the harmony of capital and labor, which lay at the basis of Schultze's scheme for coöperation, he struck at the same time a blow against all forms of non-political organization of wage earners. Perhaps the fact that he was ignorant of the British trade unions accounts for his insufficient appreciation of trade unionism. But no matter what the cause may have been, to Lassalle there was but one means of solving the labor problem—political action. When political control was finally achieved, the labor party, with the aid of state credit, would build up a network of coöperative societies into which eventually all industry would pass.

In short, the distinction between the ideas of the *Internationale* and of Lassalle consisted in the fact that the

[1] Schultze-Delizsch was a German thinker and practical reformer of the liberal school.

former advocated trade unionism prior to and underlying political organization, while the latter considered a political victory as the basis of socialism. These antagonistic starting points are apparent at the very beginning of American socialism as well as in the trade unionism and socialism of succeeding years.

Two distinct phases can be seen in the history of the *Internationale* in America. During the first phase, which began in 1866 and lasted until 1870, the *Internationale* had no important organization of its own on American soil, but tried to establish itself through affiliation with the National Labor Union. The inducement held out to the latter was of a practical nature, the international regulation of immigration. During the second phase the *Internationale* had its "sections" in nearly every large city of the country, centering in New York and Chicago, and the practical trade union part of its work receded before its activity on behalf of the propaganda of socialism.

These "sections," with a maximum membership which probably never exceeded a thousand, nearly all foreigners, became a preparatory school in trade union leadership for many of the later organizers and leaders of the American Federation of Labor: for example, Adolph Strasser, the German cigar maker, whose organization became the new model in trade unionism, and P. J. McGuire, the American-born carpenter, who founded the Brotherhood of Carpenters and Joiners and who was for many years the secretary-treasurer of the American Federation of Labor.

Fate had decreed that these sections of a handful of immigrants should play for a time high-sounding parts in the world labor movement. When, at the World Congress of the International Workingmen's Association at the Hague in 1872, the anarchist faction led by Bakunin had shown such strength that Marx and his socialist faction deemed it wise to move the General Council out of mischief's way, they removed it to New York and entrusted its powers into the hands of the faithful German Marxians on this side of the Atlantic. This spelled the end of the *Internationale* as a world organization, but enormously increased the stakes of the factional fights within the handful of American Internationalists. The organization of the workers into trade unions, the *Internationale's* first principle, was forgotten in the heat of intemperate struggles for empty honors and powerless offices. On top of that, with the panic of 1873 and the ensuing prolonged depression, the political drift asserted itself in socialism as it had in the labor movement in general and the movement, erstwhile devoted primarily to organization of trade unions, entered, urged on by the Lassalleans, into a series of political campaigns somewhat successful at first but soon succumbing to the inevitable fate of all amateurish attempts. Upon men of Strasser's practical mental grasp these petty tempests in the melting pot could only produce an impression of sheer futility, and he turned to trade unionism as the only activity worth his while. Strasser had been elected president of the Cigar Makers' International Union in 1877, in the midst of a great strike in New York against the tenement-house system.

The president of the local New York union of cigar makers was at the time Samuel Gompers, a young man of twenty-seven, who was born in England and came to America in 1862. In his endeavor to build up a model for the "new" unionism and in his almost uninterrupted headship of that movement for forty years is indicated Gompers' truly representative character. Born of Dutch-Jewish parents in England in 1850, he typifies the cosmopolitan origins of American unionism. His early contact in the union of his trade with men like Strasser, upon whom the ideas of Marx and the International Workingmen's Association had left an indelible stamp, and his thorough study of Marx gave him that grounding both in idealism and class consciousness which has produced many strong leaders of American unions and saved them from defection to other interests. Aggressive and uncompromising in a perpetual fight for the strongest possible position and power of trade unions, but always strong for collective agreements with the opposing employers, he displays the business tactics of organized labor. At the head of an organization which denies itself power over its constituent unions, he has brought and held together the most widely divergent and often antagonistic unions, while permitting each to develop and even to change its character to fit the changing industrial conditions.

The dismal failure of the strike against the tenement house system in cigar making brought home to both Strasser and Gompers the weakness of the plan of organization of their union as well as that of American trade unions in general. They consequently resolved to rebuild their union upon the pattern of the British unions, although they firmly intended that it should remain a militant organization. The change involved, first, complete authority over the local unions in the hands of the international officers; second, an increase in the membership dues for the purpose of building up a large fund; and, third, the adoption of a far-reaching benefit system in order to assure stability to the organization. This was accomplished at the convention held in August, 1879. This convention simultaneously adopted the British idea of the "equalization of funds," which gave the international officers the power to order a well-to-do local union to transfer a portion of its funds to another local union in financial straits. With the various modifications of the feature of "equalization of funds," the system of government in the Cigar Makers' International Union was later used as a model by the other national and international trade unions.

As Strasser and men of his ilk grew more and more absorbed in the practical problems of the everyday struggle of the wage-earners for better conditions of employment, the socialistic portion of their original philosophy kept receding further and further into the background until they arrived at pure trade unionism. But their trade unionism differed vastly from the "native" American trade unionism of their time, which still hankered for the haven of producers' coöperation. The philosophy which these new leaders developed might be termed a philosophy of pure wage-consciousness. It signified a labor movement reduced to an opportunistic basis, accepting the existence of capitalism and having for its object the enlarging of the bargaining power of the wage earner in the sale of his labor. Its opportunism was instrumental—its idealism was home and family and individual betterment. It also implied an attitude of aloofness from all those movements which aspire to replace the wage system by coöperation, whether voluntary or subsidized by government, whether greenbackism, socialism, or anarchism.

Perhaps the most concise definition of this philosophy

is to be found in Strasser's testimony before the Senate Committee on Education and Labor in 1883:

"*Q.* You are seeking to improve home matters first?

"*A.* Yes, sir, I look first to the trade I represent; I look first to cigars, to the interests of men who employ me to represent their interest.

"*Chairman:* I was only asking you in regard to your ultimate ends.

"*Witness:* We have no ultimate ends. We are going on from day to day. We are fighting only for immediate objects—objects that can be realized in a few years.

"By Mr. Call: *Q.* You want something better to eat and to wear, and better houses to live in?

"*A.* Yes, we want to dress better and to live better, and become better citizens generally.

"*The Chairman:* I see that you are a little sensitive lest it should be thought that you are a mere theoriser, I do not look upon you in that light at all.

"*The Witness:* Well, we say in our constitution that we are opposed to theorists, and I have to represent the organization here. We are all practical men."

Another offshoot of the same Marxian *Internationale* were the "Chicago Anarchists." [1] The *Internationale*, as we saw, emphasized trade unionism as the first step in the direction of socialism, in opposition to the political socialism of Lassalle, which ignored the trade union and would start with a political party outright. Shorn of its socialistic futurity this philosophy became non-political "business" unionism; but, when combined with a strong revolutionary spirit, it became a non-political revolutionary unionism, or syndicalism.

The organization of those industrial revolutionaries was called the International Working People's Associa-

[1] The Anarchists who were tried and executed after the Haymarket Square bomb in Chicago in May, 1886. See below, 91-93.

tion, also known as the "Black" or anarchist International, which was formed at Pittsburgh in 1883. Like
the old *Internationale* it busied itself with forming trade
unions, but insisted that they conform to a revolutionary
model. Such a "model" trade union was the Federation
of Metal Workers of America, which was organized in
1885. It said in its Declaration of Principles that the
entire abolition of the present system of society can alone
emancipate the workers, but under no consideration
should they resort to politics; "our organization should
be a school to educate its members for the new condition
of society, when the workers will regulate their own
affairs without any interference by the few. Since the
emancipation of the productive classes must come by
their own efforts, it is unwise to meddle in present politics.
. . . All *direct* struggles of the laboring masses have our
fullest sympathy." Alongside the revolutionary trade
unions were workers' armed organizations ready to usher
in the new order by force. "By force," recited the Pittsburgh Manifesto of the Black International, "our an-
cestors liberated themselves from political oppression, by
force their children will have to liberate themselves from
ecenomic bondage. It is, therefore, your right, it is your
duty, says Jefferson,—to arms!"

The following ten years were to decide whether the
leadership of the American labor movement was to be
with the "practical men of the trade unions" or with
the coöperative idealists of the Knights of Labor.

CHAPTER 4

REVIVAL AND UPHEAVAL, 1879-1887

With the return of business prosperity in 1879, the labor movement revived. The first symptom of the upward trend was a rapid multiplication of city federations of organized trades, variously known as trade councils, amalgamated trade and labor unions, trades assemblies, and the like. Practically all of these came into existence after 1879, since hardly any of the "trades' assemblies" of the sixties had survived the depression.

As was said above, the national trade unions existed during the sixties and seventies in only about thirty trades. Eighteen of these had either retained a nucleus during the seventies or were first formed during that decade. The following is a list of the national unions in existence in 1880 with the year of formation: Typographical (1850), Hat Finishers (1854), Iron Molders (1859), Locomotive Engineers (1863), Cigar Makers (1864), Bricklayers and Masons (1865), Silk and Fur Hat Finishers (1866), Railway Conductors (1868), Coopers (1870), German-American Typographia (1873), Locomotive Firemen (1873), Horseshoers (1874), Furniture Workers (1873), Iron and Steel Workers (1876), Granite Cutters (1877), Lake Seamen (1878), Cotton Mill Spinners (1878), New England Boot and Shoe Lasters (1879).

In 1880 the Western greenbottle blowers' national union was established; in 1881 the national unions of boiler makers and carpenters; in 1882, plasterers and metal workers; in 1883, tailors, lithographers, wood carvers, railroad brakemen, and silk workers.

An illustration of the rapid growth in trade union membership during this period is given in the following figures: the bricklayers' union had 303 in 1880; 1558 in 1881; 6848 in 1882; 9193 in 1883. The typographical union had 5968 members in 1879; 6520 in 1880; 7931 in 1881; 10,439 in 1882; 12,273 in 1883. The total trade union membership in the country, counting the three railway organizations and those organized only locally, amounted to between 200,000 and 225,000 in 1883 and probably was not below 300,000 in the beginning of 1885.

A distinguishing characteristic of the trade unions of this time was the predominance in them of the foreign element. The Illinois Bureau of Labor describes the ethnical composition of the trade unions of that State during 1886, and states that 21 per cent. were American, 33 per cent. German, 19 per cent. Irish, 10 per cent. British other than Irish, 12 per cent. Scandinavian, and the Poles, Bohemians, and Italians formed about 5 per cent. The strong predominance of the foreign element in American trade unions should not appear unusual, since, owing to the breakdown of the apprenticeship system, the United States had been drawing its supply of skilled labor from abroad.

The Order of the Knights of Labor, despite its "First Principles" based on the coöperative ideal, was soon forced to make concessions to a large element of its membership which was pressing for strikes. With the advent of prosperity, the Order expanded, although the Knights of Labor played but a subordinate part in the labor movement of the early eighties. The membership was

20,151 in 1879; 28,136 in 1880; 19,422 in 1881; 42,517 in 1882; 51,914 in 1883; showing a steady and rapid growth, with the exception of the year 1881. But these figures are decidedly deceptive as a means of measuring the strength of the Order, for the membership fluctuated widely; so that in the year 1883, when it reached 50,000 no less than one-half of this number passed in and out of the organization during the year. The enormous fluctuation, while reducing the economic strength of the Order, brought large masses of people under its influence and prepared the ground for the upheaval in the middle of the eighties. It also brought the Order to the attention of the public press. The labor press gave the Order great publicity, but the Knights did not rely on gratuitous newspaper publicity. They set to work a host of lecturers, who held public meetings throughout the country adding recruits and advertising the Order.

The most important Knights of Labor strike of this period was the telegraphers' strike in 1883. The telegraphers had a national organization in 1870, which soon collapsed. In 1882 they again organized on a national basis and affiliated with the Order as District Assembly 45.[1] The strike was declared on June 19, 1883, against all commercial telegraph companies in the country, among which the Western Union, with about 4000 operators, was by far the largest. The demands were one day's rest in seven, an eight-hour day shift and a seven-hour night shift, and a general increase of 15 per cent. in wages. The public and a large portion of the press gave their sympathy to the strikers, not so much on account of the oppressed condition of the telegraphers as of the general

[1] See the next chapter for the scheme of organization followed by the Order.

hatred that prevailed against Jay Gould, who then controlled the Western Union Company. This strike was the first in the eighties to call the attention of the general American public to the existence of a labor question, and received considerable attention at the hands of the Senate Committee on Education and Labor. By the end of July, over a month after the beginning of the strike, the men who escaped the blacklist went back to work on the old terms.

From 1879 till 1882 the labor movement was typical of a period of rising prices. It was practically restricted to skilled workmen, who organized to wrest from employers still better conditions than those which prosperity would have given under individual bargaining. The movement was essentially opportunistic and displayed no particular class feeling and no revolutionary tendencies. The solidarity of labor was not denied by the trade unions, but they did not try to reduce the idea to practice: each trade coped more or less successfully with its own employers. Even the Knights of Labor, the organization *par excellence* of the solidarity of labor, was at this time, in so far as practical efforts went, merely a faint echo of the trade unions.

But the situation radically changed during the depression of 1884-1885. The unskilled and the semi-skilled, affected as they were by wage reductions and unemployment even in a larger measure than the skilled, were drawn into the movement. Labor organizations assumed the nature of a real class movement. The idea of the solidarity of labor ceased to be merely verbal and took on life! General strikes, sympathetic strikes, nation-wide boycotts and nation-wide political movements became the order of the day. The effects of an unusually large immigration joined hands with the depression. The eighties were the banner decade of the entire century for immigration. The aggregate number of immigrants arriving was 5,246,613—two and a half millions larger than during the seventies and one million and a half larger than during the nineties. The eighties witnessed the highest tide of immigration from Great Britain and the North of Europe and the beginning of the tide of South and East European immigration.

However, the depression of 1883-1885 had one redeeming feature by which it was distinguished from other depressions. With falling prices, diminishing margins of profit, and decreasing wages, the amount of employment was not materially diminished. Times continued hard during 1885, a slight improvement showing itself only during the last months of the year. The years 1886 and 1887 were a period of gradual recovery, and normal conditions may be said to have returned about the middle of 1887. Except in New England, the old wages, which had been reduced during the bad years, were won again by the spring of 1887.

The year 1884 was one of decisive failure in strikes. They were practically all directed against reductions in wages and for the right of organization. The most conspicuous strikes were those of the Fall River spinners, the Troy stove mounters, the Cincinnati cigar makers and the Hocking Valley coal miners.

The failure of strikes brought into use the other weapon of labor—the boycott. But not until the latter part of 1884, when the failure of the strike as a weapon became apparent, did the boycott assume the nature of an epidemic. The boycott movement was a truly national one, affecting the South and the Far West as well as the

East and Middle West. The number of boycotts during 1885 was nearly seven times as large as during 1884. Nearly all of the boycotts either originated with, or were taken up by, the Knights of Labor.

The strike again came into prominence in the latter half of 1885. This coincided with the beginning of an upward trend in general business conditions. The strikes of 1885, even more than those of the preceding year, were spontaneous outbreaks of unorganized masses.

The frequent railway strikes were a characteristic feature of the labor movement in 1885. Most notable was the Gould railway strike in March, 1885. On February 26, a cut of 10 per cent. was ordered in the wages of the shopmen of the Wabash road. A similar reduction had been made in October, 1884, on the Missouri, Kansas & Texas. Strikes occurred on the two roads, one on February 27 and the other March 9, and the strikers were joined by the men on the third Gould road, the Missouri Pacific, at all points where the two lines touched, making altogether over 4500 men on strike. The train service personnel, that is, the locomotive engineers, firemen, brakemen, and conductors, supported the strikers and to this fact more than to any other was due their speedy victory. The wages were restored and the strikers re-employed. But six months later this was followed by a second strike. The road, now in the hands of a receiver, reduced the force of shopmen at Moberly, Missouri, to the lowest possible limit, which virtually meant a lockout of the members of the Knights of Labor in direct violation of the conditions of settlement of the preceding strike. The General Executive Board of the Knights, after a futile attempt to have a conference with the receiver, declared a boycott on Wabash rolling stock.

This order, had it been carried out, would have affected over 20,000 miles of railway and would have equalled the dimensions of the great railway strike of 1877. But Jay Gould would not risk a general strike on his lines at this time. According to an appointment made between him and the executive board of the Knights of Labor, a conference was held between that board and the managers of the Missouri Pacific and the Wabash railroads, at which he threw his influence in favor of making concessions to the men. He assured the Knights that in all troubles he wanted the men to come directly to him, that he believed in labor organizations and in the arbitration of all difficulties and that he "would always endeavor to do what was right." The Knights demanded the discharge of all new men hired in the Wabash shops since the beginning of the lockout, the reinstatement of all discharged men, the leaders being given priority, and an assurance that no discrimination against the members of the Order would be made in the future. A settlement was finally made at another conference, and the receiver of the Wabash road agreed, under pressure by Jay Gould, to issue an order conceding the demands of the Knights of Labor.

The significance of the second Wabash strike in the history of railway strikes was that the railway brotherhoods (engineers, firemen, brakemen, and conductors), in contrast with their conduct during the first Wabash strike, now refused to lend any aid to the striking shopmen, although many of the members were also Knights of Labor.

But far more important was the effect of the strike upon the general labor movement. Here a labor organization for the first time dealt on an equal footing with probably the most powerful capitalist in the country. It forced Jay Gould to recognize it as a power equal to himself, a fact which he conceded when he declared his readiness to arbitrate all labor difficulties that might arise. The oppressed laboring masses finally discovered a powerful champion. All the pent-up feeling of bitterness and resentment which had accumulated during the two years of depression, in consequence of the repeated cuts in wages and the intensified domination by employers, now found vent in a rush to organize under the banner of the powerful Knights of Labor. To the natural tendency on the part of the oppressed to exaggerate the power of a mysterious emancipator whom they suddenly found coming to their aid, there was added the influence of sensational reports in the public press. The newspapers especially took delight in exaggerating the powers and strength of the Order.

In 1885 the New York *Sun* detailed one of its reporters to "get up a story of the strength and purposes of the Knights of Labor." This story was copied by newspapers and magazines throughout the country and aided considerably in bringing the Knights of Labor into prominence. The following extract illustrates the exaggerated notion of the power of the Knights of Labor.

"Five men in this country control the chief interests of five hundred thousand workingmen, and can at any moment take the means of livelihood from two and a half millions of souls. These men compose the executive board of the Noble Order of the Knights of Labor of America. The ability of the president and cabinet to turn out all the men in the civil service, and to shift from one post to another the duties of the men in the army and navy, is a petty authority compared with that of these five

Knights. The authority of the late Cardinal was, and that of the bishops of the Methodist Church is, narrow and prescribed, so far as material affairs are concerned, in comparison with that of these five rulers.

"They can stay the nimble touch of almost every telegraph operator; can shut up most of the mills and factories, and can disable the railroads. They can issue an edict against any manufactured goods so as to make their subjects cease buying them, and the tradesmen stop selling them.

"They can array labor against capital, putting labor on the offensive or the defensive, for quiet and stubborn self-protection, or for angry, organized assault, as they will."

Before long the Order was able to benefit by this publicity in quarters where the tale of its great power could only attract unqualified attention, namely, in Congress. The Knights of Labor led in the agitation for prohibiting the immigration of alien contract laborers. The problem of contract immigrant labor rapidly came to the front in 1884, when such labor began frequently to be used to defeat strikes.

Twenty persons appeared to testify before the committee in favor of the bill, of whom all but two or three belonged to the Knights of Labor. The anti-contract labor law which was passed by Congress on February 2, 1885, therefore, was due almost entirely to the efforts of the Knights of Labor. The trade unions gave little active support, for to the skilled workingmen the importation of contract Italian and Hungarian laborers was a matter of small importance. On the other hand, to the Knights of Labor with their vast contingent of unskilled it was a strong menace. Although the law could not be enforced and had to be amended in 1887 in order to render it effective, its passage nevertheless attests the political influence already exercised by the Order in 1885.

The outcome of the Gould strike of 1885 and the dramatic exaggeration of the prowess of the Order by press and even by pulpit were largely responsible for the psychological setting that called forth and surrounded the great upheaval of 1886. This upheaval meant more than the mere quickening of the pace of the movement begun in preceding years and decades. It signalled the appearance on the scene of a new class which had not hitherto found a place in the labor movement, namely the unskilled. All the peculiar characteristics of the dramatic events in 1886 and 1887, the highly feverish pace at which organizations grew, the nation-wide wave of strikes, particularly sympathetic strikes, the wide use of the boycott, the obliteration, apparently complete, of all lines that divided the laboring class, whether geographic or trade, the violence and turbulence which accompanied the movement—all of these were the signs of a great movement by the class of the unskilled, which had finally risen in rebellion. This movement, rising as an elemental protest against oppression and degradation, could be but feebly restrained by any considerations of expediency and prudence; nor, of course, could it be restrained by any lessons from experience. But, if the origin and powerful sweep of this movement were largely spontaneous and elemental, the issues which it took up were supplied by the existing organizations, namely the trade unions and the Knights of Labor. These served also as the dykes between which the rapid streams were gathered and, if at times it seemed that they must burst under the pressure, still they gave form and direction to the move-

ment and partly succeeded in introducing order where
chaos had reigned. The issue which first brought unity
in this great mass movement was a nation-wide strike for
the eight-hour day declared for May 1, 1886.

The initiative in this strike was taken not by the Order
but by the trade unionists and on the eve of the strike
the general officers of the Knights adopted an attitude
of hostility. But if the slogan failed to arouse the enthusiasm of the national leaders of the Knights, it nevertheless found ready response in the ranks of labor. The
great class of the unskilled and unorganized, which had
come to look upon the Knights of Labor as the all-
powerful liberator of the laboring masses from oppression, now eagerly seized upon this demand as the issue
upon which the first battle with capital should be fought.

The agitation assumed large proportions in March.
The main argument for the shorter day was work for the
unemployed. With the exception of the cigar makers, it
was left wholly in the hands of local organizations. The
Knights of Labor as an organization figured far less
prominently than the trade unions, and among the latter
the building trades and the German-speaking furniture
workers and cigar makers stood in the front of the movement. Early in the strike the workingmen's cause was
gravely injured by a bomb explosion on Haymarket
Square in Chicago, attributed to anarchists, which killed
and wounded a score of policemen.

The bomb explosion on Haymarket Square connected
two movements which had heretofore marched separately,
despite a certain mutual affinity. For what many of the
Knights of Labor were practising during the upheaval in
a less drastic manner and without stopping to look for a
theoretical justification, the contemporary Chicago "an-

archists,"[1] the largest branch of the "Black International," had elevated into a well rounded-out system of thought. Both syndicalism and the Knights of Labor upheaval were related chapters in the revolutionary movement of the eighties. Whether in its conscious or unconscious form, this syndicalism was characterized by an extreme combativeness, by the ease with which minor disputes grew into widespread strikes involving many trades and large territories, by a reluctance, if not an out and out refusal, to enter into agreements with employers however temporary, and lastly by a ready resort to violence. In 1886 the membership of the Black International probably was about 5000 or 6000 and of this number about 1000 were English speaking.

The circumstances of the bomb explosion were the following. A strikers' meeting was held near the McCormick Reaper Works in Chicago, late on the third of May. About this time strike-breakers employed in these works began to leave for home and were attacked by strikers. The police arrived in large numbers and upon being received with stones, fired and killed four and wounded many. The same evening the International issued a call in which appeared the word "*Revenge*" with the appeal: "Workingmen, arm yourselves and appear in full force." A protest mass meeting met the next day on Haymarket Square and was addressed by Internationalists. The police were present in numbers and, as they formed in line and advanced on the crowd, some unknown hand hurled a bomb into their midst killing and wounding many.

It is unnecessary to describe here the period of police terror in Chicago, the hysterical attitude of the press,

[1] See above, 79-80.

or the state of panic that came over the inhabitants of the city. Nor is it necessary to deal in detail with the trial and sentence of the accused. Suffice it to say that the Haymarket bomb showed to the labor movement what it might expect from the public and the government if it combined violence with a revolutionary purpose.

Although the bomb outrage was attributed to the anarchists and not generally to the strikers for the eight-hour day, it did materially reduce the sympathy of the public as well as intimidate many strikers. Nevertheless, *Bradstreet's* estimated that no fewer than 340,000 men took part in the movement; 190,000 actually struck, only 42,000 of this number with success, and 150,000 secured shorter hours without a strike. Thus the total number of those who secured with or without strikes the eight-hour day was something less than 200,000. But even those who for the present succeeded, whether with or without striking, soon lost the concession, and *Brad-street's* estimated in January, 1887, that, so far as the payment of former wages for a shorter day's work is concerned, the grand total of those retaining the concession did not exceed, if it equalled, 15,000.

American labor movements have never experienced such a rush to organize as the one in the latter part of 1885 and during 1886. During 1886 the combined membership of labor organizations was exceptionally large and for the first time came near the million mark. The Knights of Labor had a membership of 700,000 and the trade unions at least 250,000, the former composed largely of unskilled and the latter of skilled. The Knights of Labor gained in a remarkably short time—in a few months—over 600,000 new members and grew from 1610 local assemblies with 104,066 members in good standing in July 1885, to 5892 assemblies with 702,924 members in July 1886. The greatest portion of this growth occurred after January 1, 1886. In the state of New York there were in July 1886, about 110,000 members (60,809 in District Assembly 49 of New York City alone); in Pennsylvania, 95,000 (51,557 in District Assembly 1, Philadelphia, alone); in Massachusetts, 90,000 (81,191 in District Assembly 30 of Boston); and in Illinois, 32,000.

In the state of Illinois, for which detailed information for that year is available, there were 204 local assemblies with 34,974 members, of which 65 per cent. were found in Cook County (Chicago) alone. One hundred and forty-nine assemblies were mixed, that is comprised members of different trades including unskilled and only 55 were trade assemblies. Reckoned according to country of birth the membership was 45 per cent. American, 16 per cent. German, 13 per cent. Irish, 10 per cent. British, 5 per cent. Scandinavian, and the remaining 2 per cent. scattered. The trade unions also gained many members but in a considerably lesser proportion.

The high water mark was reached in the autumn of 1886. But in the early months of 1887 a reaction became visible. By July 1, the membership of the Order had diminished to 510,351. While a share of this retrogression may have been due to the natural reaction of large masses of people who had been suddenly set in motion without experience, a more immediate cause came from the employers. Profiting by past lessons, they organized strong associations. The main object of these employers' associations was the defeat of the Knights. They were organized sectionally and nationally. In small localities, where the power of the Knights was especially great, all

employers regardless of industry joined in a single association. But in large manufacturing centers, where the
rich corporation prevailed, they included the employers
of only one industry. To attain their end these associations made liberal use of the lockout, the blacklist, and
armed guards and detectives. Often they treated agreements entered into with the Order as contracts signed
under duress. The situation in the latter part of 1886
and in 1887 had been clearly foreshadowed in the treatment accorded the Knights of Labor on the Gould railways in the Southwest in the early part of 1886.

As already mentioned, at the settlement of the strike
on the Gould system in March 1885, the employes were
assured that the road would institute no discriminations
against the Knights of Labor. However, it is apparent
that a series of petty discriminations was indulged in
by minor officials, which kept the men in a state of unrest.
It culminated in the discharge of a foreman, a member
of the Knights, from the car shop at Marshall, Texas,
on the Texas & Pacific Road, which had shortly before
passed into the hands of a receiver. A strike broke out
over the entire road on March 1, 1886. It is necessary,
however, to note that the Knights of Labor themselves
were meditating aggressive action two months before
the strike. District Assembly 101, the organization embracing the employes on the Southwest system, held a
convention on January 10, and authorized the officers to
call a strike at any time they might find opportune to
enforce the two following demands: first, the formal
"recognition" of the Order; and second, a daily wage of
$1.50 for the unskilled. The latter demand is peculiarly
characteristic of the Knights of Labor and of the feeling
of labor solidarity that prevailed in the movement. But

evidently the organization preferred to make the issue turn on discrimination against members.   Another peculiarity which marked off this strike as the beginning of a new era was the facility with which it led to a sympathetic strike on the Missouri Pacific and all leased and operated lines.   This strike broke out simultaneously over the entire system on March 6.   It affected more than 5000 miles of railway situated in Missouri, Kansas, Arkansas, Indian Territory, and Nebraska.   The strikers did not content themselves with mere picketing, but actually took possession of the railroad property and by a systematic "killing" of engines, that is removing some indispensable part, effectively stopped all the freight traffic. The number of men actively on strike was in the neighborhood of 9000, including practically all of the shopmen, yardmen, and section gangs.   The engineers, firemen, brakemen, and conductors took no active part and had to be forced to leave their posts under threats from the strikers.

The leader, one Martin Irons, accurately represented the feelings of the strikers.   Personally honest and probably well-meaning, his attitude was overbearing and tyrannical.   With him as with those who followed him, a strike was not a more or less drastic means of forcing a better labor contract, but necessarily assumed the aspect of a crusade against capital.   Hence all compromise and any policy of give and take were excluded.

Negotiations were conducted by Jay Gould and Powderly to submit the dispute to arbitration, but they failed and, after two months of sporadic violence, the strike spent itself and came to an end.   It left, however, a profound impression upon the public mind, second only to the impression made by the great railway strike of 1877; and a Congressional committee was appointed to investigate the whole matter.

The disputes during the second half of 1886 ended, for the most part, disastrously to labor. The number of men involved in six months, was estimated at 97,300. Of these, about 75,300 were in nine great lockouts, of whom 54,000 suffered defeat at the hands of associated employers. The most important lockouts were against 15,000 laundry workers at Troy, New York, in June; against 20,000 Chicago packing house workers; and against 20,000 knitters at Cohoes, New York, both in October.

The lockout of the Chicago butcher workmen attracted the most attention. These men had obtained the eight-hour day without a strike during May. A short time thereafter, upon the initiative of Armour & Company, the employers formed a packers' association and, in the beginning of October, notified the men of a return to the ten-hour day on October 11. They justified this action on the ground that they could not compete with Cincinnati and Kansas City, which operated on the ten-hour system. On October 8, the men, who were organized in District Assemblies 27 and 54, suspended work, and the memorable lockout began. The packers' association rejected all offers of compromise and on October 18 the men were ordered to work on the ten-hour basis. But the dispute in October, which was marked by a complete lack of ill-feeling on the part of the men and was one of the most peaceable labor disputes of the year, was in reality a mere prelude to a second disturbance which broke out in the plant of Swift & Company on November 2 and became general throughout the stockyards on November 6. The men demanded a return to the eight-hour day, but the packers' association, which was now joined by Swift & Company, who formerly had kept aloof, not only refused to give up the ten-hour day, but declared that they would employ no Knights of Labor in the future. The Knights retaliated by declaring a boycott on the meat of Armour & Company. The behavior of the men was now no longer peaceable as before, and the employers took extra precautions by prevailing upon the governor to send two regiments of militia in addition to the several hundred Pinkerton detectives employed by the association. To all appearances, the men were slowly gaining over the employers, for on November 10 the packers' association rescinded its decision not to employ Knights, when suddenly on November 15, like a thunderbolt out of a clear sky, a telegram arrived from Grand Master Workman Powderly ordering the men back to work. Powderly had refused to consider the reports from the members of the General Executive Board who were on the ground, but, as was charged by them, was guided instead by the advice of a priest who had appealed to him to call off the strike and thus put an end to the suffering of the men and their families.

New York witnessed an even more characteristic Knights of Labor strike and on a larger scale. This strike began as two insignificant separate strikes, one by coal-handlers at the Jersey ports supplying New York with coal and the other by longshoremen on the New York water front; both starting on January 1, 1887. Eighty-five coal-handlers employed by the Philadelphia & Reading Railroad Company, members of the Knights of Labor, struck against a reduction of $2\frac{1}{2}$ cents an hour in the wages of the "top-men" and were joined by the trimmers who had grievances of their own. Soon the strike spread to the other roads and the number of striking coal-handlers reached 3000. The longshoremen's strike was begun by 200 men, employed by the Old Dominion Steamship Company, against a reduction in wages and the hiring of cheap men by the week. The strikers were not organized, but the Ocean Association, a part of the Knights of Labor, took up their cause and was assisted by the longshoremen's union. Both strikes soon widened out through a series of sympathetic strikes of related trades and finally became united into one. The Ocean Association declared a boycott on the freight of the Old Dominion Company and this was strictly obeyed by all of the longshoremen's unions. The International Boatmen's Union refused to allow their boats to be used for "scab coal" or to permit their members to steer the companies' boats. The longshoremen joined the boatmen in refusing to handle coal, and the shovelers followed. Then the grain handlers on both floating and stationary elevators refused to load ships with grain on which there was scab coal, and the bag-sewers stood with them. The longshoremen now resolved to go out and refused to work on ships which received scab coal, and finally they decided to stop work altogether on all kinds of craft in the harbor until the trouble should be settled. The strike spirit spread to a large number of freight handlers working for railroads along the river front, so that in the last week of January the number of strikers in New York, Brooklyn, and New Jersey, reached approximately 28,000; 13,000 longshoremen, 1000 boatmen, 6000 grain handlers, 7500 coal-handlers, and 400 bag-sewers.

On February 11, August Corbin, president and receiver of the Philadelphia & Reading Railroad Company, fearing a strike by the miners working in the coal mines operated by that road, settled the strike by restoring to the eighty-five coal-handlers, the original strikers, their former rate of wages. The Knights of Labor felt impelled to accept such a trivial settlement for two reasons. The coal-handlers' strike, which drove up the price of coal to the consumer, was very unpopular, and the strike itself had begun to weaken when the brewers and stationary engineers, who for some obscure reason had been ordered to strike in sympathy, refused to come out. The situation was left unchanged, as far as the coal-handlers employed by the other companies, the longshoremen, and the many thousands of men who went out on sympathetic strike were concerned. The men began to return to work by the thousands and the entire strike collapsed.

The determined attack and stubborn resistance of the employers' associations after the strikes of May 1886, coupled with the obvious incompetence displayed by the leaders, caused the turn of the tide in the labor movement in the first half of 1887. This, however, manifested itself during 1887 exclusively in the large cities, where the movement had borne in the purest form the character of an uprising by the class of the unskilled and where the hardest battles were fought with the employers. District Assembly 49, New York, fell from its membership of 60,809 in June 1886, to 32,826 in July 1887. During the same interval, District Assembly 1, Philadelphia, decreased from 51,557 to 11,294, and District Assembly 30, Boston, from 81,197 to 31,644. In Chicago there were about 40,000 Knights immediately before the packers' strike in October 1886, and only about 17,000 on July 1, 1887. The falling off of the largest district assemblies in 10 large cities practically equalled the total loss of the Order, which amounted approximately to 191,000. At the same time the membership of the smallest district assemblies, which were for the most part located in small cities, remained stationary and, outside of the national and district trade assemblies which were formed by separation from mixed district assemblies, thirty-seven new district assemblies were formed, also mostly in rural localities. In addition, state assemblies were added in Alabama, Florida, Georgia, Indiana, Kansas, Mississippi, Nebraska, North Carolina, Ohio, West Virginia, and Wisconsin, with an average membership of about 2000 each.

It thus becomes clear that by the middle of 1887, the Great Upheaval of the unskilled and semi-skilled portions of the working class had already subsided beneath the strength of the combined employers and the unwieldiness of their own organization. After 1887 the Knights of Labor lost its hold upon the large cities with their wage-conscious and largely foreign population, and became an organization predominantly of country people, of mechanics, small merchants, and farmers,—a class of people which was more or less purely American and decidedly middle class in its philosophy.

The industrial upheaval in the middle of the eighties had, like the great strike of 1877, a political reverberation. Although the latter was heard throughout the entire country, it centered in the city of New York, where the situation was complicated by court interference in the labor struggle.

A local assembly of the Knights of Labor had declared a boycott against one George Theiss, a proprietor of a music and beer garden. The latter at first submitted and paid a fine of $1000 to the labor organization, but later brought action in court against the officers charging them with intimidation and extortion.

The judge, George C. Barrett, in his charge to the jury, conceded that striking, picketing, and boycotting as such were not prohibited by law, if not accompanied by force, threats, or intimidation. But in the case under consideration the action of the pickets in advising passers-by not to patronize the establishment and in distributing boycott circulars constituted intimidation. Also, since the $1000 fine was obtained by fear induced by a threat to continue the unlawful injury to Theiss inflicted by the "boycott," the case was one of extortion covered by the penal code. It made no difference whether the money was appropriated by the defendants for personal use or whether it was turned over to their organization. The jury, which reflected the current public opinion against boycotts, found all of the five defendants guilty of extortion, and Judge Barrett sentenced them to prison for terms ranging from one year and six months to three years and eight months.

The Theiss case, coming as it did at a time of general restlessness of labor and closely after the defeat of the eight-hour movement, greatly hastened the growth of the sentiment for an independent labor party. The New York Central Labor Union, the most famous and most influential organization of its kind in the country at the time, with a membership estimated at between 40,000 and 50,000, placed itself at the head of the movement in which both socialists and non-socialists joined. Henry George, the originator of the single tax movement, was nominated by the labor party for Mayor of New York and was allowed to draw up his own platform, which he made of course a simon-pure single tax platform. The labor demands were compressed into one plank. They were as follows: The reform of court procedure so that "the practice of drawing grand jurors from one class should cease, and the requirements of a property qualification for trial jurors should be abolished"; the stopping of the "officious intermeddling of the police with peaceful assemblages"; the enforcement of the laws for safety and the sanitary inspection of buildings; the abolition of contract labor on public work; and equal pay for equal work without distinction of sex on such work.

The George campaign was more in the nature of a religious revival than of a political election campaign. It was also a culminating point in the great labor upheaval. The enthusiasm of the laboring people reached its highest pitch. They felt that, baffled and defeated as they were in their economic struggle, they were now nearing victory in the struggle for the control of government. Mass meetings were numerous and large. Most of them were held in the open air, usually on the street corners. From the system by which one speaker followed another, speaking at several meeting places in a night, the labor campaign got its nickname of the "tailboard campaign." The common people, women and men, gathered in hundreds and often thousands around trucks from which the shifting speakers addressed the crowd. The speakers were volunteers, including representatives of the liberal professions, lawyers, physicians, teachers, ministers, and labor leaders. At such mass meetings George did most of his campaigning, making several speeches a night, once as many as eleven. The single tax and the prevailing political corruption were favorite topics. Against George and his adherents were pitted the powerful press of the city of New York, all the political power of the old parties, and all the influence of the business class. George's opponents were Abram S. Hewitt, an anti-Tammany

Democrat whom Tammany had picked for its candidate in this emergency, and Theodore Roosevelt, then as yet known only as a courageous young politician.

The vote cast was 90,000 for Hewitt, 68,000 for George, and 60,000 for Roosevelt. There is possible ground for the belief that George was counted out of thousands of votes. The nature of the George vote can be sufficiently gathered from an analysis of the pledges to vote for him. An apparently trustworthy investigation was made by a representative of the New York *Sun*. He drew the conclusion that the vast majority were not simply wage earners, but also naturalized immigrants, mainly Irish, Germans, and Bohemians, the native element being in the minority. While the Irish were divided between George and Hewitt, the majority of the German element had gone over to Henry George. The outcome was hailed as a victory by George and his supporters and this view was also taken by the general press.

In spite of this propitious beginning the political labor movement soon suffered the fate of all reform political movements. The strength of the new party was frittered away in doctrinaire factional strife between the single taxers and the socialists. The trade union element became discouraged and lost interest. So that at the next State election, in which George ran for Secretary of State, presumably because that office came nearest to meeting the requirement for a single taxer seeking a practical scope of action, the vote in the city fell to 37,000 and in the whole State amounted only to 72,000. This ended the political labor movement in New York.

Outside of New York the political labor movement was not associated either with the single tax or any other "ism." As in New York it was a spontaneous expression of dissatisfaction brought on by failure in strikes.   The movement scored a victory in Milwaukee, where it elected a mayor, and in Chicago where it polled 25,000 out of a total of 92,000.   But, as in New York, it fell to pieces without leaving a permanent trace.

CHAPTER 5

THE VICTORY OF CRAFT UNIONISM AND THE FINAL FAILURE OF PRODUCERS' COOPERATION

We now come to the most significant aspect of the Great Upheaval: the life and death struggle between two opposed principles of labor organization and between two opposed labor programs. The Upheaval offered the practical test which the labor movement required for an intelligent decision between the rival claims of Knights and trade unionists. The test as well as the conflict turned principally on "structure," that is on the difference between "craft autonomists" and those who would have labor organized "under one head," or what we would now call the "one big union" advocates.

As the issue of "structure" proved in the crucial eighties, and has remained ever since, the outstanding factional issue in the labor movement, it might be well at this point to pass in brief review the structural developments in labor organization from the beginning and try to correlate them with other important developments.

The early [1] societies of shoemakers and printers were purely local in scope and the relations between "locals" extended only to feeble attempts to deal with the competition of traveling journeymen. Occasionally, they corresponded on trade matters, notifying each other of their purposes and the nature of their demands, or expressing

[1] See Chapter 1.

fraternal greetings; chiefly for the purpose of counteracting advertisements by employers for journeymen or keeping out dishonest members and so-called "scabs." This mostly relates to printers. The shoemakers, despite their bitter contests with their employers, did even less. The Philadelphia Mechanics' Trades Association in 1827, which we noted as the first attempted federation of trades in the United States if not in the world, was organized as a move of sympathy for the carpenters striking for the ten-hour day. During the period of the "wild-cat" prosperity the local federation of trades, under the name of "Trades' Union," [1] comes to occupy the center of the stage in New York, Philadelphia, Boston, and appeared even as far "West" as Pittsburgh, Cincinnati, and Louisville. The constitution of the New York "Trades' Union" provided, among other things, that each society should pay a monthly per capita tax of $6\frac{1}{4}$ cents to be used as a strike fund. Later, when strikes multiplied, the Union limited the right to claim strike aid and appointed a standing committee on mediation. In 1835 it discussed a plan for an employment exchange or a "call room." The constitution of the Philadelphia Union required that a strike be endorsed by a two-thirds majority before granting aid.

The National Trades' Union, the federation of city trades' unions, 1834–1836, was a further development of the same idea. Its first and second conventions went little beyond the theoretical. The latter, however, passed a significant resolution urging the trade societies to observe a uniform wage policy throughout the country and

[1] In the thirties the term "union" was reserved for the city federations of trades. What is now designated as a trade union was called trade society. In the sixties the "Union" became the "trades' assembly."

should the employers combine to resist it, the unions should make "one general strike."

The last convention in 1836 went far beyond preceding conventions in its plans for solidifying the workingmen of the country. First and foremost, a "national fund" was provided for, to be made up of a levy of two cents per month on each of the members of the trades' unions and local societies represented. The policies of the National Trades' Union instead of merely advisory were henceforth to be binding. But before the new policies could be tried, as we know, the entire trade union movement was wiped out by the panic.

The city "trades' union" of the thirties accorded with a situation where the effects of the extension of the market were noticeable in the labor market, and little as yet in the commodity market; when the competitive menace to labor was the low paid out-of-town mechanic coming to the city, not the out-of-town product made under lower labor costs selling in the same market as the products of unionized labor. Under these conditions the local trade society, reënforced by the city federation of trades, sufficed. The "trades' union," moreover, served also as a source of reserve strength.

Twenty years later the whole situation was changed. The fifties were a decade of extensive construction of railways. Before 1850 there was more traffic by water than by rail. After 1860 the relative importance of land and water transportation was reversed. Furthermore, the most important railway building during the ten years preceding 1860 was the construction of East and West trunk lines; and the sixties were marked by the establishment of through lines for freight and the consolidation of connecting lines. The through freight lines greatly hastened freight traffic and by the consolidations through transportation became doubly efficient.

Arteries of traffic had thus extended from the Eastern coast to the Mississippi Valley. Local markets had widened to embrace half a continent. Competitive menaces had become more serious and threatened from a distance. Local unionism no longer sufficed. Consequently, as we saw, in the labor movement of the sixties the national trade union was supreme.

There were four distinct sets of causes which operated during the sixties to bring about nationalization; two grew out of the changes in transportation, already alluded to, and two were largely independent of such changes.

The first and most far-reaching cause, as illustrated by the stove molders, was the competition of the products of different localities side by side in the same market. Stoves manufactured in Albany, New York, were now displayed in St. Louis by the side of stoves made in Detroit. No longer could the molder in Albany be indifferent to the fate of his fellow craftsman in Louisville. With the molders the nationalization of the organization was destined to proceed to its utmost length. In order that union conditions should be maintained even in the best organized centers, it became necessary to equalize competitive conditions in the various localities. That led to a well-knit national organization to control working conditions, trade rules, and strikes. In other trades, where the competitive area of the product was still restricted to the locality, the paramount nationalizing influence was a more intensive competition for employment between migratory out-of-town journeymen and the locally organized mechanics. This describes the situation in the printing trade, where the bulk of work was newspaper and not book and job printing. Accordingly, the printers did not need to entrust their national officers with anything more than the control of the traveling journeymen and the result was that the local unions remained practically independent.

The third cause of concerted national action in a trade union was the organization of employers. Where the power of a local union began to be threatened by an employers' association, the next logical step was to combine in a national union.

The fourth cause was the application of machinery and the introduction of division of labor, which split up the established trades and laid industry open to invasion by "green hands." The shoemaking industry, which during the sixties had reached the factory stage, illustrates this in a most striking manner. Few other industries experienced anything like a similar change during this period.

Of course, none of the causes of nationalization here enumerated operated in entire isolation. In some trades one cause, in other trades other causes, had the predominating influence. Consequently, in some trades the national union resembled an agglomeration of loosely allied states, each one reserving the right to engage in independent action and expecting from its allies no more than a benevolent neutrality. In other trades, on the contrary, the national union was supreme in declaring industrial war and in making peace, and even claimed absolute right to formulate the civil laws of the trade for times of industrial peace.

The national trade union was, therefore, a response to obvious and pressing necessity. However slow or imperfect may have been the adjustment of internal organizations to the conditions of the trade, still the groove was defined and consequently the amount of possible floundering largely limited. Not so with the next step, namely the national federation of trades. In the sixties we saw the national trade unions join with other local and miscellaneous labor organizations in the National Labor Union upon a political platform of eight-hours and green-backism. In 1873 the same national unions asserted their rejection of "panaceas" and politics by attempting to create in the National Labor Congress a federation of trades of a strictly economic character. The panic and depression nipped that in the bud. When trade unionism revived in 1879 the national trade unions returned to the idea of a national federation of labor, but this time they followed the model of the British Trades Union Congress, the organization which cares for the legislative interests of British labor. This was the "Federation of Organized Trades and Labor Unions of the United States and Canada," which was set up in 1881.

It is easy to understand why the unions of the early eighties did not feel the need of a federation on economic lines. The trade unions of today look to the American Federation of Labor for the discharge of important economic functions, therefore it is primarily an economic organization. These functions are the assistance of national trade unions in organizing their trades, the adjustment of disputes between unions claiming the same "jurisdiction," and concerted action in matters of especial importance such as shorter hours, the "open-shop," or boycotts. None of these functions would have been of material importance to the trade unions of the early eighties. Existing in well-defined trades, which were not affected by technical changes, they had no "jurisdictional" disputes; operating at a period of prosperity with full employment and rising wages, they did not realize a necessity for concerted action; the era of the boycotts had not yet begun. As for having a common agency to do the work of organizing, the trade unions of the early eighties had no keen desire to organize any but the skilled workmen; and, since the competition of workmen in small towns had not yet made itself felt, each national trade union strove to organize primarily the workmen of its trade in the larger cities, a function for which its own means were adequate.

The new organization of 1881 was a loose federation of trade and labor unions with a legislative committee at the head, with Samuel Gompers of the cigar makers as a member. The platform was purely legislative and demanded legal incorporation for trade unions,[1] compulsory education for children, the prohibition of child labor under fourteen, uniform apprentice laws, the enforcement of the national eight-hour law, prison labor reform, abolition of the "truck" and "order" system, mechanics' lien, abolition of conspiracy laws as applied to labor organizations, a national bureau of labor statistics, a protective tariff for American labor, an anti-contract immigrant law, and recommended "all trade and labor organizations to secure proper representation in all law-making bodies by means of the ballot, and to use all honorable measures by which this result can be accomplished." Although closely related to the present American Federation of Labor in point of time and personnel of leadership, the Federation of Organized Trades and Labor Unions of the United States and Canada was in reality the precursor of the present state federations

[1] See below, 152-154.

of labor, which as specialized parts of the national federation now look after labor legislation.

Two or three years later it became evident that the
Federation as a legislative organization proved a failure.[1]
Manifestly the trade unions felt no great interest in national legislation. The indifference can be measured by
the fact that the annual income of the Federation never
exceeded $700 and that, excepting in 1881, none of its
conventions represented more than one-fourth of the
trade union membership of the country. Under such conditions the legislative influence of the Federation naturally was infinitesimal. The legislative committee carried
out the instructions of the 1883 convention and communi-
cated to the national committees of the Republican and
Democratic parties the request that they should define
their position upon the enforcement of the eight-hour law
and other measures. The letters were not even answered.
A subcommittee of the legislative committee appeared
before the two political conventions, but received no
greater attention.

It was not until the majority of the national trade
unions came under the menace of becoming forcibly absorbed by the Order of the Knights of Labor that a basis
appeared for a vigorous federation.

The Knights of Labor were built on an opposite principle from the national trade unions. Whereas the latter
started with independent crafts and then with hesitating
hands tried, as we saw, to erect some sort of a common
superstructure that should express a higher solidarity
of labor, the former was built from the beginning upon
a denial of craft lines and upon an absolute unity of all

[1] See below, 285-290, for a discussion why American labor looks
away from legislation.

classes of labor under one guiding head. The subdivision was territorial instead of occupational and the government centralized.

The constitution of the Knights of Labor was drawn in 1878 when the Order laid aside the veil of secrecy to which it had clung since its foundation in 1869. The lowest unit of organization was the local assembly of ten or more, at least three-fourths of whom had to be wage earners at any trade. Above the local assembly was the "district assembly" and above it the "General Assembly." The district assembly had absolute power over its local assemblies and the General Assembly was given "full and final jurisdiction" as "the highest tribunal" of the Order.[1] Between sessions of the General Assembly the power was vested in a General Executive Board, presided over by a Grand Master Workman.

The Order of the Knights of Labor in practice carried out the idea which is now advocated so fervently by revolutionary unionists, namely the "One Big Union," since it avowedly aimed to bring into one organization "all productive labor." This idea in organization was aided by the weakness of the trade unions during the long depression of the seventies, which led many to hope for better things from a general pooling of labor strength. But its main appeal rested on a view that machine technique tends to do away with all distinctions of trades by reducing all workers to the level of unskilled machine tenders. To its protagonists therefore the "one big union" stood for an adjustment to the new technique.

[1] The Constitution read as follows: "It alone possesses the power and authority to make, amend, or repeal the fundamental and general laws and regulations of the Order; to finally decide all controversies arising in the Order; to issue all charters. . . . It can also tax the members of the Order for its maintenance."

First to face the problem of adjustment to the machine technique of the factory system were the shoemakers. They organized in 1867 the Order of the Knights of St. Crispin, mainly for the purpose of suppressing the competitive menace of "green hands," that is unskilled workers put to work on shoe machines. At its height in 1872, the Crispins numbered about 50,000, perhaps the largest union in the whole world at that time. The coopers began to be menaced by machinery about the middle of the sixties, and about the same time the machinists and blacksmiths, too, saw their trade broken up by the introduction of the principle of standardized parts and quantity production in the making of machinery. From these trades came the national leaders of the Knights of Labor and the strongest advocates of the new principle in labor organization and of the interests of the unskilled workers in general. The conflict between the trade unions and the Knights of Labor turned on the question of the unskilled workers.

The conflict was held in abeyance during the early eighties. The trade unions were by far the strongest organizations in the field and scented no particular danger when here or there the Knights formed an assembly either contiguous to the sphere of a trade union or even at times encroaching upon it.

With the Great Upheaval, which began in 1884, and the inrushing of hundreds of thousands of semi-skilled and unskilled workers into the Order, a new situation was created. The leaders of the Knights realized that mere numbers were not sufficient to defeat the employers and that control over the skilled, and consequently the more strategic occupations, was required before the unskilled and semi-skilled could expect to march to victory. Hence, parallel to the tremendous growth of the Knights in 1886, there was a constantly growing effort to absorb the existing trade unions for the purpose of making them subservient to the interests of the less skilled elements. It was mainly that which produced the bitter conflict between the Knights and the trade unions during 1886 and 1887. Neither the jealousy aroused by the success of the unions nor the opposite aims of labor solidarity and trade separatism gives an adequate explanation of this conflict. The one, of course, aggravated the situation by introducing a feeling of personal bitterness, and the other furnished an appealing argument to each side. But the strugle was one between groups within the working class, in which the small but more skilled group fought for independence of the larger but weaker group of the unskilled and semi-skilled. The skilled men stood for the right to use their advantage of skill and efficient organization in order to wrest the maximum amount of concessions for themselves. The Knights of Labor endeavored to annex the skilled men in order that the advantage from their exceptional fighting strength might lift up the unskilled and semi-skilled. From the point of view of a struggle between principles, this was indeed a clash between the principle of solidarity of labor and that of trade separatism, but, in reality, each of the principles reflected only the special interest of a certain portion of the working class. Just as the trade unions, when they fought for trade autonomy, really refused to consider the unskilled men, so the Knights of Labor overlooked the fact that their scheme would retard the progress of the skilled trades.

The Knights were in nearly every case the aggressors, and it is significant that among the local organizations of the Knights inimical to trade unions, District Assembly 49, of New York, should prove the most relentless. It was this assembly which conducted the longshoremen's and coal miners' strike in New York in 1887 and which, as we saw,[1] did not hesitate to tie up the industries of the entire city for the sake of securing the demands of several hundred unskilled workingmen. Though District Assembly 49, New York, came into conflict with not a few of the trade unions in that city, its battle royal was fought with the cigar makers' unions. There were at the time two factions among the cigar makers, one upholding the International Cigar Makers' Union with Adolph Strasser and Samuel Gompers as leaders, the other calling itself the Progressive Union, which was more socialistic in nature and composed of more recent immigrants and less skilled workers. District Assembly 49 of the Knights of Labor took a hand in the struggle to support the Progressive Union and by skillful management brought the situation to the point where the latter had to allow itself to be absorbed into the Knights of Labor.

The events in the cigar making trade in New York brought to a climax the sporadic struggles that had been going on between the Order and the trade unions. The trade unions demanded that the Knights of Labor respect their "jurisdiction" and proposed a "treaty of peace" with such drastic terms that had they been accepted the trade unions would have been left in the sole possession of the field. The Order was at first more conciliatory. It would not of course cease to take part in industrial disputes and industrial matters, but it proposed a *modus vivendi* on a basis of an interchange of "working cards" and common action against employers. At the same time

[1] See above, 98-100.

it addressed separately to each national trade union a gentle admonition to think of the unskilled workers as well as of themselves. The address said: "In the use of the wonderful inventions, your organization plays a most important part. Naturally it embraces within its ranks a very large proportion of laborers of a high grade of skill and intelligence. With this skill of hand, guided by intelligent thought, comes the right to demand that excess of compensation paid to skilled above the unskilled labor. But the unskilled labor must receive attention, or in the hour of difficulty the employer will not hesitate to use it to depress the compensation you now receive. That skilled or unskilled labor may no longer be found unorganized, we ask of you to annex your grand and powerful corps to the main army that we may fight the battle under one flag."

But the trade unions, who had formerly declared that their purpose was "to protect the skilled trades of America from being reduced to beggary," evinced no desire to be pressed into the service of lifting up the unskilled and voted down with practical unanimity the proposal. Thereupon the Order declared open war by commanding all its members who were also members of the cigar makers' union to withdraw from the latter on the penalty of expulsion.

Later events proved that the assumption of the aggressive was the beginning of the undoing of the Order. It was, moreover, an event of first significance in the labor movement since it forced the trade unions to draw closer together and led to the founding in the same year, 1886, of the American Federation of Labor.

Another highly important effect of this conflict was the ascendency in the trade union movement of Samuel

Gompers as the foremost leader. Gompers had first achieved prominence in 1881 at the time of the organization of the Federation of Organized Trades and Labor Unions. But not until the situation created by the conflict with the Knights of Labor did he get his first real opportunity, both ·to demonstrate his inborn capacity for leadership and to train and develop that capacity by overcoming what was perhaps the most serious problem that ever confronted American organized labor.

The new Federation avoided its predecessor's mistake of emphasizing labor legislation above all. Its prime purpose was economic. The legislative interests of labor were for the most part given into the care of subordinate state federations of labor. Consequently, the several state federations, not the American Federation of Labor, correspond in America to the British Trades Union Congress. But in the conventions of the American Federation of Labor the state federations are represented only nominally. The Federation is primarily a federation of national and international (including Canada and Mexico) trade unions.

Each national and·international union in the new Federation was acknowledged a sovereignty unto itself, with full powers of discipline over its members and with the power of free action toward the employers without any interference from the Federation; in other words, its full autonomy was confirmed. Like the British Empire, the Federation of Labor was cemented together by ties which were to a much greater extent spiritual than they were material. Nevertheless, the Federation's authority was far from being a shadowy one. If it could not order about the officers of the constituent unions, it could so mobilize the general labor sentiment in the country on behalf of any of its constituent bodies that its good will would be sought even by the most powerful ones. The Federation guaranteed to each union a certain jurisdiction, generally coextensive with a craft, and protected it against encroachments by adjoining unions and more especially by rival unions. The guarantee worked absolutely in the case of the latter, for the Federation knew no mercy when a rival union attempted to undermine the strength of an organized union of a craft. The trade unions have learned from experience with the Knights of Labor that their deadliest enemy was, after all, not the employers' association but the enemy from within who introduced confusion in the ranks. They have accordingly developed such a passion for "regularity," such an intense conviction that there must be but one union in a given trade that, on occasions, scheming labor officials have known how to checkmate a justifiable insurgent movement by a skillful play upon this curious hypertrophy of the feeling of solidarity. Not only will a rival union never be admitted into the Federation, but no subordinate body, state or city, may dare to extend any aid or comfort to a rival union.

The Federation exacted but little from the national and international unions in exchange for the guarantee of their jurisdiction: A small annual per capita tax; a willing though a not obligatory support in the special legislative and industrial campaigns it may undertake; an adherence to its decisions on general labor policy; an undertaking to submit to its decision in the case of disputes with other unions, which however need not in every case be fulfilled; and lastly, an unqualified acceptance of the principle of "regularity" relative to labor organization. Obviously, judging from constitutional powers alone, the Federation was but a weak sort of a government. Yet the weakness was not the forced weakness of a government which was willing to start with limited powers hoping to increase its authority as it learned to stand more firmly on its own feet; it was a self-imposed weakness suggested by the lessons of labor history.

By contrast the Order of the Knights of Labor, as seen already, was governed by an all-powerful General Assembly and General Executive Board. At a first glance a highly centralized form of government would appear a promise of assured strength and a guarantee of coherence amongst the several parts of the organization. Perhaps, if America's wage earners were cemented together by as strong a class consciousness as the laboring classes of Europe, such might have been the case.

But America's labor movement lacked the unintended aid which the sister movements in Europe derived from a caste system of society and political oppression. Where the class lines were not tightly drawn, the centrifugal forces in the labor movement were bound to assert themselves. The leaders of the American Federation of Labor, in their struggle against the Knights of Labor, played precisely upon this centrifugal tendency and gained a victory by making an appeal to the natural desire for autonomy and self-determination of any distinctive group. But originally perhaps intended as a mere "strategic" move, this policy succeeded in creating a labor movement which was, on fundamentals, far more coherent than the Knights of Labor even in the heyday of their glory. The officers and leaders of the Federation, knowing that they could not command, set themselves to developing a unified labor will and purpose by means of moral suasion and propaganda. Where a bare order would breed resentment and backbiting, an appeal, which is reinforced by a carefully nurtured universal labor sentiment, will eventually bring about common consent and a willing acquiescence in the policy supported by the majority. So each craft was made a self-determining unit and "craft autonomy" became a sacred shibboleth in the labor movement without interfering with unity on essentials.

The principle of craft autonomy triumphed chiefly because it recognized the existence of a considerable amount of group selfishness. The Knights of Labor held, as was seen, that the strategic or bargaining strength of the skilled craftsman should be used as a lever to raise the status of the semi-skilled and unskilled worker. It consequently grouped them promiscuously in "mixed assemblies" and opposed as long as it could the demand for "national trade assemblies." The craftsman, on the other hand, wished to use his superior bargaining strength for his own purposes and evinced little desire to dissipate it in the service of his humbler fellow worker. To give effect to that, he felt obliged to struggle against becoming entangled with undesirable allies in the semi-skilled and unskilled workers for whom the Order spoke. Needless to say, the individual self-interest of the craft leaders worked hand in hand with the self-interest of the craft as a whole, for had they been annexed by the Order they would have become subject to orders from the General Master Workman or the General Assembly of the Order.

In addition to platonic stirrings for "self-determination" and to narrow group interest, there was a motive for craft autonomy which could pass muster both as strictly social and realistic. The fact was that the autonomous craft union could win strikes where the centralized promiscuous Order merely floundered and suffered defeat after defeat. The craft union had the advantage, on the one hand, of a leadership which was thoroughly familiar with the bit of ground upon which it operated, and, on the other hand, of handling a group of people of equal financial endurance and of identical interest. It has already been seen how dreadfully mismanaged were the great Knights of Labor strikes of 1886 and 1887. The ease with which the leaders were able to call out trade after trade on a strike of sympathy proved more a liability than an asset. Often the choice of trades to strike bore no particular relation to their strategic value in the given situation; altogether one gathers the impression that these great strikes were conducted by blundering amateurs who possessed more authority than was good for them or for the cause. It is therefore not to be wondered at if the compact craft unions led by specialists scored successes where the heterogeneous mobs of the Knights of Labor had been doomed from the first. Clearly then the survival of the craft union was a survival of the fittest; and the Federation's attachment to the principle of craft autonomy was, to say the least, a product of an evolutionary past, whatever one may hold with reference to its fitness in our own time.

Whatever reasons moved the trade unions of the skilled to battle with the Order for their separate and autonomous existence were bound sooner or later to induce those craftsmen who were in the Order to seek a similar autonomy. From the very beginning the more skilled and better organized trades in the Knights sought to separate from the mixed "district assemblies" and to create within the framework of the Order "national trade assemblies." [1] However, the national officers, who looked upon such a move as a betrayal of the great principle of the solidarity of all labor, were able to stem the tide excepting in the case of the window glass blowers, who were granted their autonomy in 1880.

The obvious superiority of the trade union form of organization over the mixed organization, as revealed by events in 1886 and 1887, strengthened the separatist tendency. Just as the struggle between the Knights of Labor and the trade unions on the outside had been fundamentally a struggle between the unskilled and the skilled portions of the wage-earning class, so the aspiration toward the national trade assembly within the Order represented the effort of the more or less skilled men for emancipation from the dominance of the unskilled. But the Order successfully fought off such attempts until after the defeat of the mixed district assemblies, or in other words of the unskilled class, in the struggle with the employers. With the withdrawal of a very large portion of this class, as shown in 1887,[2] the demand for the national trade assembly revived and there soon began a veritable rush to organize by trades. The stampede was strongest in the city of New York where the incompetence of the mixed District Assembly 49 had become patent. At the General Assembly in 1887 at Minneapolis all obstacles were removed from forming national trade assemblies, but this came too late to stem the exodus of the skilled element from the order into the American Federation of Labor.

The victory of craft autonomy over the "one big union" was decisive and complete.

[1] The "local assemblies" generally followed in practice trade lines, but the district assemblies were "mixed."
[2] See above, 100-101.

The strike activities of the Knights were confessedly a deviation from "First Principles." Yet the First Principles with their emphasis on producers' coöperation were far from forgotten even when the enthusiasm for strikes was at its highest. Whatever the actual feelings of the membership as a whole, the leaders neglected no opportunity to promote coöperation. T. V. Powderly, the head of the Order since 1878, in his reports to the annual General Assembly or convention, consistently urged that practical steps be taken toward coöperation. In 1881, while the general opinion in the Order was still undecided, the leaders did not scruple to smuggle into the constitution a clause which made coöperation compulsory.

Notwithstanding Powderly's exhortations, the Order was at first slow in taking it up. In 1882 a general coöperative board was elected to work out a plan of action, but it never reported, and a new board was chosen in its place at the Assembly of 1883. In that year, the first practical step was taken in the purchase by the Order of a coal mine at Cannelburg, Indiana, with the idea of selling the coal at reduced prices to the members. Soon thereafter a thorough change of sentiment with regard to the whole matter of coöperation took place, contemporaneously with the industrial depression and unsuccessful strikes. The rank and file, who had hitherto been indifferent, now seized upon the idea with avidity. The enthusiasm ran so high in Lynn, Massachusetts, that it was found necessary to raise the shares of the Knights of Labor Coöperative Shoe Company to $100 in order to prevent a large influx of "unsuitable members." In 1885 Powderly complained that "many of our members grow impatient and unreasonable because every avenue of the Order does not lead to coöperation."

The impatience for immediate coöperation, which seized the rank and file in practically every section of the country, caused an important modification in the official doctrine of the Order. Originally it had contemplated centralized control under which it would have taken years before a considerable portion of the membership could realize any benefit. This was now dropped and a decentralized plan was adopted. Local organizations and, more frequently, groups of members with the financial aid of their local organizations now began to establish shops. Most of the enterprises were managed by the stockholders, although, in some cases, the local organization of the Knights of Labor managed the plant.

Most of the coöperative enterprises were conducted on a small scale. Incomplete statistics warrant the conclusion that the average amount invested per establishment was about $10,000. From the data gathered it seems that coöperation reached its highest point in 1886, although it had not completely spent itself by the end of 1887. The total number of ventures probably reached two hundred. The largest numbers were in mining, cooperage, and shoes. These industries paid the poorest wages and treated their employes most harshly. A small amount of capital was required to organize such establishments.

With the abandonment of centralized coöperation in 1884, the rôle of the central coöperative board changed correspondingly. The leading member of the board was now John Samuel, one of those to whom coöperation meant nothing short of a religion. The duty of the board was to educate the members of the Order in the principles of coöperation; to aid by information and otherwise prospective and actual coöperators; in brief, to coördinate the coöperative movement within the Order. It issued forms of a constitution and by-laws which, with a few modifications, could be adopted by any locality. It also published articles on the dangers and pitfalls in coöperative ventures, such as granting credit, poor management, etc., as well as numerous articles on specific kinds of coöperation. The Knights of Labor label was granted for the use of coöperative goods and a persistent agitation was steadily conducted to induce purchasers to give a preference to coöperative products.

As a scheme of industrial regeneration, coöperation never materialized. The few successful shops sooner or later fell into the hands of an "inner group," who "froze out" the others and set up capitalistic partnerships. The great majority went on the rocks even before getting started. The causes of failure were many: Hasty action, inexperience, lax shop discipline, internal dissensions, high rates of interest upon the mortgage of the plant, and finally discriminations instigated by competitors. Railways were heavy offenders, by delaying side tracks and, on some pretext or other, refusing to furnish cars or refusing to haul them.

The Union Mining Company of Cannelburg, Indiana, owned and operated by the Order as its sole experiment of the centralized kind of coöperation, met this fate. After expending $20,000 in equipping the mine, purchasing land, laying tracks, cutting and sawing timber on the land and mining $1000 worth of coal, they were compelled to lie idle for nine months before the railway company saw fit to connect their switch with the main track. When they were ready to ship their product, it was learned that their coal could be utilized for the manufacture of gas only, and that contracts for supply of such coal were let in July, that is nine months from the time of connecting the switch with the main track. In addition, the company was informed that it must supply itself with a switch engine to do the switching of the cars from its mine to the main track, at an additional cost of $4000. When this was accomplished they had to enter the market in competition with a bitter opponent who had been fighting them since the opening of the mine. Having exhausted their funds and not seeing their way clear to securing additional funds for the purchase of a locomotive and to tide over the nine months ere any contracts for coal could be entered into, they sold out to their competitor.

But a cause more fundamental perhaps than all other causes of the failure of coöperation in the United States is to be found in the difficulties of successful entrepreneurship. In the labor movement in the United States there has been a failure, generally speaking, to appreciate the significance of management and the importance which must be imputed to it. Glib talk often commands an undeserved confidence and misleads the wage earner. Thus by 1888, three or four years after it had begun, the coöperative movement had passed the full cycle of life and succumbed. The failure, as said, was hastened by external causes and discrimination. But the experiments had been foredoomed anyway,—through the incompatibility of producers' coöperation with trade unionism. The coöperators, in their eagerness to get a market, frequently undersold the private employer expecting to recoup their present losses in future profits. In consequence, the privately employed wage earners had to bear reductions in their wages. A labor movement which endeavors to practice producers' coöperation and trade unionism at the same time is actually driving in opposite directions.

CHAPTER 6

STABILIZATION, 1888-1897

The Great Upheaval of 1886 had, as we saw, suddenly swelled the membership of trade unions; consequently, during several years following, notwithstanding the prosperity in industry, further growth was bound to proceed at a slower rate.

The statistics of strikes during the later eighties, like the figures of membership, show that after the strenuous years from 1885 to 1887 the labor movement had entered a more or less quiet stage. Most prominent among the strikes was the one of 60,000 iron and steel workers in Pennsylvania, Ohio, and the West, which was carried to a successful conclusion against a strong combination of employers. The Amalgamated Association of Iron and Steel Workers stood at the zenith of its power about this time and was able in 1889, by the mere threat of a strike, to dictate terms to the Carnegie Steel Company. The most noted and last great strike of a railway brotherhood was the one of the locomotive engineers on the Chicago, Burlington & Quincy Railroad Company. The strike was begun jointly on February 27, 1888, by the brotherhoods of locomotive engineers and locomotive firemen. The main demands were made by the engineers, who asked for the abandonment of the system of classification and for a new wage scale. Two months previously, the Knights of Labor had declared a miners' strike against the Philadelphia & Reading Railroad Company, employing 80,000 anthracite miners, and the strike had been accompanied by a sympathetic strike of engineers and firemen belonging to the Order. The members of the brotherhoods had filled their places and, in retaliation, the former Reading engineers and firemen now took the places of the Burlington strikers, so that on March 15 the company claimed to have a full contingent of employes. The brotherhoods ordered a boycott upon the Burlington cars, which was partly enforced, but they were finally compelled to submit. The strike was not officially called off until January 3, 1889. Notwithstanding the defeat of the strikers, the damage to the railway was enormous, and neither the railways of the country nor the brotherhoods since that date have permitted a serious strike of their members to occur.

The lull in the trade union movement was broken by a new concerted eight-hour movement managed by the Federation, which culminated in 1890.

Although on the whole the eight-hour movement in 1886 was a failure, it was by no means a disheartening failure. It was evident that the eight-hour day was a popular demand, and that an organization desirous of expansion might well hitch its wagon to this star. Accordingly, the convention of the American Federation of Labor in 1888 declared that a general demand should be made for the eight-hour day on May 1, 1890. The chief advocates of the resolution were the delegates of the carpenters, who announced a readiness to lead the way for a general eight-hour day in 1890.

The Federation at once inaugurated an aggressive campaign. For the first time in its history it employed special salaried organizers. Pamphlets were issued and widely distributed. On every important holiday mass meetings were held in the larger cities. On Labor Day 1889, no less than 420 such mass meetings were held throughout the country. Again the Knights of Labor came out against the plan.

The next year the plan of campaign was modified. The idea of a general strike for the eight-hour day in May 1890, was abandoned in favor of a strike trade by trade. In March 1890, the carpenters were chosen to make the demand on May 1 of the same year, to be followed by the miners at a later date.

The choice of the carpenters was indeed fortunate. Beginning with 1886, that union had a rapid growth and was now the largest union affiliated with the Federation. For several years it had been accumulating funds for the eight-hour day, and, when the movement was inaugurated in May 1890, it achieved a large measure of success. The union officers claimed to have won the eight-hour day in 137 cities and a nine-hour day in most other places.

However, the selection of the miners to follow on May 1, 1891, was a grave mistake. Less than one-tenth of the coal miners of the country were then organized. For years the miners' union had been losing ground, with the constant decline of coal prices. Some months before May 1, 1891, the United Mine Workers had become involved in a disastrous strike in the Connelsville coke region, and the plan for an eight-hour strike was abandoned. In this manner the eight-hour movement inaugurated by the convention of the Federation in 1888 came to an end. Apart from the strike of the carpenters in 1890, it had not led to any general movement to gain the eight-hour work day. Nevertheless, hundreds of thousands of workingmen had won reduced hours of labor, especially in the building trades. By 1891 the eight-hour day had been secured for all building trades in Chicago, St. Louis, Denver, Indianapolis, and San Francisco. In New York and Brooklyn the carpenters, stone-cutters, painters, and plasterers worked eight hours, while the bricklayers, masons, and plumbers worked nine. In St. Paul the bricklayers alone worked nine hours, the remaining trades eight.

In 1892 the labor movement faced for the first time a really modern manufacturing corporation with its practically boundless resources of war, namely the Carnegie Steel Company, in the strike which has become famous under the name of the Homestead Strike. The Amalgamated Association of Iron and Steel Workers, with a membership of 24,068 in 1891, was probably the strongest trade union in the entire history of the American labor movement. Prior to 1889 the relations between the union and the Carnegie firm had been invariably friendly. In January 1889, H. C. Frick, who, as owner of the largest coke manufacturing plant, had acquired a reputation of a bitter opponent of organized labor, became chairman of Carnegie Brothers and Company. In the same year, owing to his assumption of management, as the union men believed, the first dispute occurred between them and the company. Although the agreement was finally renewed for three years on terms dictated by the Association, the controversy left a disturbing impression upon the minds of the men, since during the course of the negotiations Frick had demanded the dissolution of the union.

Negotiations for the new scale presented to the company began in February 1892. A few weeks later the company presented a scale to the men providing for a reduction and besides demanded that the date of the termination of the scale be changed from July 1 to

January 1. A number of conferences were held without result; and on May 30 the company submitted an ultimatum to the effect that, if the scale were not signed by June 29, they would treat with the men as individuals. At a final conference which was held on June 23, the company raised its offer from $22 per ton to $23 as the minimum base of the scale, and the union lowered its demand from $25, the rate formerly paid, to $24. But no agreement could be reached on this point nor on others and the strike began June 29 upon the definite issue of the preservation of the union.

Even before the negotiations were broken up, Frick had arranged with the Pinkerton detective agency for 300 men to serve as guards. These men arrived at a station on the Ohio River below Pittsburgh near midnight of July 5. Here they embarked on barges and were towed up the river to Pittsburgh and taken up the Monangahela River to Homestead, which they approached about four o'clock on the morning of July 6. The workmen had been warned of their coming and, when the boat reached the landing back of the steel works, nearly the whole town was there to meet them and to prevent their landing. Passion ran high. The men armed themselves with guns and gave the Pinkertons a pitched battle. When the day was over, at least half a dozen men on both sides had been killed and a number were seriously wounded. The Pinkertons were defeated and driven away and, although there was no more disorder of any sort, the State militia appeared in Homestead on July 12 and remained for several months.

The strike which began in Homestead soon spread to other mills. The Carnegie mills at 29th and 33d Streets, Pittsburgh, went on strike. The strike at Homestead was finally declared off on November 20, and most of the men went back to their old positions as non-union men. The treasury of the union was depleted, winter was coming, and it was finally decided to consider the battle lost.

The defeat meant not only the loss by the union of the Homestead plant but the elimination of unionism in most of the mills in the Pittsburgh region. Where the great Carnegie Company led, the others had to follow. The power of the union was henceforth broken and the labor movement learned the lesson that even its strongest organization was unable to withstand an onslaught by the modern corporation. The Homestead strike stirred the labor movement as few other single events. It had its political reverberation, since it drove home to the workers that an industry protected by high tariff will not necessarily be a haven to organized labor, notwithstanding that the union had actively assisted the iron and steel manufacturers in securing the high protection granted by the McKinley tariff bill of 1890. Many of the votes which would otherwise have gone to the Republican candidate for President went in 1892 to Grover Cleveland, who ran on an anti-protective tariff issue. It is not unlikely that the latter's victory was materially advanced by the disillusionment brought on by the Homestead defeat.

In the summer of 1893 occurred the financial panic. The panic and the ensuing crisis furnished a conclusive test of the strength and stability of the American labor movement. Gompers in his presidential report at the convention of 1899, following the long depression, said: "It is noteworthy, that while in every previous industrial crisis the trade unions were literally mowed down and swept out of existence, the unions now in existence have manifested, not only the power of resistance, but of stability and permanency," and he assigned as the most prominent cause the system of high dues and benefits which had come into vogue in a large number of trade unions. He said: "Beyond doubt the superficial motive of continued membership in unions organized upon this basis was the monetary benefits the members were entitled to; but be that as it may, the results are the same, that is, *membership is maintained, the organization remains intact during dull periods of industry, and is prepared to take advantage of the first sign of an industrial revival.*" Gompers may have overstated the power of resistance of the unions, but their holding power upon the membership cannot be disputed. The aggregate membership of all unions affiliated with the Federation remained near the mark of 275,000 throughout the period of depression from 1893 to 1897. At last the labor movement had become stabilized.

The year 1894 was exceptional for labor disturbances. The number of employes involved reached nearly 750,000, surpassing even the mark set in 1886. However, in contradistinction to 1886, the movement was defensive. It also resulted in greater failure. The strike of the coal miners and the Pullman strike were the most important ones. The United Mine Workers began their strike in Ohio on April 21. The membership did not exceed 20,000, but about 125,000 struck. At first the demand was made that wages should be restored to the level at which they were in May 1893. But within a month the union in most regions was struggling to prevent a further reduction in wages. By the end of July the strike was lost.

The Pullman strike marks an era in the American

labor movement because it was the only attempt ever
made in America of a revolutionary strike on the Continental European model. The strikers tried to throw
against the associated railways and indeed against the
entire existing social order the full force of a revolutionary labor solidarity embracing the entire American wage-
earning class brought to the point of exasperation by
unemployment, wage reductions, and misery. That in
spite of the remarkable favorable conjuncture the dramatic appeal failed to shake the general labor movement
out of its chosen groove is proof positive of the comple-
tion of the stabilization process which had been going
on since the early eighties.

The Pullman strike began May 11, 1894, and grew
out of a demand of certain employes in the shops of the
Pullman Palace Car Company, situated at Pullman,
Illinois, for a restoration of the wages paid during the
previous year. In March 1894, the Pullman employes
had voted to join the American Railway Union. The
American Railway Union was an organization based on
industrial lines, organized in June 1893, by Eugene V.
Debs. Debs, as secretary-treasurer of the Brotherhood
of Locomotive Firemen, had watched the failure of
many a strike by only one trade and resigned this office
to organize all railway workers in one organization. The
American Railway Union was the result. Between June
9 and June 26 the latter held a convention in Chicago.
The Pullman matter was publicly discussed before and
after its committee reported their interviews with the
Pullman Company. On June 21, the delegates under instructions from their local unions, feeling confident after
a victory over the Great Northern in April, unanimously
voted that the members should stop handling Pullman

cars on June 26 unless the Pullman Company would consent to arbitration.

On June 26 the railway strike began. It was a purely sympathetic strike as no demands were made. The union found itself pitted against the General Managers' Association, representing twenty-four roads centering or terminating in Chicago, which were bound by contracts with the Pullman Company. The association had been organized in 1886, its main business being to determine a common policy as to traffic and freight rates, but incidentally it dealt also with wages. The strike soon spread over an enormous territory. Many of the members of the brotherhoods joined in, although their organizations were opposed to the strike. The lawless element in Chicago took advantage of the opportunity to rob, burn, and plunder, so that the scenes of the great railway strike of 1877 were now repeated. The damages in losses of property and business to the country have been estimated at $80,000,000. On July 7, E. V. Debs, president, and other principal officers of the American Railway Union were indicted, arrested, and held under $10,000 bail. On July 13 they were charged with contempt of the United States Court in disobeying an injunction which enjoined them, among other things, from compelling or inducing by threats railway employes to strike. The strike had already been weakening for some days. On July 12, at the request of the American Railway Union, about twenty-five of the executive officers of national and international labor unions affiliated with the American Federation of Labor met in conference in Chicago to discuss the situation. Debs appeared and urged a general strike by all labor organizations. But the conference decided that "it would be unwise and disastrous to the interests of labor to extend the strike any further than it had already gone," and advised the strikers to return to work. On July 13, the American Railway Union, through the Mayor of Chicago, offered the General Managers' Association to declare the strike off, provided the men should be restored to their former positions without prejudice, except in cases where they had been convicted of crime. But the Association refused to deal with the union. The strike was already virtually beaten by the combined moral effect of the indictment of the leaders and of the arrival in Chicago of United States troops, which President Cleveland sent in spite of the protest of Governor Altgeld of Illinois.

The labor organizations were taught two important lessons. First, that nothing can be gained through revolutionary striking, for the government was sufficiently strong to cope with it; and second, that the employers had obtained a formidable ally in the courts.[1]

Defeats in strikes, depression in trade, a rapidly falling labor market and court prosecutions were powerful allies of those socialistic and radical leaders inside the Federation who aspired to convert it from a mere economic organization into an economic-political one and make it embark upon the sea of independent politics.

The convention of 1893 is memorable in that it submitted to the consideration of affiliated unions a "political programme." The preamble to the "programme" recited that the English trade unions had recently launched upon independent politics "as auxiliary to their economic action." The eleven planks of the program demanded: compulsory education; the right of popular initiative in legislation; a legal eight-hour work-day;

[1] See below, 159-160.

governmental inspection of mines and workshops; abolition of the sweating system; employers' liability laws; abolition of the contract system upon public work; municipal
ownership of electric light, gas, street railway, and water
systems; the nationalization of telegraphs, telephones,
railroads, and mines; "the collective ownership by the
people of all means of production and distribution"; and
the referendum upon all legislation.

Immediately after the convention of 1893 affiliated
unions began to give their endorsement to the political
program. Not until comparatively late did any opposition make itself manifest. Then it took the form of a
demand by such conservative leaders as Gompers, Mc-
Guire, and Strasser, that plank 10, with its pledge in
favor of "the collective ownership by the people of all
means of production and distribution," be stricken out.
Notwithstanding this, the majority of national trade
unions endorsed the program.

During 1894 the trade unions were active participants
in politics. In November, 1894, the *Federationist* gave
a list of more than 300 union members candidates for
some elective office. Only a half dozen of these, however,
were elected. It was mainly to these local failures that
Gompers pointed in his presidential address at the convention of 1894 as an argument against the adoption
of the political program by the Federation. His attitude clearly foreshadowed the destiny of the program at
the convention. The first attack was made upon the preamble, on the ground that the statement therein that the
English trade unions had declared for independent political action was false. By a vote of 1345 to 861 the
convention struck out the preamble. Upon motion of
the typographical union, a substitute was adopted call-

ing for the "abolition of the monopoly system of land holding and the substitution therefor of a title of occupancy and use only." Some of the delegates seem to have interpreted this substitute as a declaration for the single tax; but the majority of those who voted in its favor probably acted upon the principle "anything to beat socialism." Later the entire program was voted down. That sealed the fate of the move for an independent labor party.

The American Federation of Labor was almost drawn into the whirlpool of partisan politics during the Presidential campaign of 1896. Three successive conventions had declared in favor of the free coinage of silver; and now the Democratic party had come out for free coinage. In this situation very many prominent trade union leaders declared publicly for Bryan. President Gompers, however, issued a warning to all affiliated unions to keep out of partisan politics. Notwithstanding this Secretary McGraith, at the next convention of the Federation, charged President Gompers with acting in collusion with the Democratic headquarters throughout the campaign in aid of Bryan's candidacy. After a lengthy secret session the convention approved the conduct of Gompers. Free silver continued to be endorsed annually down to the convention of 1898, when the return of industrial prosperity and rising prices put an end to it as a demand advocated by labor.

The depressed nineties demonstrated conclusively that a new era had arrived. No longer was the labor movement a mere plaything of the alternating waves of prosperity and depression. Formerly, as we saw, it had centered on economic or trade-union action during prosperity only to change abruptly to "panaceas" and politics with the descent of depression. Now the movement, notwithstanding possible changes in membership, and persistent political leanings in some portions of it, as a whole for the first time became stable in purpose and action. Trade unionism has won over politics.

This victory was synchronous with the first successful working out of a national trade agreement and the institutionalization of trade unionism in a leading industry, namely stove molding. While one of the earliest stable trade agreements in a conspicuous trade covering a local field was a bricklayers' agreement in Chicago in 1887, the era of trade agreements really dates from the national system established in the stove foundry industry in 1891. It is true also that the iron and steel workers had worked under a national trade agreement since 1866. However, that trade was too exceptionally strong to be typical.

The stove industry had early reached a high degree of development and organization. There had existed since 1872 the National Association of Stove Manufacturers, an organization dealing with prices and embracing in its membership the largest stove manufacturers of the country. The stove foundrymen, therefore, unlike the manufacturers in practically all other industries at that time, controlled in a large measure their own market. Furthermore, the product had been completely standardized and reduced to a piecework basis, and machinery had not taken the place of the molders' skill. It consequently was no mere accident that the stove industry was the first to develop a system of permanent industrial peace. But, on the other hand, this was not automatically established as soon as the favorable external conditions were provided. In reality, only after years of struggle, of strikes and lockouts, and after the two sides had fought each other "to a standstill," was the system finally installed.

The eighties abounded in stove molders' strikes, and in 1886 the national union began to render effective aid. The Stove Founders' National Defense Association was formed in 1886 as an employers' association of stove manufacturers. The Defense Association aimed at a national labor policy; it was organized for "resistance against any unjust demands of their workmen, and such other purposes as may from time to time prove or appear to be necessary for the benefit of the members thereof as employers of labor." Thus, after 1886, the alignment was made national on both sides. The great battle was fought the next year.

March 8, 1887, the employes of the Bridge and Beach Manufacturing Company in St. Louis struck for an advance in wages and the struggle at once became one between the International Union and the National Defense Association. The St. Louis company sent its patterns to foundries in other districts, but the union successfully prevented their use. This occasioned a series of strikes in the West and of lockouts in the East, affecting altogether about 5000 molders. It continued thus until June, when the St. Louis patterns were recalled, the Defense Association having provided the company with a sufficient number of strike-breakers. Each side was in a position to claim the victory for itself; so evenly matched were the opposing forces.

During the next four years disputes in Association plants were rare. In August 1890, a strike took place in Pittsburgh and, for the first time in the history of the industry, it was settled by a written trade agreement with the local union. This supported the idea of a national trade agreement between the two organizations. Since the dispute of 1887, negotiations with this object were from time to time conducted, the Defense Association invariably taking the initiative. Finally, the national convention of the union in 1890 appointed a committee to meet a like committee of the Defense Association. The conference took place March 25, 1891, and worked out a complete plan of organization for the stove molding industry. Every year two committees of three members each, chosen respectively by the union and the association, were to meet in conference and to draw up general laws for the year. In case of a dispute arising in a locality, if the parties immediately concerned were unable to arrive at common terms, the chief executives of both organizations, the president of the union and the president of the association, were to step in and try to effect an adjustment. If, however, they, too, failed, a conference committee composed of an equal number of members from each side was to be called in and its findings were to be final. Meanwhile the parties were enjoined from engaging in hostilities while the matter at dispute was being dealt with by the duly appointed authorities. Each organization obligated itself to exercise "police authority" over its constituents, enforcing obedience to the agreement. The endorsement of the plan by both organizations was practically unanimous, and has continued in operation without interruption for thirty years until the present day.

Since the end of the nineties the trade agreement has become one of the most generally accepted principles and aspirations of the American labor movement. However, it is not to be understood that by accepting the principle of the trade agreement the labor movement has committed itself to unlimited arbitration of industrial disputes. The basic idea of the trade agreement is that of collective bargaining rather than arbitration. The two terms are not always distinguished, but the essential difference is that in the trade agreement proper no outside party intervenes to settle the dispute and make an award. The agreement is made by direct negotiation between the two organized groups and the sanction which each holds over the head of the other is the strike or lockout. If no agreement can be reached, the labor organization as well as the employers' association, insists on its right to refuse arbitration, whether it be "voluntary" or so-called "compulsory."

The clarification of the conception of the trade agreement was perhaps the main achievement of the nineties. Without the trade agreement the labor movement could hardly come to eschew "panaceas" and to reconstitute itself upon the basis of opportunism. The coming in of the trade agreement, whether national, sectional, or local, was also the chief factor in stabilizing the movement against industrial depressions.

CHAPTER 7

TRADE UNIONISM AND THE COURTS

While it was in the nineties that trade unionists first tasted the sweets of institutionalization in industry through "recognition" by employers, it was also during the later eighties and during the nineties that they experienced a revival of suspicion and hostility on the part of the courts and a renewal of legal restraints upon their activities, which were all the more discouraging since for a generation or more they had practically enjoyed non-interference from that quarter. It was at this period that the main legal weapons against trade unionism were forged and brought to a fine point in practical application. The history of the courts' attitude to trade unionism may therefore best be treated from the standpoint of the nineties.

The subject of court interference was not altogether new in the eighties. We took occasion to point out the effect of court interference in labor disputes in the first and second decades of the nineteenth century and again in the thirties. Mention was made also of the court's decision in the Theiss boycott case in New York in 1886, which proved a prime moving factor in launching the famous Henry George campaign for Mayor. And we gave due note to the rôle of court injunctions in the Debs strike of 1894 and in other strikes. Our present interest is, however, more in the court doctrines than in their effects: more concerned with the development of the legal thought underlying the policies of the courts than with the reactions of the labor movement to the policies themselves.

The earliest case on record, namely the Philadelphia shoemakers' strike case in 1806,[1] charged two offences; one was a combination to raise wages, the other a combination to injure others; both offences were declared by the judge to be forbidden by the common law. To the public at large the prosecution seemed to rest solely upon the charge that the journeymen combined to raise wages. The defense took advantage of this and tried to make use of it for its own purposes. The condemnation of the journeymen on this ground gave rise to a vehement protest on the part of the journeymen themselves and their friends. It was pointed out that the journeymen were convicted for acts which are considered lawful when done by masters or merchants. Therefore when the next conspiracy case in New York in 1809 was decided, the court's charge to the jury was very different. Nothing was said about the illegality of the combinations to raise wages; on the contrary, the jury was instructed that this was not the question at issue. The issue was stated to be whether the defendants had combined to secure an increase in their wages by unlawful means. To the question what means were unlawful, in this case the answer was given in general terms, namely that "coercive and arbitrary" means are unlawful. The fines imposed upon the defendants were only nominal.

A third notable case of the group, namely the Pittsburgh case in 1815, grew out of a strike for higher wages, as did the preceding cases. The charges were the same as in those and the judge took the identical view that was

[1] See above, 6.

taken by the court in the New York case. However, he explained more fully the meaning of "coercive and arbitrary" action. "Where diverse persons," he said, "confederate together by direct means to impoverish or prejudice a third person, or to do acts prejudicial to the community," they are engaged in an unlawful conspiracy. Concretely, it is unlawful to "conspire to compel an employer to hire a certain description of persons," or to "conspire to prevent a man from freely exercising his trade in a particular place," or to "conspire to compel men to become members of a particular society, or to contribute toward it," or when persons "conspire to compel men to work at certain prices." Thus it was the effort of the shoemakers' society to secure a closed shop which fell chiefly under the condemnation of the court.

The counsel for the defense argued in this case that whatever is lawful for one individual is lawful also for a combination of individuals. The court, however, rejected the arguments on the ground that there was a basic difference between an individual doing a thing and a combination of individuals doing the same thing. The doctrine of conspiracy was thus given a clear and unequivocal definition.

Another noteworthy feature of the Pittsburgh case was the emphasis given to the idea that the defendants' conduct was harmful to the public. The judge condemned the defendants because they tended "to create a monopoly or to restrain the entire freedom of the trade." What a municipality is not allowed to do, he argued, a private association of individuals must not be allowed to do.

Of the group of cases which grew out of the revival of trade union activity in the twenties, the first, a case against Philadelphia master shoemakers, was decided in 1821, and the judge held that it was lawful for the masters, who had recently been forced by employes to a wage increase, to combine in order to restore wages to their "natural level." But he also held that had the employers combined to depress wages of journeymen below the level fixed by free competition, it would have been criminal.

Another Pennsylvania case resulted from a strike by Philadelphia tailors in 1827 to secure the reinstatement of six discharged members. As in previous cases the court rejected the plea that a combination to raise wages was illegal, and directed the attention of the jury to the question of intimidation and coercion, especially as it affected third parties. The defendants were found guilty.

In a third, a New York hatters' case of 1823, the charge of combining to raise wages was entirely absent from the indictment. The issue turned squarely on the question of conspiring to injure others by coercion and intimidation. The hatters were adjudged guilty of combining to deprive a non-union workman of his livelihood.

The revival of trade unionism in the middle of the thirties brought in, as we saw, another crop of court cases.

In 1829 New York State had made "conspiracy to commit any act injurious to public morals or to trade or commerce" a statutory offence, thus reënforcing the existing common law. In 1835 the shoemakers of Geneva struck to enforce the closed shop against a workman who persisted in working below the union rate. The indictment went no further than charging this offence. The journeymen were convicted in a lower court and appealed to the Supreme Court of the State. Chief Justice Savage, in his decision condemning the journeymen, broadened the charge to include a conspiracy to raise wages and condemned both as "injurious to trade or commerce" and thus expressly covered by statute.

The far-reaching effects of this decision came clearly to light in a tailor's case the next year. The journeymen were charged with practising intimidation and violence, while picketing their employers' shops during a prolonged strike against a reduction in wages. Judge Edwards, the trial judge, in his charge to the jury, stigmatized the tailors' society as an illegal combination, largely basing himself upon Judge Savage's decision. The jury handed in a verdict of guilty, but recommended mercy. The judge fined the president of the society $150, one journeyman $100, and the others $50 each. The fines were immediately paid with the aid of a collection taken up in court.

The decisions produced a violent reaction among the workingmen. They held a mass-meeting in City Hall Park, with an estimated attendance of 27,000, burned Judge Savage and Judge Edwards in effigy, and resolved to call a state convention to form a workingmen's party.

So loud, indeed, was the cry that justice had been thwarted that juries were doubtless influenced by it. Two cases came up soon after the tailors' case, the Hudson, New York, shoemakers' in June and the Philadelphia plasterers' in July 1836. In both the juries found a verdict of not guilty. Of all journeymen indicted during this period the Hudson shoemakers had been the most audacious ones in enforcing the closed shop. They not only refused to work for employers who hired non-society men, but fined them as well; yet they were acquitted.

Finally six years later, in 1842, long after the offending trade societies had gone out of existence under the stress of unemployment and depression, came the famous decision in the Massachusetts case of Commonwealth *v.* Hunt.

This was a shoemakers' case and arose out of a strike. The decision in the lower court was adverse to the defendants. However, it was reversed by the Supreme Judicial Court of Massachusetts. The decision, written by Chief Justice Shaw, is notable in that it holds trade unions to be legal organizations. In the earlier cases it was never in so many words held that trade unions were unlawful, but in all of them there were suggestions to this effect. Now it was recognized that trade unions are *per se* lawful organizations and, though men may band themselves together to effect a criminal object under the disguise of a trade union, such a purpose is not to be assumed without positive evidence. On the contrary, the court said that "when an association is formed for purposes actually innocent, and afterwards its powers are abused by those who have the control and management of it to purposes of oppression and injustice, it will be criminal in those who misuse it, or give consent thereto, but not in other members of the association." This doctrine that workingmen may lawfully organize trade unions has since Commonwealth *v.* Hunt been adopted in nearly every case.

The other doctrine which Justice Shaw advanced in this case has been less generally accepted. It was that the members of a union may procure the discharge of non-members through strikes for this purpose against their employers. This is the essence of the question of the closed shop; and Commonwealth *v.* Hunt goes the full length of regarding strikes for the closed shop as legal. Justice Shaw said that there is nothing unlawful about such strikes, if they are conducted in a peaceable manner. This was much in advance of the position which is taken by many courts upon this question even at the present day.

After Commonwealth *v.* Hunt came a forty years' lull in the courts' application of the doctrine of conspiracy to trade unions. In fact so secure did trade unionists feel from court attacks that in the seventies and early eighties their leaders advocated the legal incorporation of trade unions. The desire expressed for incorporation is of extreme interest compared with the opposite attitude of the present day. The motive behind it then was more than the usual one of securing protection for trade union funds against embezzlement by officers. A full enumeration of other motives can be obtained from the testimony of the labor leaders before the Senate Committee on Education and Labor in 1883. McGuire, the national secretary of the Brotherhood of Carpenters and Joiners, argued before the committee for a national incorporation law mainly for the reason that such a law passed by Congress would remove trade unions from the operation of the conspiracy laws that still existed though in a dormant state on the statute books of a number of States, notably New York and Pennsylvania. He pleaded that "if it (Congress) had not the power, it shall assume the power; and, if necessary, amend the constitution to do it." Adolph Strasser of the cigar makers raised the point of protection for union funds and gave as a second reason that it "will give our organization more stability, and in that manner we shall be able to avoid strikes by perhaps settling with our employers, when otherwise we should be unable to do so, because when our employers know that we are to be legally recognized that will exercise such moral force upon them that they cannot avoid recognizing us themselves." W. H. Foster, the secretary of the Legislative Committee of the Federation of Organized Trades and Labor Unions, stated that in Ohio the law provided for incorporation at a slight cost, but he wanted a national law to "legalize arbitration," by which he meant that "when a question of dispute arose between the employers and the employed, instead of having it as now, when the one often refuses to even acknowledge or discuss the question with the other, if they were required to submit the question to arbitration, or to meet on the same level before an impartial tribunal, there is no doubt but what the result would be more in our favor than it is now, when very often public opinion cannot hear our cause." He, however, did not desire to have compulsory arbitration, but merely compulsory dealing with the union, or compulsory investigation by an impartial body, both parties to remain free to accept the award, provided, however, "that once they do agree the agreement shall remain in force for a fixed period." Like Foster, John Jarrett, the President of the Amalgamated Association of Iron and Steel Workers, argued for an incorporation law before the committee solely for its effect upon conciliation and arbitration. He, too, was opposed to compulsory arbitration, but he showed that he had thought out the point less clearly than Foster.

The young and struggling trade unions of the early eighties saw only the good side of incorporation without its pitfalls; their subsequent experience with courts converted them from exponents into ardent opponents of incorporation and of what Foster termed "legalized arbitration."

During the eighties there was much legislation ap-

plicable to labor disputes. The first laws against boycotting and blacklisting and the first laws which prohibited discrimination against members who belonged to
a union were passed during this decade. At this time
also were passed the first laws to promote voluntary arbitration and most of the laws which allowed unions to
incorporate. Only in New York and Maryland were the
conspiracy laws repealed. Four States enacted such
laws and many States passed laws against intimidation.
Statutes, however, played at that time, as they do now,
but a secondary rôle. The only statute which proved of
much importance was the Sherman Anti-Trust Act.
When Congress passed this act in 1890, few people
thought it had application to labor unions. In 1893-
1894, as we shall see, however, this act was successfully
invoked in several labor controversies, notably in the
Debs case.

The bitterness of the industrial struggle during the
eighties made it inevitable that the labor movement should
acquire an extensive police and court record. It was
during that decade that charges like "inciting to riot,"
"obstructing the streets," "intimidation," and "trespass"
were first extensively used in connection with labor disputes. Convictions were frequent and penalties often
severe. What attitude the courts at that time took
toward labor violence was shown most strikingly, even if
in too extreme a form to be entirely typical, in the case of
the Chicago anarchists.[1]

But the significance of the eighties in the development
of relations of the courts to organized labor came not
from these cases which were, after all, nothing but ordinary police cases magnified to an unusual degree by the

[1] See above, 91-93.

intensity of the industrial struggle and by the excited state of public opinion, but in the new lease of life to the doctrine of conspiracy as affecting labor disputes. During the eighties and nineties there seemed to have been more conspiracy cases than during all the rest of the century. It was especially in 1886 and 1887 that organized labor found court interference a factor. At this time, as we saw, there was also passed voluminous state legislation strengthening the application of the common law doctrine of conspiracy to labor disputes. The conviction of the New York boycotters in 1886 and many similar convictions, though less widely known, of participants in strikes and boycotts were obtained upon this ground.

Where the eighties witnessed a revolution was in a totally new use made of the doctrine of conspiracy by the courts when they began to issue injunctions in labor cases. Injunctions were an old remedy, but not until the eighties did they figure in the struggles between labor and capital. In England an injunction was issued in a labor dispute as early as 1868; [1] but this case was not noticed in the United States and had nothing whatever to do with the use of injunctions in this country. When and where the first labor injunction was issued in the United States is not known. An injunction was applied for in a New York case as early as 1880 but was denied. [2] An injunction was granted in Iowa in 1884, but not until the Southwest railway strike in 1886 were injunctions used extensively. By 1890 the public had yet heard little of injunctions in connection with labor disputes, but such use was already fortified by numerous precedents.

[1] Springhead Spinning Co. *v.* Riley, L. R. 6 E. 551 (1868).
[2] Johnson Harvester Co. *v.* Meinhardt, 60 How. Pr. 171.

The first injunctions that attained wide publicity were those issued by Federal courts during the strike of engineers against the Chicago, Burlington, & Quincy Railroad [1] in 1888 and during the railway strikes of the early nineties. Justification for these injunctions was found in the provisions of the Interstate Commerce Act and the Sherman Anti-Trust Act. Often the State courts used these Federal cases as precedents, in disregard of the fact that there the issuance of injunctions was based upon special statutes. In other cases the more logical course was followed of justifying the issuance of injunctions upon grounds of equity. But most of the acts which the courts enjoined strikers from doing were already prohibited by the criminal laws. Hence organized labor objected that these injunctions violated the old principle that equity will not interfere to prevent crime. No such difficulties arose when the issuance of injunctions was justified as a measure for the protection of property. In the Debs case,[2] when the Supreme Court of the United States passed upon the issuance of injunctions in labor disputes, it had recourse to this theory.

But the theory of protection to property also presented some difficulties. The problem was to establish the principle of irreparable injury to the complainant's property. This was a simple matter when the strikers were guilty of trespass, arson, or sabotage. Then they damaged the complainant's physical property and, since they were usually men against whom judgments are worthless, any injury they might do was irreparable. But these were exceptional cases. Usually injunctions

[1] Chicago, Burlington, etc., R. R. Co. *v.* Union Pacific R. R. Co., U. S. Dist. Ct., D. Neb. (1888).
[2] In re Debs, 158 U. S. 564 (1895).

were sought to prevent not violence, but strikes, picketing, or boycotting. What is threatened by strikes and
picketing is not the employer's physical property, but the
relations he has established as an employer of labor,
summed up in his expectancy of retaining the services of
old employes and of obtaining new ones. Boycotting,
obviously, has no connection with acts of violence against
physical property, but is designed merely to undermine
the profitable relations which the employer had developed
with his customers. These expectancies are advantages
enjoyed by established businesses over new competitors
and are usually transferable and have market value. For
these reasons they are now recognized as property in the
law of good-will and unfair competition for customers,
having been first formulated about the middle of the
nineteenth century.

The first case which recognized these expectancies of
a labor market was Walker *v.* Cronin,[1] decided by the
Massachusetts Supreme Judicial Court in 1871. It held
that the plaintiff was entitled to recover damages from
the defendants, certain union officials, because they had induced his employes, who were free to quit at will, to leave
his employ and had also been instrumental in preventing
him from getting new employes. But as yet these expectancies were not considered property in the full sense
of the word. A transitional case is that of Brace Bros.
v. Evans in 1888.[2] In that case an injunction against
a boycott was justified on the ground that the value of
the complainant's physical property was being destroyed
when the market was cut off. Here the expectancies
based upon relations which customers and employes were

[1] 107 Mass. 555 (1871).
[2] 5 Pa. Co. Ct. 163 (1888).

ght of as giving value to the physical property, but they were not yet recognized as a distinct asset which in itself justifies the issuance of injunctions.

This next step was taken in the Barr [1] case in New Jersey in 1893. Since then there have been frequent statements in labor injunction cases to the effect that both the expectancies based upon the merchant-function and the expectancies based upon the employer-function are property.

But the recognition of "probable expectancies" as property was not in itself sufficient to complete the chain of reasoning that justifies injunctions in labor disputes. It is well established that no recovery can be had for losses due to the exercise by others of that which they have a lawful right to do. Hence the employers were obliged to charge that the strikes and boycotts were undertaken in pursuance of an unlawful conspiracy. Thus the old conspiracy doctrine was combined with the new theory, and "malicious" interference with "probable expectancies" was held unlawful. Earlier conspiracy had been thought of as a criminal offence, now it was primarily a civil wrong. The emphasis had been upon the danger to the public, now it was the destruction of the employer's business. Occasionally the court went so far as to say that all interference with the business of employers is unlawful. The better view developed was that interference is *prima facie* unlawful but may be justified. But even this view placed the burden of proof upon the workingmen. It actually meant that the court opened for itself the way for holding the conduct of the workingmen to be lawful only when it sympathized with their demands.

[1] Barr *v.* Trades' Council, 53 N. J. E. 101 (1894).

During the eighties, despite the far-reaching development of legal theories on labor disputes, the issuance of injunctions was merely sporadic, but a veritable crop came up during 1893-1894. Only the best-known injunctions can be here noted. The injunctions issued in the course of the Southwest railway strike in 1886 and the Burlington strike in 1888 have already received mention. An injunction was also issued by a Federal court during a miners' strike at Cœur d'Alène, Idaho, in 1892.[1] A famous injunction was the one of Judges Taft and Rickes in 1893, which directed the engineers, who were employed by connecting railways, to handle the cars of the Ann Arbor and Michigan railway, whose engineers were on strike.[2] This order elicited much criticism because it came close to requiring men to work against their will. This was followed by the injunction of Judge Jenkins in the Northern Pacific case, which directly prohibited the quitting of work.[3] From this injunction the defendants took an appeal, with the result that in Arthur v. Oakes[4] it was once for all established that the quitting of work may not be enjoined.

During the Pullman strike numerous injunctions, most sweeping in character, were issued by the Federal courts upon the initiative of the Department of Justice. Under the injunction which was issued in Chicago arose the famous contempt case against Eugene V. Debs,[5] which was carried to the Supreme Court of the United States. The decision of the court in this case is notable, because it covered the main points of doubt above mentioned and

[1] Cœur d'Alène Mining Co. v. Miners' Union, 51 Fed. 260 (1892).
[2] Toledo, etc. Co. v. Penn. Co., 54 Fed. 730 (1893).
[3] Farmers' Loan and Trust Co. v. N. P. R. Co., 60 Fed. 803 (1895).
[4] 64 Fed. 310 (1894).
[5] In re Debs, 158 U. S. 564 (1894).

placed the use of injunctions in labor disputes upon a firm legal basis.

Another famous decision of the Supreme Court growing out of the railway strikes of the early nineties was in the Lennon case [1] in 1897. Therein the court held that all persons who have actual notice of the issuance of an injunction are bound to obey its terms, whether they were mentioned by name or not; in other words, the courts had evolved the "blanket injunction."

At the end of the nineties, the labor movement, enriched on the one side by the lessons of the past and by the possession of a concrete goal in the trade agreement, but pressed on the other side by a new form of legal attack and by the growing consolidation of industry, started upon a career of new power but faced at the same time new difficulties.

[1] In re Lennon, 166 U. S. 548 (1897).

PART II
THE LARGER CAREER OF UNIONISM

CHAPTER 8

PARTIAL RECOGNITION AND NEW DIFFICULTIES, 1898-1914

When, in 1898, industrial prosperity returned, there came with it a rapid expansion of labor organization. At no time in its history, prior to the World War, not excepting the Great Upheaval in the eighties, did labor organizations make such important gains as during the following five years. True, in none of these years did the labor movement add over half a million members as in the memorable year of 1886; nevertheless, from the standpoint of permanence, the upheaval during the eighties can scarcely be classed with the one which began in the late nineties.

During 1898 the membership of the American Federation of Labor remained practically stationary, but during 1899 it increased by about 70,000 (to about 350,-000); in 1900, it increased by 200,000; in 1901, by 240,000; in 1902, by 237,000; in 1903, by 441,000; in 1904, by 210,000, bringing the total to 1,676,000. In 1905 a backward tide set in; and the membership decreased by nearly 200,000 during that year. It remained practically stationary until 1910, when the upward movement was resumed, finally bringing the membership to near the two million mark, to 1,996,000, in 1913. If we include organizations unaffiliated with the Federation, among them the bricklayers [1] and the four railway brotherhoods, with about 700,000 members, the union membership for 1913 will be brought near a total of 2,700,000.

A better index of progress is the proportion of organized workers to organizable workers. Two such estimates have been made. Professor George E. Barnett figures the organizable workers in 1900 at 21,837,000; in 1910 at 30,267,000. On this basis wage earners were 3.5 per cent. organized in 1900 and 7 per cent. in 1910.[2] Leo Wolman submits more detailed figures for 1910. Excluding employers, the salaried group, agricultural and clerical workers, persons engaged in personal or domestic service, and those below twenty years of age (unorganizable workers), the organizable total was 11,490,944. With an estimated trade union strength of 2,116,317 for 1910 the percentage of the organized was 18.4.[3] Excluding only employers and salaried persons, his percentage was 7.7, which compares closely with Professor Barnett's.

Of greater significance are Wolman's figures for organization by industries. These computations show that in 1910 the breweries had 88.8 per cent. organized, printing and book binding 34.3 per cent., mining 30.5 per cent., transportation 17.3 per cent., clothing 16.9 per cent., building trades 16.2 per cent., iron and steel 9.9 per cent., metal 4.7 per cent., and textile 3.7 per cent.[4] By separate occupations, railway conductors, brakemen, and locomotive engineers were from 50-100 per cent.

[1] The bricklayers became affiliated in 1917.
[2] "The Growth of Labor Organizations in the United States, 1897-1914," in *Quarterly Journal of Economics,* Aug., 1916, p. 780.
[3] "The Extent of Trade Unionism," in *Annals of American Academy of Political Science,* Vol. 69, p. 118.
[4] *Ibid.*

PARTIAL RECOGNITION

plasterers, from 30-50 per cent.; bakers, carpenters,
plumbers, from 15-30 per cent. organized.[1]

Accompanying the numerical growth of labor organizations was an extension of organization into heretofore
untouched trades as well as a branching out into new
geographical regions, the South and the West. On the
whole, however, though the Federation was not unmind-
ful of the unskilled, still, during the fifteen years after
1898 it brought into its fold principally the upper strata
of semi-skilled labor. Down to the "boom" period
brought on by the World War, the Federation did not
comprise to any great extent either the totally unskilled,
or the partially skilled foreign-speaking workmen, with
the exception of the miners and the clothing workers.
In other words, those below the level of the skilled trades,
which did gain admittance, were principally the same
elements which had asserted their claim to organization
during the stormy period of the Knights of Labor.[2] The
new accretions to the American wage-earning class since
the eighties, the East and South Europeans, on the one
hand, and the ever-growing contingent of "floaters" of
native and North and West European stock, on the other
hand, were still largely outside the organization.

The years of prosperity brought an intensified activity
of the trade unions on a scale hitherto unknown. Wages
were raised and hours reduced all along the line. The
new strength of the trade unions received a brilliant test

[1] "The Extent of Trade Unionism," in *Annals of American Academy
of Political Science,* Vol. 69, p. 118.
[2] The "federal labor unions" (mixed unions) and the directly
affiliated local trade unions (in trades in which a national union does
not yet exist) are forms of organization which the Federation designed for bringing in the more miscellaneous classes of labor. The
membership in these has seldom reached over 100,000.

during the hard times following the financial panic of October 1907, when they successfully fought wage reductions. As good a test is found in the conquest of the shorter day. By 1900 the eight-hour day was the rule in the building trades, in granite cutting and in bituminous coal mining. The most spectacular and costly eight-hour fight was waged by the printers. In the later eighties and early nineties, the Typographical Union had endeavored to establish a nine-hour day in the printing offices. This was given a setback by the introduction of the linotype machine during the period of depression, 1893-1897. In spite of this obstacle, however, the Typographical Union held its ground. Adopting the policy that only journeymen printers must operate the linotype machines, the union was able to meet the situation. And, furthermore, in 1898, through agreement with the United Typothetæ of America, the national association of employers in book and job printing, the union was able to gain the nine-hour day in substantially all book and job offices. In 1903 the union demanded the eight-hour day in all printing offices to become effective January 1, 1906. To gain an advantage over the union, the United Typothetæ, late in the summer of 1905, locked out all its union men. This at once precipitated a strike for the eight-hour day. The American Federation of Labor levied a special assessment on all its members in aid of the strikers. By 1907 the Typographical Union won its demand all along the line, although at a tremendous cost of money running into several million dollars, and in 1909 the United Typothetæ formally conceded the eight-hour day.

Another proof of trade union progress is found in the spread of trade agreements. The idea of a joint partnership of organized labor and organized capital in the management of industry, which, ever since the fifties, had been struggling for acceptance, finally showed definite signs of coming to be materialized.

(1) *The Miners*

In no other industry has a union's struggle for "recognition" offered a richer and more instructive picture of the birth of the new order with its difficulties as well as its promises than in coal mining. Faced in the anthracite field [1] by a small and well knitted group of employers, generally considered a "trust," and by a no less difficult situation in bituminous mining due to cutthroat competition among the mine operators, the United Mine Workers have succeeded in a space of fifteen years in unionizing the one as well as the other; while at the same time successfully and progressively solving the gigantic internal problem of welding a polyglot mass of workers into a well disciplined and obedient army.

The miners' union attained its first successes in the so-called central bituminous competitive field, including Western Pennsylvania, West Virginia, Ohio, Indiana, Michigan, and Illinois. In this field a beginning had been made in 1886 when the coal operators and the union entered into a collective agreement. However, its scope was practically confined to Ohio and even that limited agreement went under in 1890.[2] With the breakdown of

[1] A small but immensely rich area in Eastern Pennsylvania where the only anthracite coal deposits in the United States are found.

[2] At a conference at Columbus, Ohio, in January, 1886, coal operators from Western Pennsylvania, Ohio, Indiana, and Illinois met the organized miners and drew up an agreement covering the wages which were to prevail throughout the central competitive field from May 1, 1886, to April 30, 1887. The scale established would seem to have been dictated by the wish to give the markets of the central competitive field to the Ohio operators. Ohio was favored in the scale established by this first Interstate conference probably because

this agreement, the membership dwindled so that by the time of a general strike in 1894, the total paid-up membership was barely 13,000. This strike was undertaken to restore the wage-scale of 1893, but during the ensuing years of depression wages were cut still further.[1]

The turn came as suddenly as it was spectacular. In 1897, with a membership which had dropped to 10,000 and of which 7000 were in Ohio and with an empty treasury, the United Mine Workers called a general strike trusting to a rising market and to an awakenend spirit of solidarity in the majority of the unorganized after four years of unemployment and distress. In fact the leaders had not miscalculated. One hundred thousand or more coal miners obeyed the order to go on a strike. In Illinois the union had but a handful of members when the strike started, but the miners struck to a man. The tie-up was practically complete except in West Virginia. That State had early become recognized as the weakest spot in the miners' union's armor. Notwithstanding the American Federation of Labor threw almost its entire force of organizers into that limited area, which was then only beginning to assume its present day importance in the coal mining industry, barely one-third of the miners

more than half of the operators present came from that State, and because the chief strength of the miners' union also lay in that State. To prevent friction over the interpretation of the Interstate agreement, a board of arbitration and conciliation was established. This board consisted of five miners and five operators chosen at large, and one miner and operator more from each of the States of this field. Such a board of arbitration and conciliation was provided for in all of the Interstate agreements of the period of the eighties. This system of Interstate agreement, in spite of the cut-throat competition raging between operators, was maintained for Pennsylvania and Ohio practically until 1890, Illinois having been lost in 1887, and Indiana in 1888. It formed the real predecessor of the system established in 1898 and in vogue thereafter.

[1] See above, 136.

were induced to strike. A contributing factor was a more energetic interference from the courts than in other States. All marching upon the highways and all assemblages of the strikers in large gatherings were forbidden by injunctions. On one occasion more than a score of men were sentenced to jail for contempt of court by Federal Judge Goff. The handicap in West Virginia was offset by sympathy and aid from other quarters. Many unions throughout the country and even the general public sent the striking miners financial aid. In Illinois Governor John R. Tanner refused the requests for militia made by several sheriffs.

The general strike of 1897 ended in the central competitive field after a twelve-weeks' struggle. The settlement was an unqualified victory for the union. It conceded the miners a 20 per cent. increase in wages, the establishment of the eight-hour day, the abolition of company stores, semi-monthly payments, and a restoration of the system of fixing Interstate wage rates in annual joint conferences with the operators, which meant official recognition of the United Mine Workers. The operators in West Virginia, however, refused to come in.

The first of these Interstate conferences was held in January, 1898, at which the miners were conceded a further increase in wages. In addition, the agreement, which was to run for two years, established for Illinois the run-of-mine [1] system of payment, while the size of the screens of other states was regulated; and it also conceded the miners the check-off system [2] in every district,

---

[1] The run-of-mine system means payment by weight of the coal as brought out of the mine including minute pieces and impurities.
[2] The check-off system refers to collection of union dues. It means that the employer agrees to deduct from the wage of each miner the amount of his union dues, thus constituting himself the union's financial agent.

save that of Western Pennsylvania.[1] Such a comprehensive victory would not have been possible had it not been for the upward trend which coal prices had taken.

But great as was the union's newly discovered power, it was spread most unevenly over the central competitive field. Its firmest grip was in Illinois. The well-filled treasury of the Illinois district has many times been called upon for large contributions or loans, to enable the union to establish itself in some other field. The weakest hold of the United Mine Workers has been in West Virginia. At the end of the general strike of 1897, the West Virginia membership was only about 4000. Moreover, a further spread of the organization met with unusual obstacles. A large percentage of the miners of West Virginia are Negroes or white mountaineers. These have proven more difficult to organize than recent Southern and Eastern European immigrants, who formed the majority in the other districts. And yet West Virginia as a growing mining state soon assumed a high strategic importance. A lower wage scale, the better quality of its coal, and a comparative freedom from strikes have made West Virginia a formidable competitor of the other districts in the central competitive field. Consequently West Virginia operators have been able to operate their mines more days during the year than elsewhere; and despite the lower rates per ton, the West Virginia miners have earned but little less annually than union miners in other States. But above all the United Mine Workers have been handicapped in West Virginia as nowhere else by court interference in strikes and in campaigns of organization. In 1907 a temporary injunction was granted at the behest of the Hitchman Coal and Coke

[1] In that district the check-off was granted in 1902.

Company, a West Virginia concern, restraining union organizers from attempting to organize employes who signed agreements not to join the United Mine Workers while in the employ of the company. The injunction was made permanent in 1913. The decree of the District Court was reversed by the Circuit Court of Appeals in 1914, but was sustained by the United States Supreme Court in March 1917.[1] Recently the United States Steel Corporation became a dominant factor in West Virginia through its ownership of mines and lent additional strength to the already strong anti-union determination of the employers.

Very early the United Mine Workers established a reputation for strict adherence to agreements made. This faithfulness to a pledged word, which justified itself even from the standpoint of selfish motive, in as much as it gained for the union public sympathy, was urged upon all occasions by John Mitchell, the national President of the Union. The first test came in 1899, when coal prices soared up rapidly after the joint conference had adjourned. Although they might have won higher wages had they struck, the miners observed their contracts. A more severe test came in 1902 during the great anthracite strike.[2] A special union convention was then held to consider whether the bituminous miners should be called out in sympathy with the hard pressed striking miners in the anthracite field. By a large majority, however, the convention voted not to strike in violation of the agreements made with the operators. The union again gave proof of statesmanly self-control when, in 1904, taking into account the depressed condition of industry, it accepted

[1] Hitchman Coal and Coke Company v. Mitchell, 245 U. S. 232.
[2] See below, 175-177.

without a strike a reduction in wages in the central competitive field. However, as against the miners' conduct in these situations must be reckoned the many local strikes or "stoppages" in violation of agreements. The difficulty was that the machinery for the adjustment of local grievances was too cumbersome.

In 1906 the trade agreement system encountered a new difficulty in the friction which developed between the operators of the several competitive districts. On the surface, the source of the friction was the attempt made by the Ohio and Illinois operators to organize a national coal operators' association to take the place of the several autonomous district organizations. The Pittsburgh operators, however, objected. They preferred the existing system of agreements under which each district organization possessed a veto power, since then they could keep the advantage over their competitors in Ohio and Indiana with which they had started under the original agreement of 1898. The miners in this emergency threw their power against the national operators' association. A suspension throughout most districts of the central competitive field followed. In the end, the miners won an increase in wages, but the Interstate agreement system was suspended, giving place to separate agreements for each district.

In 1908 the situation of 1906 was repeated. This time the Illinois operators refused to attend the Interstate conference on the ground that the Interstate agreement severely handicapped Illinois. As said before, ever since 1897 payment in Illinois has been upon the run-of-mine basis; whereas in all other States of the central competitive field the miners were paid for screened coal only. With the operators of each State having one vote in the joint conference, it can be understood why the handicap against Illinois continued. Theoretically, of course, the Illinois operators might have voted against the acceptance of any agreement which gave an advantage to other States; however, against this weighed the fact that the union was strongest in Illinois. The Illinois operators, hence, preferred to deal separately with the United Mine Workers. Accordingly, an Interstate agreement was drawn up, applying only to Indiana, Ohio, and Pennsylvania.

In 1910, the Illinois operators again refused to enter the Interstate conference, but this time the United Mine Workers insisted upon a return to the Interstate agreement system of 1898. On April 1, 1910, operations were suspended throughout the central competitive field. By July agreements had been secured in every State save Illinois, the latter State holding out until September. This long struggle in Illinois was the first real test of strength between the operators and the miners since 1897. The miners' victory made it inevitable that the Illinois operators should eventually reënter the Interstate conference.

In 1912, after repeated conferences, the net result was the restoration of the Interstate agreement as it existed before 1906. The special burden of which the Illinois operators had been complaining was not removed; yet they were compelled by the union to remain a party to the Interstate agreement. The union justified its special treatment of the operators in Illinois on the ground that the run-of-mine rates were 40 per cent. below the screened coal rates, thus compensating them amply for the "slack" for which they had to pay under this system. The Federal report on "Restriction of Output" of 1904 substantiated the union's contention. Ultimately, the United Mine Workers unquestionably hoped to establish the run-of-mine system throughout the central competitive field.

The union, incidentally to its policy of protecting the miners, has considerably affected the market or business structure of the industry. An outstanding policy of the union has been to equalize competitive costs over the entire area of a market by means of a system of grading tonnage rates paid to the miner, whereby competitive advantages of location, thickness of vein, and the like were absorbed in higher labor costs. This doubtless tended to eliminate cut-throat competition and thus stabilize the industry. On the other hand, it may have hindered the process of elimination of unprofitable mines, and therefore may be in some measure responsible for the present-day overdevelopment in the bituminous mining industry, which results in periodic unemployment and in idle mines.

In the anthracite coal field in Eastern Pennsylvania the difficulties met by the United Mine Workers were at first far greater than in the bituminous branch of the industry. First, the working population was nearly all foreign-speaking, and the union thus lacked the fulcrum which it found in Illinois with its large proportion of English-speaking miners accustomed to organization and to carrying on a common purpose. Secondly, the employers, instead of being numerous and united only for joint dealing with labor, as in bituminous mining, were few in number besides being cemented together by a common selling policy on top of a common labor policy. In consequence, the union encountered a stone wall of opposition, which its loose ranks found for many years well-nigh impossible to overcome.

During the general strike of 1897 the United Mine Workers made a beginning in organizing the anthracite miners. In September 1900, they called a general strike. Although at that time the union had only 8000 members in this region, the strike order was obeyed by over 100,-000 miners; and within a few weeks the strike became truly general. Probably the union could not have won if it had to rely solely on economic strength. However, the impending Presidential election led to an interference by Senator Mark Hanna, President McKinley's campaign manager. Through him President John Mitchell of the United Mine Workers was informed that the operators would abolish the objectionable sliding scale system of wage payments, increase rates 10 per cent. and agree to meet committees of their employes for the adjustment of grievances. This, however, did not carry a formal recognition of the union; it was not a trade agreement but merely an unwritten understanding. A part of the same understanding was that the terms which had been agreed upon should remain in force until April, 1901. At its expiration the identical terms were renewed for another year, while the negotiations bore the same informal character.

During 1902 the essential instability of the arrangement led to sharp friction. The miners claimed that many operators violated the unwritten agreement. The operators, on their part, charged that the union was using every means for practically enforcing the closed shop, which was not granted in the understanding. In the early months of 1902 the miners presented demands for a reduction of the hours of labor from 10 to 9, for a twenty per cent. increase in wages, for payment according to the weight of coal mined, and for the recognition of the union. The operators refused to negotiate, and on May 9 the famous anthracite strike of 1902 began.

It is unnecessary to detail the events of the anthracite strike. No other strike is better known and remembered. More than 150,000 miners stood out for approximately five months. The strike was financed by a levy of one dollar per week upon all employed miners in the country, which yielded over $2,000,000. In addition several hundred thousand dollars came in from other trade unions and from the public generally. In October, when the country was facing a most serious coal famine, President Roosevelt took a hand. He called in the presidents of the anthracite railroads and the leading union officials for a conference in the White House and urged arbitration. At first he met with rebuff from the operators, but shortly afterward, with the aid of friendly pressure from New York financiers, the operators consented to accept the award of a commission to be appointed by himself. This was the well-known Anthracite Coal Strike Commission. Its appointment terminated the strike. Not until more than a half year later, however, was the award of the Commission made. It conceded the miners a 10 per cent. increase in wages, the eight and nine-hour day, and the privilege of having a union check-weighman at the scale where the coal sent up in cars by the miners is weighed. Recognition was not accorded the union, except that it was required to bear one-half of the expense connected with the maintenance of a joint arbitration board created by the Commission. When this award was announced there was much dissatisfaction with it among the miners. President Mitchell, however, put forth every effort to have the union accept the award. Upon a referendum vote the miners accepted his view.

The anthracite coal strike of 1902 was doubtless the most important single event in the history of American trade unionism until that time and has since scarcely been surpassed. To be sure, events like the great railway strike of 1877 and the Chicago Anarchist bomb and trial in 1886-1887 had equally forced the labor question into public attention. What distinguished the anthracite coal strike, however, was that for the first time a labor organization tied up for months a strategic industry and caused wide suffering and discomfort to the public without being condemned as a revolutionary menace to the existing social order calling for suppression by the government; it was, on the contrary, adjudged a force within the preserves of orderly society and entitled to public sympathy. The public identified the anthracite employers with the trust movement, which was then new and seemingly bent upon uprooting the traditional free American social order; by contrast, the striking miners appeared almost as champions of Old America. A strong contributory factor was the clumsy tactics of the employers who played into the hands of the leaders of the miners. The latter, especially John Mitchell, conducted their case with great skill.

Yet the award of the Commission fell considerably short of what the union and its sympathizers outside the ranks of labor hoped for. For by refusing to grant formal recognition, the Commission failed to constitute unionism into a publicly recognized agency in the management of industry and declared by implication that the rôle of unionism ended with a presentation of grievances and complaints.

For ten years after the strike of 1902 the union failed to develop the strength in the anthracite field which many believed would follow. Certain proof of the weakness of the union is furnished by the fact that the wage-scale in that field remained stationary until 1912 despite a rising cost of living. The wages of the anthracite miners in 1912 were slightly higher than in 1902, because coal prices had increased and the Anthracite Coal Strike Commission had reëstablished a sliding scale system of tonnage rates.

A great weakness, while the union still struggled for existence, was the lack of the "check-off." Membership would swell immediately before the expiration of the agreement but diminish with restoration of quiet. With no immediate outlook for a strike the Slav and Italian miners refused to pay union dues. The original award was to be in force until April 1, 1906. In June, 1905, the union membership was less than 39,000. But by April 1, 1906, one-half of the miners were in the union. A month's suspension of operations followed. Early in May the union and the operators reached an agreement to leave the award of the Anthracite Coal Strike Commission in force for another three years.

The following three years brought a duplication of the developments of 1903-1906. Again membership fell off only to return in the spring of 1909. Again the union demanded formal recognition, and again it was refused. Again the original award was extended for three more years.

In the winter of 1912, when the time for renewing the agreement again drew near, the entire membership in the three anthracite districts was slightly above 29,000. Nevertheless, the union demanded a twenty per cent. raise, a complete recognition of the union, the check-off, and yearly agreements, in addition to a more expeditious system of settling local grievances to replace the slow and cumbersome joint arbitration boards provided by the award of the Commission. A strike of 180,000 anthracite miners followed on April 1, 1912, during which the operators made no attempt to run their mines. The strike ended within a month on the basis of the abolition of the sliding scale, a wage increase of approximately 10 per cent., and a revision of the arbitration machinery in local disputes. This was coupled with a somewhat larger degree of recognition, but by no means a complete recognition. Nor was the check-off system granted. Strangest of all, the agreement called for a four-year contract, as against a one-year contract originally demanded by the union. In spite of the opposition of local leaders, the miners accepted the agreement. President White's chief plea for acceptance was the need to rebuild the union before anything ambitious could be attempted.

After 1912 the union entered upon the work of organization in earnest. In the following two years the membership was more than quadrupled. With the stopping of immigration due to the European War, the power of the union was greatly increased. Consequently, in 1916, when the agreement was renewed, the miners were accorded not only a substantial wage increase and the eight-hour day but also full rcognition. The United Mine Workers have thus at last succeeded in wresting a share of industrial control from one of the strongest capitalistic powers of the country; while demonstrating beyond doubt that, with intelligent preparation and with sympathetic treatment, the polyglot immigrant masses from Southern and Eastern Europe, long thought to be impervious to the idea of labor organization, can be changed into reliable material for unionism.

The growth of the union in general is shown by the following figures. In 1898 it was 33,000; in 1900, 116,000; in 1903, 247,000; in 1908, 252,000; and in 1913, 378,000.[1]

(2) *The Railway Men*

The railway men are divided into three groups. One group comprises the Brotherhood of Locomotive Engineers, the Order of Railroad Conductors, the Brotherhood of Firemen and Enginemen, and the Brotherhood of Railroad Trainmen. These are the oldest and strongest railway men's organizations and do not belong to the American Federation of Labor. A second group are the shopmen, comprising the International Association of Machinists; the International Brotherhood of Blacksmiths, Drop Forgers, and Helpers; the Brotherhood of Railway Carmen of America; the Amalgamated Sheet Metal Workers' International Alliance; the Brotherhood of Boilermakers and Iron Ship Builders and Helpers of America; the International Brotherhood of Electrical Workers; and the International Brotherhood of Stationary Firemen and Oilers. A third and more miscellaneous group are the Brotherhood of Railway Clerks, the Order of Railway Telegraphers, the Switchmen's Union of North America, the International Brotherhood of Maintenance of Way Employes and Railroad Shop Laborers, and the Brotherhood of Railway Signalmen. The organizations comprised in the latter two groups

[1] The actual membership of the union is considerably above these figures, since they are based upon the dues-paying membership, and miners out on strike are exempted from the payment of all dues. The number of miners who always act with the union is much larger still. Even in non-union fields the United Mine Workers have always been successful in getting thousands of miners to obey their order to strike.

belong to the American Federation of Labor. For the period from 1898 to the outbreak of the War, the organizations, popularly known as the "brotherhoods," namely, those of the engineers, conductors, firemen, and trainmen, are of outstanding importance.

The brotherhoods were unique among American labor organizations in that for many years they practically reproduced in most of their features the sort of unionism typified by the great "Amalgamated" unions of the fifties and sixties in England.[1] Like these unions the brotherhoods stressed mutual insurance and benefits and discouraged when they did not actually prohibit striking. It should, however, be added that the emphasis on insurance was due not to "philosophy," but to the practical consideration that, owing to the extra hazardous nature of their occupations, the men could get no insurance protection from ordinary commercial insurance companies.

By the end of the eighties the brotherhoods began to press energetically for improvements in employment conditions and found the railways not disinclined to grant their demands in a measure. This was due in great measure to the strategic position of these trades, which have it in their power completely to tie up the industry when on strike, causing enormous losses to the carriers.[2] Accordingly, they were granted wages which fairly placed them among the lower professional groups in society as well as other privileges, notably "seniority" in promotion, that is promotion based on length of service and not on a free selection by the officials. Seniority was all the more important since the train personnel service is so

[1] See Webb, *History of Trade Unionism,* p. 205 ff.
[2] This was demonstrated in the bitterly fought strike on the Chicago, Burlington and Quincy Railroad in 1888. (See above, 130-131.)

organized that each employe will pass several times in the regular course of his career from a lower to a higher rung on the industrial ladder.[1] For instance, a typical passenger train engineer starts as fireman on a freight train, advances to a fireman on a passenger train, then to engineer on a freight train, and finally to engineer on a passenger train. A similar sequence is arranged in advancing from brakeman to conductor. Along with seniority the brotherhoods received the right of appeal in cases of discharge, which has done much to eliminate discrimination. Since they were enjoying such exceptional advantages relative to income, to the security of the job, and to the stability of their organization, it is not surprising, in view of the limited class solidarity among American laboring men in general, that these groups of workers should have chosen to stand alone in their wage bargaining and that their refusal to enter "entangling alliances" with other less favored groups should have gone even to the length of staying out of the American Federation of Labor.

This condition of relative harmony between employer and employe, notwithstanding the energetic bargaining, continued for about fiften years until it was disturbed by factors beyond the control of either railway companies or brotherhoods. The steady rise in the cost of living forced the brotherhoods to intensify their demands for increased wages. At the same time an ever tightening regulation of railway rates by the Federal government since 1906 practically prevented a shift of increased costs to the shipper. "Class struggles" on the railways began in earnest.

[1] Seniority also decides the assignment to "runs," which differ greatly in desirability, and it gives preference over junior employes in keeping the job when it is necessary to lay men off.

The new situation was brought home to the brotherhoods in the course of several wage arbitration cases in which they figured.[1] The outcome taught them that the public will give them only limited support in their efforts to maintain their real income at the old high level compared with other classes of workers.

A most important case arose from a "concerted movement" in 1912[2] of the engineers and firemen on the 52 Eastern roads for higher wages. Two separate arbitration boards were appointed. The engineers' board consisted of seven members, one each for the interests involved and five representing the public. The award was unsatisfactory to the engineers, first, because of the meager raise in wages and, second, because it contained a strong plea to Congress and the country to have all wages of all railway employes fixed by a government commission, which implied a restriction of the right to strike. The award in the firemen's case, which was decided practically simultaneously with the engineers', failed to satisfy either side.

The conductors and trainmen on the Eastern roads were next to move "in concert" for increased wages. The roads refused and the brotherhoods decided by a good majority to quit work. This threatened strike occasioned the passage of the so-called Newlands bill as an amendment to the Erdman Act, with increased powers to the government in mediation and with more specified condi-

[1] The first arbitration act was passed by Congress in 1888. In 1898 it was superseded by the well known Erdman Act, which prescribed rules for mediation and voluntary arbitration.

[2] Concerted movements began in 1905 as joint demands upon all railways in a single section of the country, like the East or the West, by a single group of employes; after 1912 two or more brotherhoods initiated common concerted movements, first in one section only, and at last covering all the railways of the country.

tions relative to the work of the arbitration boards chosen
for each occasion. Whereupon both sides agreed to submit to arbitration.

The award allowed an increase in wages of seven per
cent., or less than one-half of that demanded, but dis-
allowed a plea made by the men for uniformity of the
wage scales East and West, and denied the demanded
time and a half for overtime. The men accepted but
the decision added to their growing opposition to the
principle of arbitration.

Another arbitration case, in 1914, involving the engineers and firemen on the Western roads led the brotherhoods to come out openly against arbitration. The
award was signed only by the representatives on the board
of the employers and the public. A characteristic after-
math of this case was an attack made by the unions upon
one of the "neutrals" on the board. His impartiality
was questioned because of his relations with several con-
cerns which owned large amounts of railroad securities.
Therefore, when in 1916 the four brotherhoods together
demanded the eight-hour day, they categorically refused
to consider arbitration.[1] The evolution to a fighting
unionism had become complete.

While the brotherhoods of the train service personnel
were thus shifting their tactics, they kept drawing nearer
to the position held by the other unions in the railway
service. These had rarely had the good fortune to bask
in the sunshine of their employers' approval and "recognition." Some railways, of the more liberal sort, made
agreements with the machinists and with the other shop
unions. On the whole, however, the hold of these organizations upon their industry was of a precarious sort.

[1] See below, 230-233.

To meet their strong opponents on a basis nearer to equality, they started about 1904 a movement for "system federations," [1] that is, federations of all organized trades through the length of a given railway system as, for instance, the Pennsylvania Railroad or the Illinois Central Railroad. In turn the creation of system federations sharpened the employers' antagonism. Some railway systems, like the Illinois Central, might be willing to enter into agreements with the separate crafts, but refused to deal with a federation of crafts. In 1912, stimulated by a dispute on the Illinois Central Railroad and on the Harriman lines in general, involving the issue of system federations, a Federation of System Federations was formed by forty systems upon an aggressive program. In 1908 a weak and rather tentative Railway Employes' Department had been launched by the American Federation of Labor. The Federation of Federations was thus a rival organization and "illegal" or, at best, "extra-legal" from the standpoint of the American Federation of Labor. The situation, however, was too acute to permit the consideration of "legality" to enter. An adjustment was made and the Federation of System Federations was "legitimatized" through fusion with the "Department," to which it gave its constitution, officers, and fighting purpose, and from which it took only its name. This is the now well-known Railway Employes' Department of the American Federation of Labor (embracing all important national unions of the railway workers excepting the four brotherhoods), and which, as we shall see, came into its own when the government took over the

[1] Long before this, about the middle of the nineties, the first system federations were initiated by the brotherhoods and were confined to them only; they took up adjustment of grievances and related matters.

railways from their private owners eight months after America's entry into the World War.

(3) *The Machinery and Metal Trades*

Unlike the miners and the railway brotherhoods, the unions in the machinery and metal trades met with small success in their efforts for "recognition" and trade agreements. The outstanding unions in the industry are the International Association of Machinists and the International Molders' Union, with a half dozen smaller and very small unions.[1] The molders' International united in the same union the stove molders, who as was seen had been "recognized" in 1891, and the molders of parts of machinery and other foundry products. The latter found the National Founders' Association as their antagonist or potential "co-partner" in the industry.

The upward swing in business since 1898, combined with the growth of trade unionism and with the successful negotiation of the Interstate agreement in the soft coal mining industry, created an atmosphere favorable to trade agreements. For a time "recognition" and its implications seemed to all concerned, the employer, the unions, and the public, a sort of cure-all for industrial disputes. Accordingly, in March 1899, the National Founders' Association (organized in the previous year and comprising foundrymen engaged principally in machinery manufacturing and jobbing) and the International Molders' Union of North America met and drew

[1] The International Brotherhood of Blacksmiths, the Brotherhood of Boilermakers and Iron Shipbuilders, the Pattern Makers' League, the International Union of Stove Mounters, the International Union of Metal Polishers, Platers, Brass and Silver Workers, the International Federation of Draftsmen's Unions, and the International Brotherhood of Foundry Employes.

up the following tersely worded agreement which became known as the New York Agreement:

"That in event of a dispute arising between members of the respective organizations, a reasonable effort shall be made by the parties directly at interest to effect a satisfactory adjustment of the difficulty; failing to do which, either party shall have the right to ask its reference to a Committee of Arbitration which shall consist of the President of the National Founders' Association and the President of the Iron Molders' Union or their representatives, and two other representatives from each organization appointed by the respective Presidents.

"The finding of this Committee of Arbitration by majority vote shall be considered final in so far as the future action of the respective organizations is concerned.

"Pending settlement by the Committee, there shall be no cessation of work at the instance of either party to the dispute. The Committee of Arbitration shall meet within two weeks after reference of dispute to them."

The agreement was a triumph for the principle of pure conciliation as distinct from arbitration by a third party. Both sides preferred to run the risk of a possible deadlock in the conciliation machinery to throwing decisions into the hands of an umpire, who would be an uncertain quantity both as regards special bias and understanding of the industry.

The initial meeting of the arbitration committee was held in Cleveland, in May 1899, to consider the demand by the unions at Worcester, Massachusetts, and Providence, Rhode Island, for a minimum wage which the employers had refused. In each city one member of the National Founders' Association was involved and the men in these firms went to work pending the arbitration decision, while the others stayed out on strike.

The meeting ended inauspiciously. The founders and molders seemed not to be able to settle their difficulties. Each side stood fast on its own principles and the arbitration committees regularly became deadlocked. The question of a minimum wage was the most important issue. From 1899 to 1902 several joint conventions were held to discuss the wage question. In 1899 a settlement was made, which, however, proved of short duration. In November 1902, the two organizations met, differed, and arranged for a sub-committee to meet in March 1903. The sub-committee met but could reach no agreement.

The two organizations clashed also on the question of apprentices. The founders contended that, because there were not enough molders to fill the present demand, the union restrictions as to the employment of apprentices should be removed. The union argued that a removal of the restriction would cause unlimited competition among molders and eventually the founders could employ them at their own price. They likewise failed to agree on the matter of classifying molders.

Owing to the stalling of the conciliation machinery many strikes occurred in violation at least of the spirit of the agreement. July 1, 1901, the molders struck in Cleveland for an increase in wages; arbitration committees were appointed but failed to make a settlement. In Chicago and San Francisco strikes occurred for the same reason.

It was at last becoming evident that the New York agreement was not working well. In the autumn of 1903 business prosperity reached its high watermark and then came a sharp depression which lessened the demand for molders. Early in 1904 the National Founders' Association took advantage of this situation to reduce wages and finally practically abrogated the New York agreement. In April, 1904, the founders and molders tried to reach a decision as to how the agreement could be made effective, but gave it up after four days and nights of constant consideration. The founders claimed that the molders violated the agreement in 54 out of the 96 cases that came up during the five years of its life; and further justified their action on the ground that the union persistently refused to submit to arbitration by an impartial outsider the issues upon which the agreement was finally wrecked.

An agreement similar to the New York one was concluded in 1900 between the National Metal Trades' Association and the International Association of Machinists. The National Metal Trades' Association had been organized in 1899 by members of the National Founders' Association, whose foundries formed only a part of their manufacturing plants. The spur to action was given by a strike called by the machinists in Chicago and other cities for the nine-hour day. After eight weeks of intense struggle the Association made a settlement granting a promise of the shorter day. Although hailed as one of the big agreements in labor history, it lasted only one year, and broke up on the issue of making the nine-hour day general in the Association shops. The machinists continued to make numerous agreements with individual firms, especially the smaller ones, but the general agreement was never renewed. Thereafter the National Metal Trades' Association became an uncompromising enemy of organized labor.

In the following ten years both molders and machinists went on fighting for control and engaged in strikes with more or less success. But the industry as a whole never again came so near to embracing the idea of a joint copartnership between organized capital and labor as in 1900.

(4) *The Employers' Reaction*

With the disruption of the agreement systems in the machinery producing and foundry industries, the idea of collective bargaining and union recognition suffered a setback; and the employers' uneasiness, which had already steadily been feeding on the unions' mounting pressure for control, now increased materially. As long, however, as business remained prosperous and a rising demand for labor favored the unions, most of the agreements were permitted to continue. Therefore, it was not until the industrial depression of 1907-1908 had freed the employers' hands that agreements were disrupted wholesale. In 1905 the Structural Erectors' Association discontinued its agreements with the Structural Iron Workers' Union, causing a dispute which continued over many years. In the course of this dispute the union replied to the victorious assaults of the employers by tactics of violence and murder, which culminated in the fatal explosion in the *Los Angeles Times* Building in 1911. In 1906 the employing lithographers discontinued their national agreement with the lithographers' union. In 1907 the United Typothetæ broke with the pressmen, and the stove founders with the stove mounters and stove polishers. In 1908 the agreements between the Lake Carriers and Lumber Carriers (both operating on the Great Lakes) and the seafaring and water front unions were terminated.

In the operation of these unsuccessful agreements the most serious stumbling blocks were the union "working rules," that is to say, the restrictive rules which unions strove to impose on employers in the exercise of their managerial powers in the shop, and for which the latter adopted the sinister collective designation of "restriction of output."

Successful trade unionism has always pressed "working rules" on the employer. As early as the first decade of the nineteenth century, the trade societies then existing tried to impose on the masters the closed shop and restrictions on apprenticeship along with higher wages and shorter hours. As a union advances from an ephemeral association to a stable organization more and more the emphasis is shifted from wages to working rules. Unionists have discovered that on the whole wages are the unstable factor, going up or down, depending on fluctuating business conditions and cost of living; but that once they have established their power by making the employer accept their working rules, high wages will ultimately follow.

These working rules are seldom improvisations of the moment, but, crude and one-sided as they often are, they are the product of a long labor experience and have taken many years to be shaped and hammered out. Since their purpose is protective, they can best be classified with reference to the particular thing in the workingman's life which they are designed to protect: the standard of living of the trade group, health, the security of the worker's job, equal treatment in the shop and an equal chance with other workmen in promotion, the bargaining power of the trade group, as a whole, and the safety of the union from the employer's attempts to undermine it. We shall mention only a few of these rules by way of illustration. Thus all rules relating to methods of wage payment, like the prohibition of piece work and of bonus systems (including those associated with scientific management systems), are primarily devices to protect the wage earner's rate of pay against being "nibbled away" by the employer; and in part also to protect his health against undue exertion. Other rules like the normal (usually the eight-hour) day with a higher rate for overtime; the rule demanding a guarantee of continuous employment for a stated time or a guarantee of minimum earnings, regardless of the quantity of work available in the shop; again the demand for the sharing of work in slack times among all employes; and further, when lay-offs become necessary, the demand of recognition by the employer of a right to continuous employment based on "seniority" in the shop;—all these have for their common aim chiefly the protection of the job. Another sort of rules, like the obstruction to the splitting up of trades and the restrictions on apprenticeship, have in view the protection of the bargaining power of the craft group—through artificially maintaining an undiminished demand for skilled labor, as well as through a reduction of the number of competitors, present and future, for jobs. The protection of the union against the employer's designs, actual or potential, is sought by an insistence on the closed union shop, by the recognition of the right of appeal to grievance boards in cases of discharge to prevent anti-union discrimination, and through establishing a seniority right in promotion which binds the worker's allegiance to his union rather than to the employer.

With these rigid rules, partly already enforced on the employer by strikes or threats to strike and partly as yet unrealized but energetically pushed, trade unionism enters the stage of the trade agreement. The problem of industrial government then becomes one of steady adjustment of the conflicting claims of employer and union for the province of shop control staked out by these working rules. When the two sides are approximately equal in bargaining strength (and lasting agreements are possible only when this condition obtains), a promising line of compromise, as recent experience has shown, has been to extend to the unions and their members in some form that will least obstruct shop efficiency the very same kind of guarantees which they strive to obtain through rules of their own making. For instance, an employer might induce a union to give up or agree to mitigate its working rules designed to protect the job by offering a *quid pro quo* in a guarantee of employment for a stated number of weeks during the year; and likewise, a union might hope to counteract the employer's natural hankering for being "boss in his own business," free of any union working rules, only provided it guaranteed him a sufficient output per unit of labor time and wage investment.

However, compromises of this sort are pure experiments even at present—fifteen to twenty years after the dissolution of those agreements; and they certainly require more faith in government by agreement and more patience than one could expect in the participants in these earlier agreements. It is not surprising, therefore, that the short period of agreements after 1898 should in many industries have formed but a prelude to an "open-shop" movement.[1]

---

[1] Professor Barnett attributes the failure of these agreements chiefly to faulty agreement machinery. The working rules, he points out, are rules made by the national union and therefore can be changed by the national union only. At the same time the agreements were national only in so far as they provided for national conciliation machinery; the fixing of wages was left to local bodies. Consequently, the national employers' associations lacked the power to offer the unions an indispensable *quid pro quo* in higher wages

After their breach with the union, the National Founders' Association and the National Metal Trades' Association have gone about the business of union wrecking in a systematic way. They have maintained a so-called "labor bureau," furnishing men to their members whenever additional help was needed, and keeping a complete card system record of every man in the employ of members. By this system occasion was removed for employers communicating with the business agents of the various unions when new men were wanted. The associations have had in their regular pay a large number of non-union men, or "strike-breakers," who were sent to the shop of any member whose employes were on strike.

In addition to these and other national organizations, the trade unions were attacked by a large and important class of local employers' associations. The most influential association of this class was the Employers' Association of Dayton, Ohio. This association had a standing strike committee which, in trying to break a strike, was authorized to offer rewards to the men who continued at work, and even to compensate the employer for loss of production to the limit of one dollar per day for each man on strike. Also a system was adopted of issuing cards to all employes, which the latter, in case of changing employment, were obliged to present to the new employer and upon which the old employer inscribed his recommendation. The extreme anti-unionism of the Dayton Association is best attested by its policy of taking into membership employers who were threatened with strikes, notwithstanding the heavy financial obligations involved.

for a compromise on working rules. ("National and District Systems of Collective Bargaining in the United States," in *Quarterly Journal of Economics,* May, 1912, pp. 425 ff.)

Another class of local associations were the "Citizens' Alliances," which did not restrict membership to employers but admitted all citizens, the only qualification being that the applicant be not a member of any labor organization. These organizations were frequently started by employers and secured coöperation of citizens generally. In some places there were two associations, an employers' and a Citizens' Alliance. A good example of this was the Citizens' Alliances of Denver, Colorado, organized in 1903. These "Citizens' Alliances," being by virtue of mixed membership more than a mere employers' organization, claimed in time of strikes to voice the sentiment of the community in general.

So much for the employers' counter attacks on trade unions on the strictly industrial front. But there were also a legal front and a political front. In 1902 was organized the American Anti-Boycott Association, a secret body composed mainly of manufacturers. The purpose of the organization was to oppose by legal proceedings the boycotts of trade unions, and to secure statutory enactments against the boycott. The energies of the association have been devoted mainly to taking certain typical cases to the courts in order thereby to create legal precedents. The famous Danbury Hatters' Case, in which the Sherman Anti-Trust law was invoked against the hatters' union, was fought in the courts by this Association.

The employers' fight on the political front was in charge of the National Association of Manufacturers. This association was originally organized in 1895 for the pursuit of purely trade interests, but about 1903, under the influence of the Dayton, Ohio, group of employers, turned to combating trade unions. It closely coöperated with other employers' associations in the industrial and legal field, but its chief efforts lay in the political or legislative field, where it has succeeded through clever lobbying and manipulations in nullifying labor's political influence, especially in Congress. The National Association of Manufacturers saw to it that Congress and State Legislatures might not weaken the effect of court orders, injunctions and decisions on boycotts, closed shop, and related matters.

The "open-shop movement" in its several aspects, industrial, legal, and political, continued strong from 1903 to 1909. Nevertheless, despite most persistent effort and despite the opportunity offered by the business depression which followed the financial panic of 1907, the results were not remarkable. True, it was a factor in checking the rapid rate of expansion of unionism, but it scarcely compelled a retrogression from ground already conquered. It is enough to point out that the unions managed to prevent wage reductions in the organized trades notwithstanding the unemployment and distress of 1907-1908. On the whole trade unionism held its own against employers in strictly competitive industry. Different, however, was the outcome in industries in which the number of employers had been reduced by monopolistic or semi-monopolistic mergers.

The steel industry is the outstanding instance.[1] The disastrous Homestead strike of 1892 [2] had eliminated unionism from the steel plants of Pittsburgh. However, the Carnegie Steel Company was only a highly efficient and powerful corporation, not yet a "trust." The panic

---

[1] The following account is taken from Chapter X of the *Steel Workers* by John A. Fitch, published by the Russell Sage Foundation.
[2] See above, 133-135.

of 1893 dealt another blow to the Amalgamated Association of Iron & Steel Workers. The steel mills of Alleghany County, outside Pittsburgh, were all put upon a non-union basis before 1900. In Pittsburgh, the iron mills, too, became non-union between 1890 and 1900. There remained to the organization only the iron mills west of Pittsburgh, the large steel mills of Illinois, and a large proportion of the sheet, tin, and iron hoop mills of the country. In 1900 there began to be whisperings of a gigantic consolidation in the steel industry. The Amalgamated officials were alarmed. In any such combination the Carnegie Steel Company, an old enemy of unionism, would easily be first and would, they feared, insist on driving the union out of every mill in the combination. Then it occurred to President Shaffer and his associates that it might be a propitious time to press for recognition while the new corporation was forming. Anxious for public confidence and to float their securities, the companies could not afford a labor controversy.

Accordingly, when the new scales were to be signed in July 1901, the Amalgamated Association demanded of the American Tin Plate Company that it sign a scale not only for those mills that had been regarded as union but for all of its mills. This was agreed, provided the American Sheet Steel Company would agree to the same. The latter company refused, and a strike was started against the American Tin Plate Company, the American Sheet Steel Company, and the American Steel Hoop Company. In conferences held on July 11, 12, and 13 these companies offered to sign for all tin mills but one, for all the sheet mills that had been signed for in the preceding year and for four other mills that had been non-union, and for all the hoop mills that had been signed for in the preceding year. This highly advantageous offer was foolishly rejected by the representatives of the union; they demanded all the mills or none. The strike then went on in earnest. In August, President Shaffer called on all the men working in mills of the United States Steel Corporation to come out on strike.

By the middle of August it was evident that the Association had made a mistake. Instead of finding their task easier because the United States Steel Corporation had just been formed, they found that corporation ready to bring all its tremendous power to bear against the organization. President Shaffer offered to arbitrate the whole matter, but the proposal was rejected; and at the end of August the strike was declared at an end.

The steel industry was apparently closed to unionism.[1]

(5) *Legislation, Courts, and Politics*

While trade unionism was thus on the whole holding its ground against the employers and even winning victories and recognition, its influence on National and State legislation failed for many years to reflect its growing economic strength. The scant success with legislation resulted, on the one hand, from the very expansion of the Federation into new fields, which absorbed nearly all its means and energy; but was due in a still greater measure to a solidification of capitalist control in the Republican party and in Congress, against which President Roosevelt directed his spectacular campaign. A good illustration is

[1] The opposition of the Steel Corporation to unionism was an important factor in the disruption of the agreement systems in the structural iron-erecting industry in 1905 and in the carrying industry on the Great Lakes in 1908; in each of these industries the Corporation holds a place of considerable control.

furnished by the attempt to get a workable eight-hour law on government work.

In the main the leaders of the Federation placed slight reliance upon efforts to shorten the working day through legislation. The movement for shorter hours by law for women, which first attained importance in the nineties, was not the work of organized labor but of humanitarians and social workers. To be sure, the Federation has supported such laws for women and children workers, but so far as adult male labor was concerned, it has always preferred to leave the field clear for the trade unions. The exception to the rule was the working day on public work.

The Federal eight-hour day law began to receive attention from the Federation towards the end of the eighties. By that time the status of the law of 1868 which decreed the eight-hour day on Federal government work [1] had been greatly altered. In a decision rendered in 1887 the Supreme Court held that the eight-hour day law of 1868 was merely directory to the officials of the Federal government, but did not invalidate contracts made by them not containing an eight-hour clause. To counteract this decision a special law was passed in 1888, with the support of the Federation, establishing the eight-hour day in the United States Printing Office and for letter carriers. In 1892 a new general eight-hour law was passed, which provided that eight-hours should be the length of the working day on all public works of the United States, whether directed by the government or under contract or sub-contract. Within the next few years interpretations rendered by attorney generals of the United States practically rendered the law useless.

[1] See above, 47-49.

In 1895 the Federation began to press in earnest for a satisfactory eight-hour law. In 1896 its eight-hour bill passed the House of Representatives unanimously. In the Senate it was introduced by Senator Kyle, the chairman of the committee on Education and Labor. After its introduction, however, hearings upon the bill were delayed so long that action was prevented during the long session. In the short session of 1898-1899 the bill met the cruel fate of having its introducer, Senator Kyle, submit a minority report against it. Under the circumstances no vote upon the bill could be had in the Senate. In the next Congress, 1899-1901, the eight-hour bill once more passed the House of Representatives only to be lost in the Senate by failure to come to a vote. In 1902, the bill again unanimously passed the House, but was not even reported upon by the Senate committee. In the hearings upon the eight-hour bill in that year the opposition of the National Manufacturers' Association was first manifested. In 1904 the House Labor Committee sidetracked a similar bill by recommending that the Department of Commerce and Labor should investigate its merits. Secretary Metcalf, however, declared that the questions submitted to his Department with reference to the eight-hour bill were "well-nigh unintelligible." In 1906 the House Labor Committee, at a very late stage in the session, reported "favorably" upon the eight-hour bill. At the same time it eliminated all chances of passage of the bill through the failure of a majority of the members of the committee to sign the "favorable" report made. This session of Congress, also, allowed a "rider" to be added to the Panama Canal bill, exempting the canal construction from the provisions of the eight-hour law. In the next two Congresses no report could be obtained from the labor committees of either House upon the general eight-hour day bill, despite the fact that President Roosevelt and later President Taft recommended such legislation. In the sessions of the Congress of 1911-1913 the American Federation of Labor hit upon a new plan. This was the attachment of "riders" to departmental appropriation bills requiring that all work contracted for by these departments must be done under the eight-hour system. The most important "rider" of this character was that attached to the naval appropriation bill. Under its provisions the Attorney-General held that in all work done in shipyards upon vessels built for the Federal government the eight-hour rule must be applied. Finally, in June 1912, a Democratic House and a Republican Senate passed the eight-hour bill supported by the American Federation of Labor with some amendments, which the Federation did not find seriously objectionable; and President Taft signed it.

Still better proof of the slight influence of the Federation upon government is furnished by the vicissitudes of its anti-injunction bills in Congress. The Federation had been awakened to the seriousness of the matter of the injunction by the Debs case. A bill of its sponsoring providing for jury trials in "indirect" contempt cases passed the Senate in 1896 only to be killed in the House. In 1900 only eight votes were recorded in the House against a bill exempting labor unions from the Sherman Anti-Trust Act; it failed, however, of passage in the Senate. In 1902 an anti-injunction bill championed by the American Federation of Labor passed the House of Representatives. That was the last time, however, for many years to come when such a bill was even reported out of committee. Thereafter, for a decade, the controlling powers in Congress had their faces set against removal by law of the judicial interference in labor's use of its economic strength against employers.

In the meantime, however, new court decisions made the situation more and more critical. A climax was reached in 1908-1909. In February 1908, came the Supreme Court decision in the Danbury Hatters' case, which held that members of a labor union could be held financially responsible to the full amount of their individual property under the Sherman Anti-Trust Act for losses to business occasioned by an interstate boycott.[1] By way of contrast, the Supreme Court within the same week held unconstitutional the portion of the Erdman Act which prohibited discrimination by railways against workmen on account of their membership in a union.[2] One year later, in the Buck's Stove and Range Company boycott case, Gompers, Mitchell, and Morrison, the three most prominent officials of the American Federation of Labor, were sentenced by a lower court in the District of Columbia to long terms in prison for violating an injunction which prohibited all mention of the fact that the plaintiff firm had ever been boycotted.[3] " Even though neither these nor subsequent court decisions had the paralyzing effect upon American trade unionism which its enemies hoped for and its friends feared, the situation called for a change in tactics. It thus came about that the Federation, which, as was seen, by the very principles of its program wished to let government alone,—as it

---

[1] Loewe v. Lawlor, 208 U. S. 274 (1908).

[2] Adair v. U. S., 208 U. S. 161 (1908).

[3] 36 Wash. Law Rep. 436 (1909). Gompers was finally sentenced to imprisonment for thirty days and the other two defendants were fined $500 each. These penalties were later lifted by the Supreme Court on a technicality, 233 U. S. 604 (1914).

indeed expected little good of government,—was obliged to enter into competition with the employers for controlling government; this was because one branch of the government, namely the judicial one, would not let it alone.

A growing impatience with Congress was manifested in resolutions adopted by successive conventions. In 1902 the convention authorized the Executive Council to take "such further steps as will secure the nomination—and the election—of only such men as are fully and satisfactorily pledged to the support of the bills" championed by the Federation. Accordingly, the Executive Council prepared a series of questions to be submitted to all candidates for Congress in 1904 by the local unions of each district.

The Federation was more active in the Congressional election of 1906. Early in the year the Executive Council urged affiliated unions to use their influence to prevent the nomination in party primaries or conventions of candidates for Congress who refused to endorse labor's demands, and where both parties nominated refractory candidates to run independent labor candidates. The labor campaign was placed in the hands of a Labor Representation Committee, which made use of press publicity and other standard means. Trade union speakers were sent into the districts of the most conspicuous enemies of labor's demands to urge their defeat. The battle royal was waged against Congressman Littlefield of Maine. A dozen union officials, headed by President Gompers, invaded his district to tell the electorate of his insults to organized labor. However, he was reëlected, although with a reduced plurality over the preceding election. The only positive success was the election of McDermott of the commercial telegraphers' union in Chicago. President Gompers, however, insisted that the cutting down of the majorities of the conspicuous enemies of labor's demands gave "more than a hint" of what organized labor "can and may do when thoroughly prepared to exercise its political strength." Nevertheless the next Congress was even more hostile than the preceding one. The convention of the Federation following the election approved the new tactics, but was careful at the same time to declare that the Federation was neither allied with any political party nor had any intention of forming an independent labor party.

In the Presidential election of 1908, however, the Federation virtually entered into an alliance with the Democrats. At a "Protest Conference" in March, 1908, attended by the executive officers of most of the affiliated national unions as well as by the representatives of several farmers' organizations, the threat was uttered that organized labor would make a determined effort in the coming campaign to defeat its enemies, whether "candidates for President, for Congress, or other offices." The next step was the presentation of the demands of the Federation to the platform committees of the conventions of both parties. The wording of the proposed anti-injunction plank suggests that it had been framed after consultation with the Democratic leaders, since it omitted to demand the sweeping away of the doctrine of malicious conspiracy or the prohibition of the issuance of injunctions to protect business rights, which had regularly been asked by the American Federation of Labor since 1904. In its place was substituted an indefinite statement against the issuance of injunctions in labor disputes where none would be allowed if no labor dispute existed and a declaration in favor of jury trial on the charge of contempt of court.

The Republicans paid scant attention to the planks of the Federation. Their platform merely reiterated the recognized law upon the allowance of equity relief; and as if to leave no further doubt in the minds of the labor leaders, proceeded to nominate for President, William H. Taft, who as a Federal judge in the early nineties was responsible for some of the most sweeping injunctions ever issued in labor disputes. A year earlier Gompers had characterized Taft as "the injunction standard-bearer" and as an impossible candidate. The Democratic platform, on the other hand, *verbatim* repeated the Federation plank on the injunction question and nominated Bryan.

After the party conventions had adjourned the *American Federationist* entered on a vigorous attack upon the Republican platform and candidate. President Gompers recognized that this was equivalent to an endorsement of Bryan, but pleaded that "in performing a solemn duty at this time in support of a political party, labor does not become partisan to a political party, but partisan to a principle." Substantially, all prominent non-Socialist trade-union officials followed Gompers' lead. That the trade unionists did not vote solidly for Bryan, however, is apparent from the distribution of the vote. On the other hand, it is true that the Socialist vote in 1908 in almost all trade-union centers was not materially above that of 1904, which would seem to warrant the conclusion that Gompers may have "delivered to Bryan" not a few labor votes which would otherwise have gone to Debs.

In the Congressional election of 1910 the Federation repeated the policy of "reward your friends, and punish your enemies." However, it avoided more successfully the appearance of partisanship. Many progressive Republicans received as strong support as did Democratic candidates. Nevertheless the Democratic majority in the new House meant that the Federation was at last "on the inside" of one branch of the government. In addition, fifteen men holding cards of membership in unions, were elected to Congress, which was the largest number on record. Furthermore William B. Wilson, Ex-Secretary of the United Mine Workers, was appointed chairman of the important House Committee on Labor.

The Congress of 1911-1913 with its Democratic House of Representatives passed a large portion of the legislation which the Federation had been urging for fifteen years. It passed an eight-hour law on government contract work, as already noted, and a seaman's bill, which went far to grant to the sailors the freedom of contract enjoyed by other wage earners. It created a Department of Labor with a seat in the Cabinet. It also attached a "rider" to the appropriation bill for the Department of Justice enjoining the use of any of the funds for purposes of prosecuting labor organizations under the Sherman Anti-Trust Law and other Federal laws. In the presidential campaign of 1912 Gompers pointed to the legislation favorable to labor initiated by the Democratic House of Representatives and let the workers draw their own conclusions. The corner stone of the Federation's legislative program, the legal exemption of trade unions from the operation of anti-trust legislation and from court interference in disputes by means of injunctions, was yet to be laid. By inference, therefore, the election of a Democratic administration was the logical means to that end.

At last, with the election of Woodrow Wilson as President and of a Democratic Congress in 1912, the political friends of the Federation controlled all branches of government. William B. Wilson was given the place of Secretary of Labor. Hereafter, for at least seven years, the Federation was an "insider" in the national government. The road now seemed clear to the attainment by trade unions of freedom from court interference in struggles against employers—a judicial *laissez-faire*. The political program initiated in 1906 seemed to be bearing fruit.

The drift into politics, since 1906, has differed essentially from that of earlier periods. It has been a movement coming from "on top," not from the masses of the laborers themselves. Hard times and defeats in strikes have not very prominently figured. Instead of a movement led by local unions and by city centrals as had been the case practically in all preceding political attempts, the Executive Council of the American Federation of Labor now became the directing force. The rank and file seem to have been much less stirred than the leaders; for the member who held no union office felt less intensely the menace from injunctions than the officials who might face a prison sentence for contempt of court. Probably for this reason the "delivery" of the labor vote by the Federation has ever been so largely problematical. That the Federation leaders were able to force the desired concessions from one of the political parties by holding out a *quid pro quo* of such an uncertain value is at once a tribute to their political sagacity as well as a mark of the instability of the general political alignment in the country.

CHAPTER 9

RADICAL UNIONISM AND A "COUNTER-REFORMATION"

For ten years after 1904, when it reached its high point, the American Federation of Labor was obliged to stay on the defensive—on the defensive against the "open-shop" employers and against the courts. Even the periodic excursions into politics were in substance defensive moves. This turn of events naturally tended to detract from the prestige of the type of unionism for which Gompers was spokesman; and by contrast raised the stock of the radical opposition.

The opposition developed both in and outside the Federtion. Inside it was the socialist "industrialist" who advocated a political labor party on a socialist platform, such as the Federation had rejected when it defeated the "program" of 1893,[1] together with a plan of organization by industry instead of by craft. Outside the Federation the opposition marched under the flag of the Industrial Workers of the World, which was launched by socialists but soon after birth fell into the hands of syndicalists.

However, fully to understand the issue between conservatives and radicals in the Federation after 1905, one needs to go back much earlier for the "background."

The socialist movement, after it had unwittingly assisted in the birth of the opportunistic trade unionism of

[1] See above, 139-141.

208

Strasser and Gompers,[1] did not disappear, but remained throughout the eighties a handful of "intellectuals" and "intellectualized" wage earners, mainly Germans. These never abandoned the hope of better things for socialism in the labor movement. With this end in view, they adopted an attitude of enthusiastic coöperation with the Knights of Labor and the Federation in their wage struggle, which they accompanied, to be sure, by a persistent though friendly "nudging" in the direction of socialism. During the greater part of the eighties the socialists were closer to the trade unionists than to the Knights, because of the larger proportion of foreign born, principally Germans, among them. The unions in the cigar making, cabinet making, brewing, and other German trades counted many socialists, and socialists were also in the lead in the city federations of unions in New York, Chicago, Cleveland, St. Louis, Milwaukee, and other cities. In the campaign of Henry George for Mayor of New York in 1886, the socialists coöperated with him and the labor organizations. When, however, the campaign being over, they fell out with George on the issue of the single tax, they received more sympathy from the trade unionists than George; though one should add that the internal strife caused the majority of the trade unionists to lose interest in either faction and in the whole political movement. The socialist organization went by the name of the Socialist Labor party, which it had kept since 1877. Its enrolled membership was under 10,000, and its activities were non-political (since it refrained from nominating its own tickets) but entirely agitational and propagandist. The socialist press was chiefly in German and was led by a daily in New York. So it

[1] See above, 76-79.

continued until there appeared on the scene an imperious figure, one of those men who, had he lived in a country with conditions more favorable to socialism than the United States, would doubtless have become one of the world's outstanding revolutionary leaders. This man was Daniel DeLeon.

DeLeon was of South American ancestry, who early immigrated to New York. For a time he was teacher of languages at Columbia College; later he devoted himself thoroughly to socialist propaganda. He established his first connection with the labor movement in the George campaign in 1886 and by 1890 we find him in control of the socialist organization. DeLeon was impatient with the policy of slow permeation carried on by the socialists. A convinced if not fanatical Marxian, his philosophy taught him that the American labor movement, like all national labor movements, had, in the nature of things, to be socialist. He formed the plan of a supreme and last effort to carry socialism into the hosts of the Knights and the Federation, failing which, other and more drastic means would be used.

By 1895 he learned that he was beaten in both organizations; not, however, without temporarily upsetting the groups in control. For, the only time when Samuel Gompers was defeated for President of the Federation was in 1894, when the socialists, angered by his part in the rejection of the socialist program at the convention,[1] joined with his enemies and voted another man into office. Gompers was reëlected the next year and the Federation seemed definitely shut to socialism. DeLeon was now ready to go to the limit with the Federation. If the established unions refused to assume the part of the grave-

[1] See above, 139-141.

diggers of capitalism, designed for them, as he believed, by the very logic of history, so much the worse for the established trade unions.

Out of this grew the Socialist Trade and Labor Alliance as a life and death rival to the Federation. From the standpoint of socialism no more unfortunate step could have been taken. It immediately stamped the socialists as wilful destroyers of the unity of labor. To the trade unionists, yet fresh from the ordeal of the struggle against the Knights of Labor, the action of the socialists was an unforgivable crime. All the bitterness which has characterized the fight between socialist and anti-socialist in the Federation verily goes back to this gross miscalculation by DeLeon of the psychology of the trade union movement. DeLeon, on his part, attributed the action of the Federation to a hopelessly corrupt leadership and, since he failed to unseat it by working from within, he now felt justified in striking at the entire structure.

The Socialist Trade and Labor Alliance was a failure from the outset. Only a small portion of even the socialist-minded trade unionists were willing to join in the venture. Many trade union leaders who had been allied with the socialists now openly sided with Gompers. In brief, the socialist "revolution" in the American labor world suffered the fate of all unsuccessful revolutions: it alienated the moderate sympathizers and forced the victorious majority into taking up a more uncompromising position than heretofore.

Finally, the hopelessness of DeLeon's tactics became obvious. One faction in the Socialist Labor party, which had been in opposition ever since he assumed command, came out in revolt in 1898. A fusion took place between it and another socialist group, the so-called Debs-Berger Social Democracy,[1] which took the name of the Social Democratic Party. Later, at a "Unity Congress" in 1901, it became the Socialist Party of America. What distinguished this party from the Socialist Labor party (which, although it had lost its primacy in the socialist movement, has continued side by side with the Socialist party of America), was well expressed in a resolution adopted at the same "Unity" convention: "We recognize that trade unions are by historical necessity organized on neutral grounds as far as political affiliation is concerned." With this program, the socialists have been fairly successful in extending their influence in the American Federation of Labor so that at times they have controlled about one-third of the votes in the conventions. Nevertheless the conservatives have never forgiven the socialists their "original sin." In the country at large socialism made steady progress until 1912, when nearly one million votes were cast for Eugene V. Debs, or about 1/16 of the total. After 1912, particularly since 1916, the socialist party became involved in the War and the difficulties created by the War and retrogressed.

For a number of years DeLeon's failure kept possible imitators in check. However, in 1905, came another attempt in the shape of the Industrial Workers of the World. As with its predecessor, impatient socialists

[1] Eugene V. Debs, after serving his sentence in prison for disobeying a court injunction during the Pullman strike of 1894, became a convert to socialism. It is said that his conversion was due to Victor Berger of Milwaukee. Berger had succeeded in building up a strong socialist party in that city and in the State of Wisconsin upon the basis of a thorough understanding with the trade unions and was materially helped by the predominance of the German-speaking element in the population. In 1910 the Milwaukee socialists elected a municipal ticket, the first large city to vote the socialists into office.

helped to set it afoot, but unlike the Alliance, it was at the same time an outgrowth of a particular situation in the actual labor movement, namely, of the bitter fight which was being waged by the Western Federation of Miners since the middle nineties.

Beginning with a violent clash between miners and mine owners in the silver region of Cœur d'Alène, Idaho, in the early nineties, the mining States of the West became the scene of many labor struggles which were more like civil wars than like ordinary labor strikes.

A most important contributing cause was a struggle, bolder than has been encountered elsewhere in the United States, for control of government in the interest of economic class. This was partly due to the absence of a neutral middle class, farmers or others, who might have been able to keep matters within bounds.

The Western Federation of Miners was an organization of workers in and around the metaliferous mines. It also included workers in smelters. It held its first convention in 1893 in Butte, Montana. In 1894 the men employed in the Cripple Creek, Colorado, gold fields demanded a minimum wage of three dollars for an eight-hour day. After four months the strike resulted in a victory for the union. Other strikes occurred in 1896 and 1897 at Leadville, in 1899 in the Cœur d'Alène mining district, and in 1901 at Rossland and Fernie, British Columbia, and also in the San Juan district in California.

The most important strike of the Western Federation of Miners, however, began in 1903 at Colorado City, where the mill and smeltermen's union quit work in order to compel better working conditions. As the sympathetic strike was a recognized part of the policy of the Western Federation of Miners, all the miners in the Cripple Creek

region were called out. The eight-hour day in the smelters was the chief issue. In 1899 the Colorado legislature had passed an eight-hour law which was declared
unconstitutional by the Supreme Court of the State. To
overcome this difficulty, an amendment to the State constitution was passed in 1902 by a large majority, but
the legislature, after having thus received a direct command to establish the eight-hour law, adjourned without
taking action. Much of the subsequent disorder and
bloodshed in the Cripple Creek region during 1903-1904
is traceable to this failure on the part of the legislature
to enact the eight-hour law. The struggle in Colorado
helped to convince the Western miners that agreements
with their employers were futile, that constitutional
amendments and politics were futile, and from this they
drew the conclusion that the revolutionary way was the
only way. William D. Haywood, who became the central
figure in the revolutionary movement of the Industrial
Workers of the World since its launching in 1905, was a
former national officer of the Western Federation of
Miners and a graduate of the Colorado school of industrial experience.[1]

Even before 1905 the Western Federation of Miners,
which was out of touch with the American Federation of
Labor for reasons of geography and of difference in
policy and program, attempted to set up a national labor
federation which would reflect its spirit. An American
Labor Union was created in 1902, which by 1905 had
a membership of about 16,000 besides the 27,000 of the

[1] In 1907 Haywood was tried and acquitted with two other officers
of the Western Federation of Miners at Boisé, Idaho, on a murder
charge which grew out of the same labor struggle. This was one of
the several sensational trials in American labor history, on a par with
the Molly Maguires' case in the seventies, the Chicago Anarchists' in
1887, and the McNamaras' case in 1912.

miners' federation. It was thus the precursor of the Industrial Workers of the World in 1905. In the latter the revolutionary miners from the West joined hands with radical socialists from the East and Middle West of both socialist parties, the Socialist party of America and DeLeon's Socialist Labor party.

We shall forbear tracing here the complicated internal history of the I. W. W., that is the friction which immediately arose between the DeLeonites and the other socialists and later on the struggle between the socialists and the syndicalist-minded labor rebels from the West. Suffice it to say that the Western Federation of Miners, which was its very heart and body, convinced of the futility of it all, seceded in 1907. In 1911 it joined the American Federation of Labor and after several hardfought strikes, notably in Michigan in 1913, it practically became assimilated to the other unions in the American Federation of Labor.

The remnant of the I. W. W. split in 1908 into two rival Industrial Workers of the World, with headquarters in Detroit and Chicago, respectively, on the issue of revolutionary political versus non-political or "direct" action. As a rival to the Federation of Labor the I. W. W. never materialized, but on the one hand, as an instrument of resistance by the migratory laborers of the West and, on the other hand, as a prod to the Federation to do its duty to the unorganized and unskilled foreignspeaking workers of the East, the I. W. W. will for long have a part to play.

In fact, about 1912, it seemed as though the I. W. W. were about to repeat the performance of the Knights of Labor in the Great Upheaval of 1885-1887. Its clamorous appearance in the industrial East, showing in the strikes by the non-English-speaking workers in the textile mills of Lawrence, Massachusetts, Paterson, New Jersey, and Little Falls, New York, on the one hand, and on the other, the less tangible but no less desperate strikes of casual laborers which occurred from time to time in the West, bore for the observer a marked resemblance to the Great Upheaval. Furthermore, the trained eyes of the leaders of the Federation espied in the Industrial Workers of the World a new rival which would best be met on its own ground by organizing within the Federation the very same elements to which the I. W. W. especially addressed itself. Accordingly, at the convention of 1912, held in Rochester, the problem of organizing the unskilled occupied a place near the head of the list. But after the unsuccessful Paterson textile strikes in 1912 and 1913, the star of the Industrial Workers of the World set as rapidly as it had risen and the organization rapidly retrogressed. At no time did it roll up a membership of more than 60,000 as compared with the maximum membership of 750,000 of the Knights of Labor.

The charge made by the I. W. W. against the Federation of Labor (and it is in relation to the latter that the I. W. W. has any importance at all) is mainly two-fold: on aim and on method. "Instead of the conservative motto, 'A fair day's wage for a fair day's work,'" reads the Preamble, "We must inscribe on our banner the revolutionary watchword, 'Abolition of the wage system.' It is the historic mission of the working class to do away with capitalism. The army of production must be organized, not only for the every-day struggle with capitalists, but to carry on production when capitalism shall have been overthrown." Then on method: "We find that the centering of management in industries into fewer and fewer hands makes the trade union unable to cope with the ever-growing power of the employing class. The trade unions foster a state of affairs which allows one set of the workers to be pitted against another set of workers in the same industry, thereby helping to defeat one another in wage wars. . . . These conditions must be changed and the interest of the working class upheld only by an organization founded in such a way that all its members in any one industry, or in all industries, if necessary, cease work whenever a strike or a lockout is in any department thereof, thus making an injury to one an injury to all." Lastly, "By organizing industrially we are forming the structure of the new society within the shell of the old."

This meant "industrialism" versus the craft autonomy of the Federation. "Industrialism" was a product of the intense labor struggles of the nineties, of the Pullman railway strike in 1894, of the general strike of the bituminous miners of 1898, and of a decade long struggle and boycott in the beer-brewing industry. Industrialism meant a united front against the employers in an industry regardless of craft; it meant doing away with the paralyzing disputes over jurisdiction amongst the several craft unions; it meant also stretching out the hand of fellowship to the unskilled worker who knowing no craft fitted into no craft union. But over and above these changes in structure there hovered a new spirit, a spirit of class struggle and of revolutionary solidarity in contrast with the spirit of "business unionism" of the typical craft union. Industrialism signified a challenge to the old leadership, to the leadership of Gompers and his associates, by a younger generation of leaders who were more in tune with the social ideas of the radical intellectuals and the labor movements of Europe than with the traditional policies of the Federation.

But there is industrialism and industrialism, each answering the demands of a *particular stratum* of the wage-earning class. The class lowest in the scale, the unskilled and "floaters," for which the I. W. W. speaks, conceives industrialism as "one big union," where not only trade but even industrial distinctions are virtually ignored with reference to action against employers, if not also with reference to the principle of organization. The native floater in the West and the unskilled foreigner in the East are equally responsive to the appeal to storm capitalism in a successive series of revolts under the banner of the "one big union." Uniting in its ranks the workers with the least experience in organization and with none in political action, the "one big union" pins its faith upon assault rather than "armed peace," upon the strike without the trade agreement, and has no faith whatsoever in political or legislative action.

Another form of industrialism is that of the middle stratum of the wage-earning group, embracing trades which are moderately skilled and have had considerable experience in organization, such as brewing, clothing, and mining. They realize that, in order to attain an equal footing with the employers, they must present a front coextensive with the employers' association, which means that all trades in an industry must act under one direction. Hence they strive to assimilate the engineers and machinists, whose labor is essential to the continuance of the operation of the plant. They thus reproduce on a minor scale the attempt of the Knights of Labor during the eighties to engulf the more skilled trade unions.

At the same time the relatively unprivileged position of

these trades makes them keenly alive to the danger from below, from the unskilled whom the employer may break into their jobs in case of strikes. They therefore favor taking the unskilled into the organization. Their industrialism is consequently caused perhaps more by their own trade consideration than by an altruistic desire to uplift the unskilled, although they realize that the organization of the unskilled is required by the broader interests of the wage-earning class. However, their long experience in matters of organization teaches them that the "one big union" would be a poor medium. Their accumulated experience likewise has a moderating influence on their economic activity, and they are consequently among the strongest supporters inside the American Federation of Labor of the trade agreement. Nevertheless, opportunistic though they are in the industrial field, their position is not sufficiently raised above the unskilled to make them satisfied with the wage system. Hence, they are mostly controlled by socialists and are strongly in favor of political action through the Socialist party. This form of industrialism may consequently be called "socialist industrialism." In the annual conventions of the Federation, industrialists are practically synonymous with socialists.

The best examples of the "middle stratum" industrialism are the unions in the garment industries. Enthusiastic admirers have proclaimed them the harbingers of a "new unionism" in America. One would indeed be narrow to withhold praise from organizations and leaders who in spite of a most chaotic situation in their industry have succeeded so brilliantly where many looked only for failure. Looking at the matter, however, from the wider standpoint of labor history, the contribution of this so-called "new unionism" resides chiefly, first, in that it has rationalized and developed industrial government by collective bargaining and trade agreements as no other unionism, and second, in that it has applied a spirit of broadminded all-inclusiveness to all workers in the industry. To put it in another way, its merit is in that it has made supreme use of the highest practical acquisition of the American Federation of Labor—namely, the trade agreement—while reinterpreting and applying the latter in a spirit of a broader labor solidarity than the "old unionism" of the Federation. As such the clothing workers point the way to the rest of the labor movement.

The first successful application of the "new unionism" in the clothing trades was in 1910 by the workers on cloaks and suits in the International Ladies' Garment Workers Union of America, a constituent union of the American Federation of Labor. They established machinery of conciliation from the shop to the industry, which in spite of many tempests and serious crises, will probably live on indefinitely. Perhaps the greatest achievement to their credit is that they have jointly with the employers, through a Joint Board of Sanitary Control, wrought a revolution in the hygienic conditions in the shops.

The Amalgamated Clothing Workers of America have won great power in the men's clothing industry, through aggressive but constructive leadership. The nucleus of the union seceded from the United Garment Workers, an A. F. of L. organization, in 1914. The socialistic element within the organization was and still is numerically dominating. But in the practical process of collective bargaining, this union's revolutionary principles have served more as a bond to hold the membership together

than as a severe guide in its relations with the employers.[1]
As a result, the Amalgamated Clothing Workers attained
trade agreements in all the large men's clothing centers.
The American Federation of Labor, however, in spite of
this union's success, has persistently refused to admit it
to affiliation, on account of its original secessionist origin
from a chartered international union.

The unions of the clothing workers have demonstrated
how immigrants (the majority in the industry are Russian and Polish Jews and Italians) may be successfully
organized on the basis of a broad minded industrialism.
On the issue of industrialism in the American Federation
of Labor the last word has not yet been said. It appears,
though, that the matter is being solved slowly but surely
by a silent "counter-reformation" by the old leaders. For
industrialism, or the adjustment of union structure to
meet the employer with ranks closed on the front of an
entire industry, is not altogether new even in the most
conservative portion of the Federation, although it has
never been called by that name.

Long before industrialism entered the national arena
as the economic creed of socialists, the unions of the
skilled had begun to evolve an industrialism of their own.
This species may properly be termed craft industrialism,
as it sought merely to unite on an efficient basis the
fighting strength of the unions of the skilled trades by
devising a method for speedy solution of jurisdictional
disputes between overlapping unions and by reducing the
sympathetic strike to a science. The movement first
manifested itself in the early eighties in the form of local
building trades' councils, which especially devoted them-

[1] The same applies to the International Ladies' Garment Workers'
Union.

selves to sympathetic strikes. This local industrialism grew, after a fashion, to national dimensions in the form of the International Building Trades' Council organized in St. Louis in 1897. The latter proved, however, ineffective, since, having for its basic unit the local building trades' council, it inevitably came into conflict with the national unions in the building trades. For the same reason it was barred from recognition of the American Federation of Labor. The date of the real birth of craft industrialism on a national scale, was therefore deferred to 1903, when a Structural Building Trades' Alliance was founded. The formation of the Alliance marks an event of supreme importance, not only because it united for the first time for common action all the important national unions in the building industry, but especially because it promulgated a new principle which, if generally adopted, was apparently destined to revolutionize the structure of American labor organizations. The Alliance purported to be a federation of the "basic" trades in the industry, and in reality it did represent an *entente* of the big and aggressive unions. The latter were moved to federate not only for the purpose of forcing the struggle against the employers, but also of expanding at the expense of the "non-basic" or weak unions, besides seeking to annihilate the last vestiges of the International Building Trades' Council. The Brotherhood of Carpenters and Joiners, probably the most aggressive union in the American Federation of Labor, was the leader in this movement. From the standpoint of the Federation, the Structural Alliance was at best an extra-legal organization, as it did not receive the latter's formal sanction, but the Federation could scarcely afford to ignore it as it had ignored the International Building Trades' Council. Thus in 1908 the Alliance was "legitimatized" and made a "Department" of the American Federation of Labor, under the name of the Building Trades' Department, with the settlement of jurisdictional disputes as its main function. It was accompanied by departments of metal trades, of railway employes, of miners, and by a "label" department.

It is not, however, open to much doubt that the Department was not a very successful custodian of the trade autonomy principle. Jurisdictional disputes are caused either by technical changes, which play havoc with official "jurisdiction," or else by a plain desire on the part of the stronger union to encroach upon the province of the weaker one. When the former was the case and the struggle happened to be between unions of equal strength and influence, it generally terminated in a compromise. When, however, the combatants were two unions of unequal strength, the doctrine of the supremacy of the "basic" unions was generally made to prevail in the end. Such was the outcome of the struggle between the carpenters and joiners on the one side and the wood workers on the other and also between the plumbers and steam fitters. In each case it ended in the forced amalgamation of the weaker union with the stronger one, upon the principle that there must be only one union in each "basic" trade. In the case of the steam fitters, which was settled at the convention at Rochester in 1912, the Federation gave what might be interpreted as an official sanction of the new doctrine of one union in a "basic" trade.

Notwithstanding these official lapses from the principle of craft autonomy, the socialist industrialists [1] are still compelled to abide by the letter and the spirit of craft autonomy. The effect of such a policy on the coming

[1] Except the miners, brewers, and garment workers.

American industrialism may be as follows: The future development of the "department" may enable the strong "basic" unions to undertake concerted action against employers, while each retains its own autonomy. Such indeed is the notable "concerted movement" of the railway brotherhoods, which since 1907 has begun to set a type for craft industrialism. It is also probable that the majority of the craft unions will sufficiently depart from a rigid craft standard for membership to include helpers and unskilled workers working alongside the craftsmen.

The clearest outcome of this silent "counter-reformation" in reply to the socialist industrialists is the Railway Employes' Department as it developed during and after the war-time period.[1] It is composed of all the railway men's organizations except the brotherhoods of engineers, firemen, conductors, trainmen, telegraphers, and several minor organizations, which on the whole coöperate with the Department. It also has a place for the unskilled laborers organized in the United Brotherhood of Maintenance of Way Employes and Railroad Shop Laborers. The Railway Employes' Department therefore demonstrates that under craft unionism the unskilled need not be left out in the cold. It also meets the charge that craft unionism renders it easy for the employers to defeat the unions one by one, since this Department has consolidated the constituent crafts into one bargaining and striking union [2] practically as well as could be done by an industrial union. Finally, the Railway Employes' Department has an advantage over an industrial union in that many of its constituent unions, like the machinists',

---

[1] See above, 185-186.
[2] This refers particularly to the six shopmen's unions.

blacksmiths', boilermakers', sheet metal workers', and electrical workers', have large memberships outside the railway industry, which might by their dues and assessments come to the aid of the railway workers on strike. To be sure, the solidarity of the unions in the Department might be weakened through jurisdictional disputes, which is something to be considered. However, when unions have gone so far as to confederate for joint collective bargaining, that danger will probably never be allowed to become too serious.

CHAPTER 10

THE WAR-TIME BALANCE SHEET

The outbreak of the War in Europe in August 1914 found American labor passing through a period of depression. The preceding winter had seen much unemployment and considerable distress and in the summer industrial conditions became scarcely improved. In the large cities demonstrations by the unemployed were daily occurrences. A long and bloody labor struggle in the coal fields of Colorado, which was slowly drawing to an unsuccessful end in spite of sacrifices of the heaviest kind, seemed only to set into bold relief the generally inauspicious outlook. Yet the labor movement could doubtless find solace in the political situation. Owing to the support it had given the Democratic party in the Presidential campaign of 1912, the Federation could claim return favors. The demand which it was now urging upon its friends in office was the long standing one for the exemption of labor unions from the operation of the anti-trust legislation and for the reduction to a minimum of interference by Federal Courts in labor disputes through injunction proceedings.

During 1914 the anti-trust bill introduced in the House by Clayton of Alabama was going through the regular stages preliminary to enactment and, although it finally failed to embody all the sweeping changes demanded by the Federation's lobbyists, it was pronounced at the time satisfactory to labor. The Clayton Act starts with the declaration that "The labor of a human being is not a commodity or article of commerce" and specifies that labor organizations shall not be construed as illegal combinations or conspiracies in restraint of trade under Federal anti-trust laws. It further proceeds to prescribe the procedure in connection with the issuance of injunctions in labor disputes as, for instance, limiting the time of effectiveness of temporary injunctions, making notice obligatory to persons about to be permanently enjoined, and somewhat limiting the power of the courts in contempt proceedings. The most vital section of the Act relating to labor disputes is Section 20, which says "that no such restraining order or injunction shall prohibit any person or persons, whether singly or in concert, from terminating any relation of employment, or from ceasing to perform any work or labor or from recommending, advising, or persuading others by peaceful means so to do; or from attending at any place where any such person or persons may lawfully be, for the purpose of peacefully persuading any person to work or to abstain from working, or from recommending, advising, or persuading others by peaceful and lawful means so to do; or from paying or giving to, or withholding from, any person employed in such dispute, any strike benefits or other moneys or things of value; or from peacefully assembling in a lawful manner, or for lawful purposes, or from doing any act or things which might lawfully be done in the absence of such dispute by any party thereto; nor shall any of the acts specified in this paragraph be considered or held to be violations of any law of the United States."

The government was also rendering aid to organized labor in another, though probably little intended, form, namely through the public hearings conducted by the

United States Commission on Industrial Relations. This Commission had been authorized by Congress in 1912 to investigate labor unrest after a bomb explosion in the *Los Angeles Times* Building, which was set off at the order of some of the national officers of the structural iron workers' union, incidental to a strike. The hearings which were conducted by the able and versatile chairman, Frank P. Walsh, with a particular eye for publicity, centering as they did around the Colorado outrages, served to popularize the trade union cause from one end of the country to the other. The report of the Commission or rather the minority report, which was signed by the chairman and the three labor members, and was known as the "staff" report, named *trade unionism* as the paramount remedy—not compulsory arbitration which was advocated by the employer members, nor labor legislation and a permanent governmental industrial commission proposed by the economist on the commission. The immediate practical effects of the commission were *nil*, but its agitational value proved of great importance to labor. For the first time in the history of the United States the employing class seemed to be arrayed as a defendant before the bar of public opinion. Also, it was for the first time that a commission representing the government not only unhesitatingly pronounced the trade union movement harmless to the country's best interests but went to the length of raising it to the dignity of a fundamental and indispensable institution.

The Commission on Industrial Relations on the whole reflected the favorable attitude of the Administration which came to power in 1912. The American Federation of Labor was given full sway over the Department of Labor and a decisive influence in all other government departments on matters relating to labor. Without a political party of its own, by virtue only of its "bargaining power" over the old parties, the American Federation of Labor seemed to have attained a position not far behind that of British labor after more than a decade of independent political action. Furthermore, fortunately for itself, labor in America had come into a political patrimony at a time when the country was standing on the threshold of a new era, during which government was destined to become the arbiter of industry.

The War in Europe did not immediately improve industrial conditions in America. The first to feel its effects were the industries directly engaged in the making of munitions. The International Association of Machinists, the organization of the now all-important munition workers, actually had its membership somewhat decreased during 1915, but in the following year made a 50 per cent. increase. The greater part of the new membership came from the "munitions towns," such as Bridgeport, Connecticut, where, in response to the insatiable demand from the Allied nations, new enormous plants were erected during 1915 and shipment of munitions in mass began early the next year. Bridgeport and surrounding towns became a center of a successful eight-hour movement, in which the women workers newly brought into the industry took the initiative. The Federation as a whole lost three per cent. of its membership in 1915 and gained seven per cent. during 1916.

On its War policy the Federation took its cue completely from the national government. During the greater part of the period of American neutrality its attitude was that of a shocked lover of peace who is desirous to maintain the strictest neutrality if the belligerents will persist in refusing to lend an ear to reason. To prevent a repetition of a similar catastrophe, the Federation did the obvious thing, pronouncing for open and democratized diplomacy; and proposed to the several national trade union federations that an international labor congress meet at the close of the war to determine the conditions of peace. However, both the British and Germans declined. The convention in 1915 condemned the German-inspired propaganda for an embargo on shipments to all belligerents and the fomenting of strikes in munitions-making plants by German agents. The Federation refused to interpret neutrality to mean that the American wage earner was to be thrown back into the dumps of depression and unemployment, from which he was just delivered by the extensive war orders from the Allied governments.

By the second half of 1916 the war prosperity was in full swing. Cost of living was rising rapidly and movements for higher wages became general. The practical stoppage of immigration enabled common labor to get a larger share than usual of the prosperity. Many employers granted increases voluntarily. Simultaneously, a movement for the eight-hour day was spreading from strictly munitions-making trades into others and was meeting with remarkable success. But 1916 witnessed what was doubtless the most spectacular move for the eight-hour day in American history—the joint eight-hour demand by the four railway brotherhoods, the engineers, firemen, conductors, and trainmen. The effectiveness acquired by trade unionism needs no better proof than the remarkable success with which these four organizations, with the full support of the whole labor movement at their back and aided by a not unfriendly attitude on the part of the national Administration, brought to bay the greatest single industry of the country and overcame the opposition of the entire business class.

The four brotherhoods made a joint demand for an eight-hour day early in 1916.[1] The railway officials claimed that the demand for the reduction of the work-day from ten to eight hours with ten hours' pay and a time and a half rate for overtime was not made in good faith. Since, they said, the employes ought to have known that the railways could not be run on an eight-hour day, the demand was but a covert attempt to gain a substantial increase in their wages, which were already in advance of any of the other skilled workers. On the other hand, the brotherhoods stoutly maintained during their direct negotiations with the railway companies and in the public press that their demand was a *bona fide* demand and that they believed that the railway business did admit of a reorganization substantially on an eight-hour basis. The railway officials offered to submit to arbitration the demand of the men together with counter demands of their own. The brotherhoods, however, fearing prejudice and recalling to mind past disappointments, declined the proposal and threatened to tie up the whole transportation system of the country by a strike on Labor Day.

When the efforts at mediation by the United States Board of Mediation and Conciliation came to naught, President Wilson invited to Washington the executives of the several railway systems and a convention of the several hundred division chairmen of the brotherhoods and attempted personal mediation. He urged the railway executives to accept the eight-hour day and pro-

[1] For the developments which led up to this joint move see above, 182-184.

posed that a commission appointed by himself should investigate the demand for time and a half for overtime. This the employes accepted, but the executives objected to giving the eight-hour day before an investigation was made. Meantime the brotherhoods had issued their strike order effective on Labor Day and the crisis became imminent. To obviate the calamity of a general strike, at a time when the country was threatened with troubles on the Mexican frontier and with the unsettled submarine controversy with Germany ready to flare up any moment, the President went before Congress and asked for a speedy enactment of an eight-hour law for train operatives without a reduction in wages but with no punitive overtime. He coupled it with a request for an authorization of a special commission to report on the operation of such law for a period of six months, after which the subject might be reopened. Lastly, he urged an amendment to the Newlands Act making it illegal to call a strike or a lockout pending an investigation of a controversy by a government commission. Spurred on by the danger of the impending strike, Congress quickly acceded to the first two requests by the President and passed the so-called Adamson law.[1] The strike was averted, but in the immediately following Presidential campaign labor's "hold-up" of the national government became one of the trump issues of the Republican candidate.

This episode of the summer of 1916 had two sequels, one in the courts and the other one in a negotiated agreement between the railways and the brotherhoods. The former brought many suits in courts against the govern-

[1] Congress ignored the last-named recommendation which would have introduced in the United States the Canadian system of "Compulsory Investigation."

ment and obtained from a lower court a decision that the Adamson law was unconstitutional. The case was then taken to the United States Supreme Court, but the decision was not ready until the spring of 1917. Meantime the danger of a strike had been renewed. However, on the same day when the Supreme Court gave out its decision, the railways and brotherhoods had signed, at the urging of the National Council of Defense, an agreement accepting the conditions of the Adamson law regardless of the outcome in court. When the decision became known it was found to be in favor of the Adamson law. The declaration of war against Germany came a few days later and opened a new era in the American labor situation.

Previous to that, on March 12, 1917, when war seemed inevitable, the national officers of all important unions in the Federation met in Washington and issued a statement on "American Labor's Position in Peace or in War." They pledged the labor movement and the influence of the labor organizations unreservedly in support of the government in case of war. Whereas, they said, in all previous wars "under the guise of national necessity, labor was stripped of its means of defense against enemies at home and was robbed of the advantages, the protections, and guarantees of justice that had been achieved after ages of struggle"; and "labor had no representatives in the councils authorized to deal with the conduct of the war"; and therefore "the rights, interests and welfare of workers were autocratically sacrificed for the slogan of national safety"; in this war "the government must recognize the organized labor movement as the agency through which it must coöperate with wage earners." Such recognition will imply first "representation on all agencies de-

termining and administering policies of national defense"
and "on all boards authorized to control publicity during
war time." Second, that "service in government factories and private establishments, in transportation agencies, all should conform to trade union standards"; and
that "whatever changes in the organization of industry are
necessary upon a war basis, they should be made in ac-
cord with plans agreed upon by representatives of the
government and those engaged and employed in the industry." Third, that the government's demand of sacrifice
of their "labor power, their bodies or their lives" be accompanied by "increased guarantees and safe-guards,"
the imposing of a similar burden on property and the
limitation of profits. Fourth, that "organization for industrial and commercial service" be "upon a different
basis from military service" and "that military service
should be carefully distinguished from service in industrial disputes," since "the same voluntary institutions
that organized industrial, commercial and transportation
workers in times of peace will best take care of the same
problems in time of war." For, "wrapped up with the
safety of this Republic are ideals of democracy, a heritage
which the masses of the people received from our forefathers, who fought that liberty might live in this country
—a heritage that is to be maintained and handed down to
each generation with undiminished power and usefulness."

We quote at such length because this document gives
the quintessence of the wise labor statesmanship which
this crisis brought so clearly to light. Turning away from
the pacifism of the Socialist party, Samuel Gompers and
his associates believed that victory over world militarism
as well as over the forces of reaction at home depended
on labor's unequivocal support of the government. And

in reality, by placing the labor movement in the service of the war-making power of the nation they assured for it, for the time being at least, a degree of national prestige and a freedom to expand which could not have been conquered by many years of the most persistent agitation and strikes.

The War, thus, far from being a trial for organized labor, proved instead a great opportunity. For the War released organized labor from a blind alley, as it were. The American Federation of Labor, as we saw, had made but slow progress in organization after 1905. At that time it had succeeded in organizing the skilled and some of the semi-skilled workers. Further progress was impeded by the anti-union employers especially in industries commonly understood to be dominated by "trusts." In none of the "trustified" industries, save anthracite coal, was labor organization able to make any headway. And yet the American Federation of Labor, situated as it is, is obliged to stake everything upon the power to organize.[1] The war gave it that all-important power. Soon after the Federal government became the arbiter of industry—by virtue of being the greatest consumer, and by virtue of a public opinion clearly outspoken on the subject—we see the Taft-Walsh War Labor Board [2] embody "the right to organize" into a code of rules for the guidance of the relations of labor and capital during War-time, along with the basic eight-hour day and the right to a living wage. In return for these gifts American labor gave up nothing so vital as British labor had done in the identical situation. The right to strike was left unmolested and remained a permanent threat hanging

[1] See below, 283-287.
[2] See below, 238-240.

over slow moving officialdom and recalcitrant employers. And the only restraint accepted by labor was a promise of self-restraint. The Federation was not to strike until all other means for settlement had been tried, nor was it to press for the closed shop where such had not existed prior to the War declaration. But at the same time no employer was to interpose a check to its expansion into industries and districts heretofore unorganized. Nor could an employer discipline an employe for joining a union or inducing others to join.

In 1916, when the President established the National Council of Defense, he appointed Samuel Gompers one of the seven members composing the Advisory Commission in charge of all policies dealing with labor and chairman of a committee on labor of his own appointment. Among the first acts of the Council of Defense was an emphatic declaration for the preservation of the standards of legal protection of labor against the ill-advised efforts for their suspension during War-time. The Federation was given representation on the Emergency Construction Board, the Fuel Administration Board, on the Woman's Board, on the Food Administration Board, and finally on the War Industries Board. The last named board was during the war the recognized arbiter of the country's industries, all labor matters being handled by its labor representative. The Department of Labor, which in the War emergency could rightly be considered the Federation's arm in the Administration, was placed in supreme charge of general labor administration. Also, in connection with the administration of the military conscription law, organized labor was given representation on each District Exemption Board. But perhaps the strongest expression of the official recognition of the labor move-

ment was offered by President Wilson when he took time
from the pressing business in Washington to journey to
Buffalo in November 1917, to deliver an address before
the convention of the American Federation of Labor.

In addition to representation on boards and commis-
sions dealing with general policies, the government entered with the Federation into a number of agreements
relative to the conditions of direct and indirect employment by the government. In each agreement the prevalent trade union standards were fully accepted and provision was made for a three-cornered board of adjustment
to consist of a representative of the particular government department, the public and labor. Such agreements
were concluded by the War and Navy departments and
by the United States Emergency Fleet Corporation. The
Shipping Board sponsored a similar agreement between
the shipping companies and the seafaring unions ; and the
War Department between the leather goods manufacturers and leather workers' union. When the government
took over the railways on January 1, 1918, it created
three boards of adjustment on the identical principle of
a full recognition of labor organizations. The spirit with
which the government faced the labor problem was shown
also in connection with the enforcement of the eight-
hour law. The ‘law of 1912 provided for an eight-hour
day on contract government work but allowed exceptions
in emergencies. In 1917 Congress gave the President
the right to waive the application of the law, but provided
that in such event compensation be computed on a "basic"
eight-hour day. The War and Navy departments enforced these provisions not only to the letter but generally
gave to them a most liberal interpretation.

The taking over of the railways by the government

revolutionized the railway labor situation. Under private management, as was seen, the four brotherhoods alone, the engineers, firemen, conductors, and trainmen enjoyed universal recognition, the basic eight-hour day (since 1916), and high wages. The other organizations of the railway workers, the shopmen, the yardmen, the maintenance of way men, the clerks, and the telegraphers were, at best, tolerated rather than recognized. Under the government administration the eight-hour day was extended to all grades of workers, and wages were brought up to a minimum of 68 cents per hour, with a considerable though not corresponding increase in the wages of the higher grades of labor. All discrimination against union men was done away with, so that within a year labor organization on the railways was nearing the hundred per cent. mark.

The policies of the national railway administration of the open door to trade unionism and of recognition of union standards were successfully pressed upon other employments by the National War Labor Board. On March 29, 1918, a National War Labor Conference Board, composed of five representatives of the Federation of Labor, five representatives of employers' associations and two joint chairmen, William H. Taft for the employers and Frank P. Walsh for the employes, reported to the Secretary of Labor on "Principles and Policies to govern Relations between Workers and Employers in War Industries for the Duration of the War." These "principles and policies," which were to be enforced by a permanent War Labor Board organized upon the identical principle as the reporting board, included a voluntary relinquishment of the right to strike and lockout by employes and employers, respectively, upon the following conditions: First, there was a recognition of the equal right of employes and employers to organize into associations and trade unions and to bargain collectively. This carried an undertaking by the employers not to discharge workers for membership in trade unions or for legitimate trade union activities, and was balanced by an undertaking of the workers, "in the exercise of their right to organize," not to "use coercive measures of any kind to induce persons to join their organizations, nor to induce employers to bargain or deal therewith." Second, both sides agreed upon the observance of the *status quo ante bellum* as to union or open shop in a given establishment and as to union standards of wages, hours, and other conditions of employment. This carried the express stipulation that the right to organize was not to be curtailed under any condition and that the War Labor Board could grant improvement in labor conditions as the situation warranted. Third, the understanding was that if women should be brought into industry, they must be allowed equal pay for equal work. Fourth, it was agreed that "the basic eight-hour day was to be recognized as applying in all cases in which the existing law required it, while in all other cases the question of hours of labor was to be settled with due regard to government necessities and the welfare, health, and proper comfort of the workers." Fifth, restriction of output by trade unions was to be done away with. Sixth, in fixing wages and other conditions regard was to be shown to trade union standards. And lastly came the recognition of "the right of all workers, including common laborers, to a living wage" and the stipulation that in fixing wages, there will be established "minimum rates of pay which will insure the subsistence of the worker and his family in health and reasonable comfort."

The establishment of the War Labor Board did not mean that the country had gone over to the principle of compulsory arbitration, for the Board could not force any party to a dispute to submit to its arbitration or by an umpire of its appointment. However, so outspoken was public opinion on the necessity of avoiding interruptions in the War industries and so far-reaching were the powers of the government over the employer as the administrator of material and labor priorities and over the employes as the administrator of the conscription law that the indirect powers of the Board sufficed to make its decision prevail in nearly every instance.

The packing industry was a conspicuous case of the "new course" in industrial relations. This industry had successfully kept unionism out since an ill-considered strike in 1904, which ended disastrously for the strikers. Late in 1917, 60,000 employes in the packing houses went on strike for union recognition, the basic eight-hour day, and other demands. Intervention by the government led to a settlement, which, although denying the union formal recognition, granted the basic eight-hour day, a living wage, and the right to organize, together with all that it implied, and the appointment of a permanent arbitrator to adjudicate disputes. Thus an industry which had prohibited labor organization for fourteen years was made to open its door to trade unionism.[1] Another telling gain for the basic eight-hour day was made by the timber workers in the Northwest, again at the insistence of the government.

What the aid of the government in securing the right to organize meant to the strength of trade unionism may

[1] The unions again lost their hold upon the packing industry in the autumn of 1921.

be derived from the following figures. In the two years from 1917 to 1919 the organization of the meat cutters and butcher workmen increased its membership from less than 10,000 to over 66,000; the boilermakers and iron shipbuilders from 31,000 to 85,000; the blacksmiths from 12,000 to 28,000; the railway clerks from less than 7000 to over 71,000; the machinists from 112,000 to 255,000; the maintenance of way employes from less than 10,000 to 54,000; the railway carmen from 39,000 to 100,000; the railway telegraphers from 27,000 to 45,000; and the electrical workers from 42,000 to 131,000. The trades here enumerated—mostly related to shipbuilding and railways—accounted for the greater part of the total gain in the membership of the Federation from two and a half million members in 1917 to over three and a third in 1919.

An important aspect of the coöperation of the government with the Federation was the latter's eager self-identification with the government's foreign policy, which went to the length of choosing to play a lone hand in the Allied labor world. Labor in America had an implicit faith in the national government, which was shared by neither English nor French labor. Whereas the workers in the other Allied Nations believed that their governments needed to be prodded or forced into accepting the right road to a democratic peace by an international labor congress, which would take the entire matter of war and peace out of the diplomatic chancellories into an open conference of the representatives of the workers, the American workers were only too eager to follow the leadership of the head of the American nation. To this doubtless was added the usual fervor of a new convert to any cause (in this instance the cause of the War against Germany) and a strong distrust of German socialism, which American labor leaders have developed during their drawn-out struggle against the German-trained socialists inside the Federation who have persistently tried to "capture" the organization.

When on January 8, 1918, President Wilson enunciated his famous Fourteen Points, the Federation of course gave them an enthusiastic endorsement. In the autumn of 1918 Gompers went to Europe and participated in an Inter-Allied labor conference. He refused, however, to participate in the first International Labor and Socialist Congress called since the War, which met at Berne, Switzerland, in March 1919, since he would not sit with the Germans while their country was not formally at peace with the United States. The convention of the Federation in June 1919 gave complete endorsement to the League of Nations Pact worked out at Versailles,—on general grounds and on the ground of its specific provisions for an international regulation of labor conditions designed to equalize labor standards and costs. Contrasting with this was the position of British labor, which regarded the Pact with a critical eye, frankly confessing disillusionment, but was willing to accept it for the sake of its future possibilities, when the Pact might be remodelled by more liberal and more democratic hands.

The contrast in outlook between the mild evolutionism of the American Federation of Labor and the social radicalism of British labor stood out nowhere so strongly as in their respective programs for Reconstruction after the War. The chief claim of the British Labor party for recognition at the hands of the voter at the General Election in December 1918, was its well-thought-out reconstruction program put forth under the telling title of "Labour and the New Social Order." This program was above all a legislative program. It called for a thoroughgoing governmental control of industry by means of a control of private finance, natural resources, transportation, and international trade. To the workingmen such control would mean the right to steady employment, the right to a living wage, and the appropriation of economic surpluses by the state for the common good—be they in the form of rent, excessive profits, or overlarge personal incomes. Beyond this minimum program loomed the coöperative commonwealth with the private capitalist totally eliminated.

Such was the program of British labor. What of the Reconstruction program of American labor? First of all, American labor thought of Reconstruction as a program to be carried out by the trade union, not by the government. Moreover, it did not see in Reconstruction the great break with the past which that meant to British labor. The American Federation of Labor applied to Reconstruction the same philosophy which lies at the basis of its ordinary, everyday activity. It concerned itself not with any far-reaching plan for social reorganization, but with a rising standard of living and an enlarged freedom for the union. The American equivalent of a government-guaranteed right to employment and a living wage was the "right to organize." Assure to labor that right, free the trade unions of court interference in strikes and boycotts, prevent excessive meddling by the government in industrial relations—and the stimulated activities of the "legitimate" organizations of labor, which will result therefrom, will achieve a far better Reconstruction than a thousand paper programs however beautiful. So reasoned the leaders of the American Federation of Labor.

During the period of War, they of course gladly accepted directly from the government the basic eight-hour day and the high wages, which under other circumstances they could have got only by prolonged and bitter striking. But even more acceptable than these directly bestowed boons was the indirect one of the right to organize free from anti-union discriminations by employers. Having been arrested in its expansion, as we saw, by anti-union employers and especially "trusts," the American Federation of Labor took advantage of the War situation to overflow new territory. Once entrenched and the organization well in hand, it thought it could look to the future with confidence.

CHAPTER 11

RECENT DEVELOPMENTS

The Armistice with Germany came suddenly and unexpectedly. To the organized workers the news was as welcome as to other citizens. But, had they looked at the matter from a special trade union standpoint, they would probably have found a longer duration of the War not entirely amiss. For coal had been unionized already before the War, the railways first during the War, but the third basic industry, steel, was not touched either before or during the War. However, it was precisely in the steel industry that opposition to unionism has found its chief seat, not only to unionism in that industry alone but to unionism in related or subsidiary industries as well.

The first three months after the Armistice the general expectation was for a set-back in business conditions due to the withdrawal of the enormous government War-time demand. Employers and trade unions stood equally undecided. When, however, instead of the expected slump, there came a prosperity unknown even during the War, the trade unions resumed their offensive, now unrestrained by any other but the strictly economic consideration. As a matter of fact, the trade unions were not at all free agents, since their demands, frequent and considerable though they were, barely sufficed to keep wages abreast of the soaring cost of living. Through 1919 and the first half of 1920 profits and wages were going up by leaps and bounds; and the forty-four hour week,—no longer the mere eight-hour day,—became a general slogan and a partial reality. Success was especially notable in clothing, building, printing, and the metal trades. One cannot say the same, however, of the three basic industries, steel, coal, and railways. In steel the twelve-hour day and the seven-day week continued as before for approximately one-half of the workers and the unions were preparing for a battle with the "Steel Trust." While on the railways and in coal mining the unions now began to encounter opposition from an unexpected quarter, namely, the government.

When in the summer of 1919 the railway shopmen demanded an increase in their wages, which had not been raised since the summer of 1918, President Wilson practically refused the demand, urging the need of a general deflation but binding himself to use all the powers of the government immediately to reduce the cost of living. A significant incident in this situation was a spontaneous strike of shopmen on many roads unauthorized by international union officials, which disarranged the movement of trains for a short time but ended with the men returning to work under the combined pressure of their leaders' threats and the President's plea.

In September 1919, the United States Railroad Administration and the shopmen's unions entered into national agreements, which embodied the practices under the Administration as well as those in vogue on the more liberal roads before 1918, including recognition and a large number of "working rules." These "national agreements" became an important issue one year later, when their abolition began to be pressed by the railway executives before the Railroad Labor Board, which was established under the Transportation Act of 1920.

In the summer of 1919 employers in certain industries, like clothing, grew aware of a need of a more "psychological" handling of their labor force than heretofore in order to reduce a costly high labor turnover and no less costly stoppages of work. This created a veritable Eldorado for "employment managers" and "labor managers," real and spurious. Universities and colleges, heretofore wholly uninterested in the problem of labor or viewing training in that problem as but a part of a general cultural education, now vied with one another in establishing "labor management" and "labor personnel" courses. One phase of the "labor personnel" work was a rather wide experimentation with "industrial democracy" plans. These plans varied in form and content, from simple provision for shop committees for collective dealing, many of which had already been installed during the War under the orders of the War Labor Board, to most elaborate schemes, some modelled upon the Constitution of the United States. The feature which they all had in common was that they attempted to achieve some sort of collective bargaining outside the channels of the established trade unions. The trade unionists termed the new fashioned expressions of industrial democracy "company unions." This term one may accept as technically correct without necessarily accepting the sinister connotation imputed to it by labor.

The trade unions, too, were benefiting as organizations. The Amalgamated Clothing Workers' Union firmly established itself by formal agreement on the men's clothing "markets" of Chicago, Rochester, Baltimore, and New

York. The membership of the Amalgamated Clothing Workers' Union rose to 175,000. Employers in general were complaining of increased labor unrest, a falling off of efficiency in the shop, and looked askance at the rapid march of unionization. The trade unions, on their part, were aware of their opportunity and eager for a final recognition as an institution in industry. As yet uncertainty prevailed as to whether enough had survived of the War-time spirit of give and take to make a struggle avoidable, or whether the issue must be solved by a bitter conflict of classes.

A partial showdown came in the autumn of 1919. Three great events, which came closely together, helped to clear the situation: The steel strike, the President's Industrial Conference, and the strike of the soft coal miners. The great steel strike, prepared and directed by a Committee representing twenty-four national and international unions with William Z. Foster as Secretary and moving spirit, tried in September 1919 to wrest from the owners of the steel mills what the railway shopmen had achieved in 1918 by invitation of the government, namely, "recognition" and the eight-hour day. Three hundred thousand men went out on strike at the call of the committee. The industry came to a practical standstill. But in this case the twenty-four allied unions were not dealing with a government amenable to political pressure, nor with a loosely joined association of employers competing among themselves. Furthermore, the time had passed when the government had either the will or the power to interfere and order both sides to arbitrate their dispute. On the contrary, the unions were now dealing unaided with the strongest capitalist aggregation in the world.

At the request of President Wilson, Gompers had urged the strike committee to postpone the strike until after the meeting of the national industrial conference called by the President in October, but the committee claimed that it could not have kept the men back after a summer of agitation and feverish organization had they even tried. The President's conference, modelled upon a similar conference which met earlier in Great Britain, was composed of three groups of representatives equal in number, one for capital, one for labor, and one for the general public. Decisions, to be held effective, had to be adopted by a majority in each group. The labor representation, dominated of course by Gompers, was eager to make the discussion turn on the steel strike. It proposed a resolution to this effect which had the support of the public group, but fearing a certain rejection by the employer group the matter was postponed. The issue upon which the alignment was effected was industrial control and collective bargaining. All three groups, the employer and public groups and of course the labor group, advocated collective bargaining,—but with a difference. The labor group insisted that collective bargaining is doomed to be a farce unless the employes are allowed to choose as their spokesmen representatives of the national trade union. In the absence of a powerful protector in the national union, they argued, the workers in a shop can never feel themselves on a bargaining equality with their employer, nor can they be represented by a spokesman of the necessary ability if their choice be restricted to those working in the same plant. The employers, now no longer dominated by the War-time spirit which caused them in 1917 to tolerate an expansion of unionism, insisted that no employer must be obliged to meet for the purpose of collec-

tive bargaining with other than his own employes.[1] After
two weeks of uncertainty, when it had become clear that a
resolution supported by both labor and public groups,
which restated the labor position in a milder form, would
be certain to be voted down by the employer group, the
labor group withdrew from the conference, and the conference broke up. The period of the coöperation of
classes had definitely closed.

Meantime the steel strike continued. Federal troops
patrolled the steel districts and there was no violence.
Nevertheless, a large part of the country's press pic-
tured the strike by the steel workers for union recognition
and a normal workday as an American counterpart of the
Bolshevist revolution in Russia. Public opinion, unbal-
anced and excited as it was over the whirlpool of world
events, was in no position to resist. The strike failed.

Nothing made so clear to the trade unionists the
changed situation since the War ended as the strike of
the bituminous coal miners which began November 1. The
miners had entered, in October 1917, into a wage agreement with the operators for the duration of the War.
The purchasing power of their wages having become
greatly reduced by the ever rising cost of living, discontent was general in the union. A further complication
arose from the uncertain position of the United States
with reference to War and Peace, which had a bearing on
the situation. The miners claimed that the Armistice
had ended the War. The War having ended, the disad-

[1] The most plausible argument in favor of the position taken by
the employing group is that no employer should be forced to decide
matters as intimately connected with the welfare of his business
as the ones relating to his labor costs and shop discipline with
national union leaders, since the latter, at best, are interested in the
welfare of the trade as a whole but rarely in the particular success
of *his own* particular establishment.

vantageous agreement expired with it. So argued the miners and demanded a sixty per cent. increase in tonnage rates, a corresponding one for yardmen and others paid by the day or hour, and a thirty-hour week to spread employment through the year. The operators maintained that the agreement was still in force, but intimated a readiness to make concessions if they were permitted to shift the cost to the consumer. At this point, the Fuel Administration, a War-time government body, already partly in the process of dissolution, intervened and attempted to dictate a settlement at a fourteen per cent. increase, which was entirely unacceptable to the union. The strike continued and the prospect of a dire coal famine grew nearer. To break the deadlock, on motion of Attorney-General Palmer, Judge Anderson of Indianapolis, under the War-time Lever Act, issued an injunction forbidding the union officials to continue conducting the strike. The strike continued, the strikers refusing to return to work, and a Bituminous Coal Commission appointed by the President finally settled it by an award of an increase of twenty-seven per cent. But that the same Administration which had given the unions so many advantages during the War should now have invoked against them a War-time law, which had already been considered practically abrogated, was a clear indication of the change in the times. In a strike by anthracite coal miners in the following year an award was made by a Presidential board of three, representing the employers, the union, and the public. The strikers, however, refused to abide by it and inaugurated a "vacation-strike," the individual strikers staying away on a so-called vacation, nominally against the will of the union officers. They finally returned to work.

Both the steel and coal strikes furnished occasions for considerable anti-union propaganda in the press. Public sentiment long favorable to labor became definitely hostile.[1] In Kansas the legislature passed a compulsory arbitration law and created an Industrial Relations Court to adjudicate trade disputes. Simultaneously an "anti-Red" campaign inaugurated by Attorney-General Palmer contributed its share to the public excitement and helped to prejudice the cause of labor more by implication than by making direct charges. It was in an atmosphere thus surcharged with suspicion and fear that a group of employers, led by the National Association of Manufacturers and several local employers' organizations, launched an open-shop movement with the slogan of an "American plan" for shops and industries. Many employers, normally opposed to unionism, who in War-time had permitted unionism to acquire scope, were now trying to reconquer their lost positions. The example of the steel industry and the fiasco of the President's Industrial Conference crystallized this reviving anti-union sentiment into action.

Meanwhile the railway labor situation remained unsettled and fraught with danger. The problem was bound up with the general problem as to what to do with the railways. Many plans were presented to Congress, from an immediate return to private owners to permanent government ownership and management. The railway labor organizations, that is, the four brotherhoods of the train service personnel and the twelve unions united in

[1] The turn in public sentiment really dated from the threat of a strike for the eight-hour day by the four railway brotherhoods in 1916, which forced the passage of the Adamson law by Congress. The law was a victory for the brotherhoods, but also extremely useful to the enemies of organized labor in arousing public hostility to unionism.

the Railway Employes' Department of the American Federation of Labor, came before Congress with the so-called Plumb Plan, worked out by Glenn E. Plumb, the legal representative of the brotherhoods. This plan proposed that the government take over the railways for good, paying a compensation to the owners, and then entrust their operation to a board composed of government officials, union representatives, and representatives of the technical staffs.[1] So much for ultimate plans. On the more immediate wage problem proper, the government had clearly fallen down on its promise made to the shopmen in August 1919, when their demands for higher wages were refused and a promise was made that the cost of living would be reduced. Early in 1920 President Wilson notified Congress that he would return the roads to the owners on March 1, 1920. A few days before that date the Esch-Cummins bill was passed under the name of the Transportation Act of 1920. Strong efforts were made to incorporate in the bill a prohibition against strikes and lockouts. In that form it had indeed passed the Senate. In the House bill, however, the compulsory arbitration feature was absent and the final law contained a provision for a Railroad Labor Board, of railway, union, and public representatives, to be appointed by the President, with the power of conducting investigations and issuing awards, but with the right to strike or lockout unimpaired either before, during, or after the investigation. It was the first appointed board of this description which was to pass on the clamorous demands by the railway employes for higher wages.[2]

[1] See below, 259-261, for a more detailed description of the Plan.
[2] The Transportation Act included a provision that prior to September 1, 1920, the railways could not reduce wages.

No sooner had the roads been returned under the new law, and before the board was even appointed, than a strike broke out among the switchmen and yardmen, whose patience had apparently been exhausted. The strike was an "outlaw" strike, undertaken against the wishes of national leaders and organized and led by "rebel" leaders risen up for the occasion. For a time it threatened not only to paralyze the country's railway system but to wreck the railway men's organizations as well. It was finally brought to an end through the efforts of the national leaders, and a telling effect on the situation was produced by an announcement by the newly constituted Railroad Labor Board that no "outlaw" organization would have standing before it. The Board issued an award on July 20, retroactive to May 1, increasing the total annual wage bill of the railways by $600,000,000. The award failed to satisfy the union, but they acquiesced.

When the increase in wages was granted to the railway employes, industry in general and the railways in particular were already entering a period of slump. With the depression the open-shop movement took on a greater vigor. With unemployment rapidly increasing employers saw their chance to regain freedom from union control. A few months later the tide also turned in the movement of wages. Inside of a year the steel industry reduced wages thirty per cent., in three like installments; and the twelve-hour day and the seven-day week, which had figured among the chief causes of the strike of 1919 and for which the United States Steel Corporation was severely condemned by a report of a Committee of the Interchurch World Movement,[1] has largely continued as

---

[1] A Protestant interdenominational organization of influence, which investigated the strike and issued a report.

before. In the New York "market" of the men's clothing industry, where the union faces the most complex and least stable condition mainly owing to the heterogeneous character of the employing group, the latter grasped the opportunity to break with the Amalgamated Clothing Workers' Union. By the end of the spring of 1921 the clothing workers won their struggle, showing that a union built along new lines was at least as efficient a fighting machine as any of the older unions. It was this union also and several local branches of the related union in the ladies' garment industry, which realized the need of assuring to the employer at least a minimum of labor efficiency if the newly established level of wages was not to be materially lowered. Hence the acceptance of the principle of "standards of production" fixed with the aid of scientific managers employed jointly by the employers and the union.

The spring and summer of 1921 were a time of widespread "readjustment" strikes, or strikes against cuts in wages, especially in the building trades. The building industry went through in 1921 and 1922 one of its periodic upheavals against the tyranny of the "walking delegates" and against the state of moral corruption for which some of the latter shared responsibility together with an unscrupulous element among the employers. In San Francisco, where the grip of the unions upon the industry was strongest, the employers turned on them and installed the "open-shop" after the building trades' council had refused to accept an award by an arbitration committee set up by mutual agreement. The union claimed, however, in self-justification that the Committee, by awarding a *reduction* in the wages of fifteen crafts while the issue as originally submitted turned on a demand by these crafts for a *raise* in wages, had gone outside its legitimate scope. In New York City an investigation by a special legislative committee uncovered a state of reeking corruption among the leadership in the building trades' council and among an element in the employing group in connection with a successful attempt to establish a virtual local monopoly in building. Some of the leading corruptionists on both sides were given court sentences and the building trades' council accepted modifications in the "working rules" formulated by the counsel for the investigating committee. In Chicago a situation developed in many respects similar to the one in San Francisco. In a wage dispute, which was submitted by both sides to Federal Judge K. M. Landis for arbitration, the award authorized not only a wage reduction but a revision of the "working rules" as well. Most of the unionists refused to abide by the award and the situation developed into literal warfare. In Chicago the employers' side was aggressively upheld by a "citizens' committee" formed to enforce the Landis award. The committee claimed to have imported over 10,000 out-of-town building mechanics to take the places of the strikers.

In the autumn of 1921 the employers in the packing industry discontinued the arrangement whereby industrial relations were administered by an "administrator," [1] Judge Alschuler of Chicago, whose rulings had materially restricted the employers' control in the shop. Some of the employers put into effect company union plans. This led to a strike, but in the end the unions lost their foothold in the industry, which the War had enabled them to acquire. By that time, however, the

---

[1] The union had not been formally "recognized" at any time.

open-shop movement seemed already passing its peak, without having caused an irreparable breach in the position of organized labor. Evidently, the long years of preparation before the War and the great opportunity during the War itself, if they have failed to give trade unionism the position of a recognized national institution, have at least made it immune from destruction by employers, however general or skillfully managed the attack. In 1920 the total organized union membership, including the 871,000 in unions unaffiliated with the American Federation of Labor, was slightly short of 5,000,000, or over four million in the Federation itself. In 1921 the membership of the Federation declined slightly to 3,906,000, and the total organized membership probably in proportion. In 1922 the membership of the Federation declined to about 3,200,000, showing a loss of about 850,000 since the high mark of 1920.

The legal position of trade unions has continued as uncertain and unsatisfactory to the unions, as if no Clayton Act had been passed. The closed shop has been condemned as coercion of non-unionists. Yet in the Coppage case [1] the United States Supreme Court found that it is not coercion when an employer threatens discharge unless union membership is renounced. Similarly, it is unlawful for union agents to attempt organization, even by peaceful persuasion, when employes have signed contracts not to join the union as a condition of employment.[2] A decision which arouses strong doubt whether the Clayton Act made any change in the status of trade unions was given by the Supreme Court in the recent

[1] Coppage v. Kansas, 236 U. S. 1 (1915).
[2] Hitchman Coal and Coke Co. v. Mitchell et al, 245 U. S. 229 (1917).

Duplex Printing case.[1] In this decision the union rested its defense squarely on the immunities granted by the Clayton Act. Despite this, the injunction was confirmed and the boycott again declared illegal, the court holding that the words "employer and employes" in the Act restrict its benefits only to "parties standing in proximate relation to a controversy," that is to the employes who are immediately involved in the dispute and not to the national union which undertakes to bring the employer to terms by causing its out-of-town members to refuse to set up his products.

The prevailing judicial interpretation of unlawful union methods is briefly as follows: Strikes are illegal when they involve defamation, fraud, actual physical violence, threats of physical violence, or inducement of breach of contract. Boycotts are illegal when they bring third parties into the dispute by threats of strikes, or loss of business, publication of "unfair lists," [2] or by interference with Interstate commerce. Picketing is illegal when accompanied by violence, threats, intimidation, and coercion. In December 1921 the Supreme Court declared mere numbers in groups constituted intimidation and, while admitting that circumstances may alter cases, limited peaceful picketing to one picket at each point of ingress or egress of the plant.[3] In another case the Court held unconstitutional an Arizona statute, which reproduced *verbatim* the labor clauses of the Clayton Act; [4] this on the ground that concerted action by the union would be illegal if the means used were illegal and

[1] Duplex Printing Press Co. *v.* Deering, 41 Sup. Ct. 172 (1921).
[2] Montana allows the "unfair list" and California allows all boycotts.
[3] American Steel Foundries of Granite City, Illinois, *v.* Tri-City Central Trades' Council, 42 Sup. Ct. 72 (1921).
[4] Truax et al. *v.* Corrigan, 42 Sup. Ct. 124 (1921).

therefore the law which operated to make them legal deprived the plaintiff of his property without due process of law.   In June 1922, in the Coronado case, the Court held that unions, although unincorporated, are in every respect like corporations and are liable for damages in their corporate capacity, including triple damages under the Sherman Anti-Trust law, and which may be collected from their funds.

We have already pointed out that since the War ended the American labor movement has in the popular mind become linked with radicalism.   The steel strike and the coal miners' strike in 1919, the revolt against the national leaders and "outlaw" strikes in the printing industry and on the railways in 1920, the advocacy by the organizations of the railway men of the Plumb Plan for nationalization of railways and its repeated endorsement by the conventions of the American Federation of Labor, the resolutions in favor of the nationalization of coal mines passed at the conventions of the United Mine Workers, the "vacation" strike by the anthracite coal miners in defiance of a government wage award, the sympathy expressed for Soviet Russia in a number of unions, notably of the clothing industry, have led many to see, despite the assertions of the leaders of the American Federation of Labor to the contrary, an apparent drift in the labor movement towards radicalism, or even the probability of a radical majority in the Federation in the not distant future.

The most startling shift has been, of course, in the railway men's organizations, which have changed from a pronounced conservatism to an advocacy of a socialistic plan of railway nationalization under the Plumb Plan. The Plumb Plan raises the issue of socialism in its American form. In bare outline the Plan proposes government acquisition of the railroads at a value which excludes rights and privileges not specifically granted to the roads in their charters from the States. The government would then lease the roads to a private operating corporation governed by a tri-partite board of directors equally representing the consuming public, the managerial employes, and the classified employes. An automatic economy-sharing scheme was designed to assure efficient service at low rates calculated to yield a fixed return on a value shorn of capitalized privileges.

The purpose of the Plumb Plan is to equalize the opportunities of labor and capital in using economic power to obtain just rewards for services rendered to the public. In this respect it resembles many of the land reform and other "panaceas" which are scattered through labor history. Wherein it differs is in making the trade unions the vital and organized representatives of producers' interests entitled to participate in the direct management of industry. An ideal of copartnership and self-employment was thus set up, going beyond the boundaries of self-help to which organized labor had limited itself in the eighties.

But it is easy to overestimate the drift in the direction of radicalism. The Plumb Plan has not yet been made the *sine qua non* of the American labor program. Although the American Federation of Labor endorsed the principle of government ownership of the railways at its conventions of 1920 and 1921, President Gompers, who spoke against the Plan, was reëlected and again reëlected. And in obeying instructions to coöperate with brotherhood leaders, he found that they also thought it inopportune to press Plumb Plan legislation actively. So far as the railway men themselves are concerned, after the Railroad Labor Board set up under the Esch-Cummins act had begun to pass decisions actually affecting wages and working rules, the pressure for the Plumb Plan subsided. Instead, the activities of the organizations, though scarcely lessened in intensity, have become centered upon the issues of conditions of employment.

The drift towards independent labor politics, which many anticipate, also remains quite inconclusive. A Farmer-Labor party, launched in 1920 by influential labor leaders of Chicago (to be sure, against the wishes of the national leaders), polled not more than 350,000 votes. And in the same election, despite a wide dissatisfaction in labor circles with the change in the government's attitude after the passage of the War emergency and with a most sweeping use of the injunction in the coal strike, the vote for the socialist candidate for President fell below a million, that is behind the vote of 1912, notwithstanding a doubling of the electorate with women's suffrage. Finally, the same convention of the American Federation of Labor, which showed so much sympathy for the ideas of the Plumb Plan League, approved a rupture with the International Trade Union Federation, with headquarters in Amsterdam, Holland, mainly on account of the revolutionary character of the addresses issued by the latter.

PART III
CONCLUSIONS AND INFERENCES

CHAPTER 12

AN ECONOMIC INTERPRETATION

To interpret the labor movement means to offer a theory of the struggle between labor and capital in our present society. According to Karl Marx, the founder of modern socialism, the efficient cause in all the class struggles of history has been technical progress. Progress in the mode of making a living or the growth of "productive forces," says Marx, causes the coming up of new classes and stimulates in each and all classes a desire to use their power for a maximum class advantage. Referring to the struggle between the class of wage earners and the class of employers, Marx brings out that modern machine technique has concentrated the social means of production under the ownership of the capitalist, who thus became absolute master. The laborer indeed remains a free man to dispose of his labor as he wishes, but, having lost possession of the means of production, which he had as a master-workman during the preceding handicraft stage of industry, his freedom is only an illusion and his bargaining power is no greater than if he were a slave.

But capitalism, Marx goes on to say, while it debases the worker, at the same time produces the conditions of his ultimate elevation. Capitalism with its starvation wages and misery makes the workers conscious of their common interests as an exploited class, concentrates them in a limited number of industrial districts, and forces them to organize for a struggle against the exploiters. The struggle is for the complete displacement of the capitalists both in government and industry by the revolutionary labor class. Moreover, capitalism itself renders effective although unintended aid to its enemies by developing the following three tendencies: First, we have the tendency towards the concentration of capital and wealth in the hands of a few of the largest capitalists, which reduces the number of the natural supporters of capitalism. Second, we observe a tendency towards a steady depression of wages and a growing misery of the wage-earning class, which keeps revolutionary ardor alive. And lastly, the inevitable and frequent economic crises under capitalism disorganize it and hasten it on towards destruction. The last and gravest capitalistic industrial crisis will coincide with the social revolution which will bring capitalism to an end. The wage-earning class must under no condition permit itself to be diverted from its revolutionary program into futile attempts to "patch-up" capitalism. The labor struggle must be for the abolition of capitalism.

American wage earners have steadily disappointed several generations of Marxians by their refusal to accept the Marxian theory of social development and the Marxian revolutionary goal. In fact, in their thinking, most American wage earners do not start with any general theory of industrial society, but approach the subject as bargainers, desiring to strike the best wage bargain possible. They also have a conception of what the bargain ought to yield them by way of real income, measured in terms of their customary standard of living, in terms of security for the future, and in terms of freedom in the shop or "self-determination." What impresses them is not so much the fact that the employer owns the employment opportunities but that he possesses a high degree of bargaining advantage over them. Viewing the situation as bargainers, they are forced to give their best attention to the menaces they encounter as bargainers, namely, to the competitive menaces; for on these the employer's own advantage as a bargainer rests. Their impulse is therefore not to suppress the employer, but to suppress those competitive menaces, be they convict labor, foreign labor, "green" or untrained workers working on machines, and so forth. To do so they feel they must organize into a union and engage in a "class struggle" against the employer.

It is the employer's purpose to bring in ever lower and lower levels in competition among laborers and depress wages; it is the purpose of the union to eliminate those lower levels and to make them stay eliminated. That brings the union men face to face with the whole matter of industrial control. They have no assurance that the employer will not get the best of them in bargaining unless they themselves possess enough control over the shop and the trade to check him. Hence they will strive for the "recognition" of the union by the employer or the associated employers as an acknowledged part of the government of the shop and the trade. It is essential to note that in struggling for recognition, labor is struggling not for something absolute, as would be a struggle for a complete dispossession of the employer, but for the sort of an end that admits of relative differences and gradations. Industrial control may be divided in varying proportions,[1] reflecting at any one time the relative

[1] The struggle for control, as carried on by trade unions, centers on such matters as methods of wage determination, the employer's right of discharge, hiring and lay-off, division of work, methods of

ratio of bargaining power of the contesting sides. It is labor's aim to continue increasing its bargaining power and with it its share of industrial control, just as it is the employer's aim to maintain a *status quo* or better. Although this presupposes a continuous struggle, it is not a revolutionary but an "opportunist" struggle.

Once we accept the view that a broadly conceived aim to control competitive menaces is the key to the conduct of organized labor in America, light is thrown on the causes of the American industrial class struggles. In place of looking for these causes, with the Marxians, in the domain of technique and production, we shall look for them on the market, where all developments which affect labor as a bargainer and competitor, of which technical change is one, are sooner or later bound to register themselves. It will then become possible to account for the long stretch of industrial class struggle in America prior to the factory system, while industry continued on the basis of the handicraft method of production. Also we shall be able to render to ourselves a clearer account of the changes, with time, in the intensity of the struggle, which, were we to follow the Marxian theory, would appear hopelessly irregular.

We shall take for an illustration the shoe industry.[1] The ease with which shoes can be transported long distances, due to the relatively high money value contained in small bulk, rendered the shoe industry more sensitive to changes in marketing than other industries. Indeed

enforcing shop discipline, introduction of machinery and division of labor, transfers of employes, promotions, the union or non-union shop, and similar subjects.

[1] The first trade societies were organized by shoemakers. (See above, 4-7.)

we may say that the shoe industry epitomized the general economic evolution of the country.[1]

We observe no industrial class struggle during Colonial times when the market remained purely local and the work was custom-order work. The journeyman found his standard of life protected along with the master's own through the latter's ability to strike a favorable bargain with the consumer. This was done by laying stress upon the quality of the work. It was mainly for this reason that during the custom-order stage of industry the journeymen seldom if ever raised a protest because the regulation of the craft, be it through a guild or through an informal organization, lay wholly in the hands of the masters. Moreover, the typical journeyman expected in a few years to set up with an apprentice or two in business for himself—so there was a reasonable harmony of interests.

A change came when improvements in transportation, the highway and later the canal, had widened the area of competition among masters. As a first step, the master began to produce commodities in advance of the demand, laying up a stock of goods for the retail trade. The result was that his bargaining capacity over the consumer was lessened and so prices eventually had to be reduced, and with them also wages. The next step was even more serious. Having succeeded in his retail business, the master began to covet a still larger market,— the wholesale market. However, the competition in this wider market was much keener than it had been in the custom-order or even in the retail market. It was inevitable that both prices and wages should suffer in the proc-

[1] See Chapter on "American Shoemakers," in *Labor and Administration*, by John R. Commons (Macmillan, 1913).

ess. The master, of course, could recoup himself by lowering the quality of the product, but when he did that he lost a telling argument in bargaining with the consumer or the retail merchant. Another result of this new way of conducting the business was that an increased amount of capital was now required for continuous operation, both in raw material and in credits extended to distant buyers.

The next phase in the evolution of the market rendered the separation of the journeymen into a class by themselves even sharper as well as more permanent. The market had grown to such dimensions that only a specialist in marketing and credit could succeed in business, namely, the "merchant-capitalist." The latter now interposed himself permanently between "producer" and consumer and by his control of the market assumed a commanding position. The merchant-capitalist ran his business upon the principle of a large turn-over and a small profit per unit of product, which, of course, made his income highly speculative. He was accordingly interested primarily in low production and labor costs. To depress the wage levels he tapped new and cheaper sources of labor supply, in prison labor, low wage country-town labor, woman and child labor; and set them up as competitive menaces to the workers in the trade. The merchant-capitalist system forced still another disadvantage upon the wage earner by splitting up crafts into separate operations and tapping lower levels of skill. In the merchant-capitalist period we find the "team work" and "task" system. The "team" was composed of several workers: a highly skilled journeyman was in charge, but the other members possessed varying degrees of skill down to the practically unskilled "finisher." The team was generally paid a lump wage, which was divided by an understanding among the members. With all that the merchant-capitalist took no appreciable part in the productive process. His equipment consisted of a warehouse where the raw material was cut up and given out to be worked up by small contractors, to be worked up in small shops with a few journeymen and apprentices, or else by the journeyman at his home,—all being paid by the piece. This was the notorious "sweat-shop system."

The contractor or sweatshop boss was a mere labor broker deriving his income from the margin between the piece rate he received from the merchant-capitalist and the rate he paid in wages. As any workman could easily become a contractor with the aid of small savings out of wages, or with the aid of money advanced by the merchant-capitalist, the competition between contractors was of necessity of the cut-throat kind. The industrial class struggle was now a three-cornered one, the contractor aligning himself here with the journeymen, whom he was forced to exploit, there with the merchant-capitalist, but more often with the latter. Also, owing to the precariousness of the position of both contractor and journeyman, the class struggle now reached a new pitch of intensity hitherto unheard of. It is important to note, however, that as yet the tools of production had not undergone any appreciable change, remaining hand tools as before, and also that the journeyman still owned them. So that the beginning of class struggles had nothing to do with machine technique and a capitalist ownership of the tools of production. The capitalist, however, had placed himself across the outlets to the market and dominated by using all the available competitive menaces to both contractor and wage earner. Hence the bitter class struggle.

The thirties witnessed the beginning of the merchant-capitalist system in the cities of the East. But the situation grew most serious during the forties and fifties. That was a period of the greatest disorganization of industry. The big underlying cause was the rapid extension of markets outrunning the technical development of industry. The large market, opened first by canals and then by railroads, stimulated the keenest sort of competition among the merchant-capitalists. But the industrial equipment at their disposal had made no considerable progress. Except in the textile industry, machinery had not yet been invented or sufficiently perfected to make its application profitable. Consequently industrial society was in the position of an antiquated public utility in a community which persistently forces ever lower and lower rates. It could continue to render service only by cutting down the returns to the factors of production,—by lowering profits, and especially by pressing down wages.

In the sixties the market became a national one as the effect of the consolidation into trunk lines of the numerous and disconnected railway lines built during the forties and fifties. Coincident with the nationalized market for goods, production began to change from a handicraft to a machine basis. The former sweatshop boss having accumulated some capital, or with the aid of credit, now became a small "manufacturer," owning a small plant and employing from ten to fifty workmen. Machinery increased the productivity of labor and gave a considerable margin of profits, which enabled him to begin laying a foundation for his future independence of the middleman. As yet he was, however, far from independent.

The wider areas over which manufactured products were now to be distributed, called more than ever before for the services of the specialist in marketing, namely, the wholesale-jobber. As the market extended, he sent out his traveling men, established business connections, and advertised the articles which bore his trade mark. His control of the market opened up credit with the banks, while the manufacturer, who with the exception of his patents possessed only physical capital and no market opportunities, found it difficult to obtain credit. Moreover, the rapid introduction of machinery tied up all of the manufacturers' available capital and forced him to turn his products into money as rapidly as possible, with the inevitable result that the merchant was given an enormous bargaining advantage over him. Had the extension of the market and the introduction of machinery proceeded at a less rapid pace, the manufacturer probably would have been able to obtain greater control over the market opportunities, and the larger credit which this would have given him, combined with the accumulation of his own capital, might have been sufficient to meet his needs. However, as the situation really developed, the merchant obtained a superior bargaining power and, by playing off the competing manufacturers one against another, produced a cut-throat competition, low prices, low profits, and consequently a steady and insistent pressure upon wages. This represents the situation in the seventies and eighties.

For labor the combination of cut-throat competition among employers with the new machine technique brought serious consequences. In this era of machinery the forces of technical evolution decisively joined hands with the older forces of marketing evolution to depress the conditions of the wage bargain. It is needless to dilate upon the effects of machine technique on labor conditions— they have become a commonplace of political economy. The shoemakers were first among the organized trades to feel the effects. In the later sixties they organized what was then the largest trade union in the world, the Order of the Knights of St. Crispin,[1] to ward off the menace of "green hands" set to work on machines. With the machinists and the metal trades in general, the invasion of unskilled and little skilled competitors began a decade later. But the main and general invasion came in the eighties, the proper era from which to date machine production in America. It was during the eighties that we witness an attempted fusion into one organization, the Order of the Knights of Labor, of the machine-menaced mechanics and the hordes of the unskilled.[2]

With the nineties a change comes at last. The manufacturer finally wins his independence. Either he reaches out directly to the ultimate consumer by means of chains of stores or other devices, or else, he makes use of his control over patents and trade marks and thus succeeds in reducing the wholesale-jobber to a position which more nearly resembles that of an agent working on a commission basis than that of the *quondam* industrial ruler. The immediate outcome is, of course, a considerable increase in the manufacturer's margin of profit. The industrial class struggle begins to abate in intensity. The employer, now comparatively free of anxiety that he may be forced to operate at a loss, is able to diminish pres-

[1] See Don D. Lescohier, *The Order of the Knights of St. Crispin.*
[2] See above, 114-116.

sure on wages. But more than this: the greater certainty about the future, now that he is a free agent, enables him to enter into time agreements with a trade union. At first he is generally disinclined to forego any share of his newly acquired freedom by tying himself up with a union. But if the union is strong and can offer battle, then he accepts the situation and "recognizes" it. Thus the class struggle instead of becoming sharper and sharper with the advance of capitalism and leading, as Marx predicted, to a social revolution, in reality, grows less and less revolutionary and leads to a compromise or succession of compromises,—namely, collective trade agreements.

But the manufacturer's emancipation from the middleman need not always lead to trade agreements. In the shoe industry this process did not do away with competition. In other industries such an emancipation was identical with the coming in of the "trust," or a combination of competing manufacturers into a monopoly. As soon as the "trust" becomes practically the sole employer of labor in an industry, the relations between labor and capital are thrown almost invariably back into the state of affairs which characterized the merchant-capitalist system at its worst, but with one important difference. Whereas under the merchant-capitalist system the employer was *obliged* to press down on wages and fight unionism to death owing to cut-throat competition, the "trust," its strength supreme in both commodity and labor market, can do so and usually does so *of free choice*.

The character of the labor struggle has been influenced by cyclical changes in industry as much as by the permanent changes in the organization of industry and market.

In fact, whereas reaction to the latter has generally been slow and noticeable only over long periods of time, with a turn in the business cycle, the labor movement reacted surely and instantaneously.

We observed over the greater part of the history of American labor an alternation of two planes of thought and action, an upper and a lower. On the upper plane, labor thought was concerned with ultimate goals, self-employment or coöperation, and problems arising therefrom, while action took the form of politics. On the lower plane, labor abandoned the ultimate for the proximate, centering on betterments within the limits of the wage system and on trade-union activity. Labor history in the past century was largely a story of labor's shifting from one plane to another, and then again to the first. It was also seen that what determined the plane of thought and action at any one time was the state of business measured by movements of wholesale and retail prices and employment and unemployment. When prices rose and margins of employers' profits were on the increase, the demand for labor increased and accordingly also labor's strength as a bargainer; at the same time, labor was compelled to organize to meet a rising cost of living. At such times trade unionism monopolized the arena, won strikes, increased membership, and forced "cure-alls" and politics into the background. When, however, prices fell and margins of profit contracted, labor's bargaining strength waned, strikes were lost, trade unions faced the danger of extinction, and "cure-alls" and politics received their day in court. Labor would turn to government and politics only as a last resort, when it had lost confidence in its ability to hold its own in industry. This phenomenon, noticeable also in other countries, came out with particular clearness in America.

For, as a rule, down to the World War, prices both wholesale and retail, fluctuated in America more violently than in England or the Continent. And twice, once in the thirties and again in the sixties, an irredeemable paper currency moved up the water mark of prices to tremendous heights followed by reactions of corresponding depth. From the war of 1812, the actual beginning of an industrial America, to the end of the century, the country went through several such complete industrial and business cycles. We therefore conveniently divide labor and trade union history into periods on the basis of the industrial cycle. It was only in the nineties, as we saw, that the response of the labor movement to price fluctuations ceased to mean a complete or nearly complete abandonment of trade unionism during depressions. A continuous and stable trade union movement consequently dates only from the nineties.

The coöperative movement which was, as we saw, far less continuous than trade unionism, has also shown the effects of the business cycle. The career of distributive coöperation in America has always been intimately related to the movements of retail prices and wages. If, in the advance of wages and prices during the ascending portion of the industrial cycle, the cost of living happened to outdistance wages by a wide margin, the wage earners sought a remedy in distributive coöperation. They acted likewise during the descending portion of the industrial cycle, when retail prices happened to fall much less slowly than wages.

Producers' coöperation in the United States has generally been a "hard times" remedy. When industrial prosperity has passed its high crest and strikes have begun to fail, producers' coöperation has often been used as a retaliatory measure to bring the employer to terms by menacing to underbid him in the market. Also, when in the further downward course of industry the point has been reached where cuts in wages and unemployment have become quite common, producers' coöperation has sometimes come in as an attempt to enable the wage earner to obtain both employment and high earnings bolstered through coöperative profits.

CHAPTER 13

THE IDEALISTIC FACTOR

The puzzling fact about the American labor movement is, after all, its limited objective. As we saw before, the social order which the typical American trade unionist considers ideal is one in which organized labor and organized capital possess equal bargaining power. The American trade unionist wants, first, an equal voice with the employer in fixing wages and, second, a big enough control over the productive processes to protect job, health, and organization. Yet he does not appear to wish to saddle himself and fellow wage earners with the trouble of running industry without the employer.

But materialistic though this philosophy appears, it is nevertheless the product of a long development to which the spiritual contributed no less than the material. In fact the American labor movement arrived at an opportunist trade unionism only after an endeavor spread over more than seventy years to realize a more idealistic program.

American labor started with the "ideology" of the Declaration of Independence in 1776. Intended as a justification of a political revolution, the Declaration was worded by the authors as an expression of faith in a social revolution. To controvert the claims of George III, Thomas Jefferson quoted Rousseau. To him Rousseau was in all probability little more than an abstract "beau idéal," but Rousseau's abstractions were no mere abstractions to the pioneer American farmer. To the latter the doctrine that all men are born free and equal seemed to have grown directly out of experience. So it appeared, two or three generations later, to the young workmen when they for the first time achieved political consciousness. And, if reality ceased to square with the principles of the Declaration, it became, they felt, the bounden duty of every true American to amend reality.

Out of a combination of the principles of individual rights, individual self-determination, equality of opportunity, and political equality enumerated and suggested in the Declaration, arose the first and most persistent American labor philosophy. This philosophy differed in no wise from the philosophy of the old American democracy except in emphasis and particular application, yet these differences are highly significant. Labor read into the Declaration of Independence a condemnation of the wage system as a permanent economic régime; sooner or later in place of the wage system had to come *self-employment*. Americanism to them was a social and economic as well as a political creed. Economic self-determination was as essential to the individual as political equality. Just as no true American will take orders from a king, so he will not consent forever to remain under the orders of a "boss." It was the *uplifting* force of this social ideal as much as the propelling force of the changing economic environment that molded the American labor program.

We find it at work at first in the decade of the thirties at the very beginning of the labor movement. It then took the form of a demand for a free public school system. These workingmen in Philadelphia and New York discovered that in the place of the social democracy of the

Declaration, America had developed into an "aristocracy." They thought that the root of it all lay in "inequitable" legislation which fostered "monopoly," hence the remedy lay in democratic legislation. But they further realized that a political and social democracy must be based on an educated and intelligent working class. No measure, therefore, could be more than a palliative until they got a "Republican" system of education. The workingmen's parties of 1828-1831 failed as parties, but humanitarians like Horace Mann took up the struggle for free public education and carried it to success.

If in the thirties the labor program was to restore a social and political democracy by means of the public school, in the forties the program centered on economic democracy, on equality of economic opportunity. This took the form of a demand of a grant of public land free of charge to everyone willing to brave the rigors of pioneer life. The government should thus open an escape to the worker from the wage system into self-employment by way of free land. After years of agitation, the same cry was taken up by the Western States eager for more settlers to build up their communities and this combined agitation proved irresistible and culminated in the Homestead law of 1862.

The Homestead law opened up the road to self-employment by way of free land and agriculture. But in the sixties the United States was already becoming an industrial country. In abandoning the city for the farm, the wage earner would lose the value of his greatest possession—his skill. Moreover, as a homesteader, his problem was far from solved by mere access to free land. Whether he went on the land or stayed in industry, he needed access to reasonably free credit. The device invented by workingmen to this end was the bizarre "green-back" idea which held their minds as if in a vise for nearly twenty years. "Greenbackism" left no such permanent trace on American social and economic structure as "Republican education" or "free land."

The lure of "greenbackism" was that it offered an opportunity for self-employment. But already in the sixties, it became clear that the workingman could not expect to attain self-employment as an individual, but if at all, it had to be sought on the basis of producers' coöperation. In the eighties, it became doubly clear that industry had gone beyond the one-man-shop stage; self-employment had to stand or fall with the coöperative or self-governing workshop. The protagonist of this most interesting and most idealistic striving of American labor was the "Noble Order of the Knights of Labor," which reached its height in the middle of the eighties.

The period of the greatest enthusiasm for coöperation was between 1884 and 1887; and by 1888 the coöperative movement had passed the full cycle of life and succumbed. The failure of coöperation proved a turning point in the evolution of the American labor program. Whatever the special causes of failure, the idealistic unionism, for which the ideas of the Declaration of Independence served as a fountain head, suffered in the eyes of labor, a degree of discredit so overwhelming that to regain its old position was no longer possible. The times were ripe for the opportunistic unionism of Gompers and the trade unionists.

These latter, having started in the seventies as Marxian socialists, had been made over into opportunistic unionists by their practical contact with American conditions. Their philosophy was narrower than that of the Knights and their concept of labor solidarity narrower still. However, these trade unionists demonstrated that they could win strikes. It was to this practical trade unionism, then, that the American labor movement turned, about 1890, when the idealism of the Knights of Labor had failed. From groping for a coöperative economic order or self-employment, labor turned with the American Federation of Labor to developing bargaining power for use against employers. This trade unionism stood for a strengthened group consciousness. While it continued to avow sympathy with the "anti-monopoly" aspirations of the "producers," who fought for the opportunity of self-employment, it also declared that the interests of democracy will be best served if the wage earners organized by themselves.

This opportunist unionism, now at last triumphant over the idealistic unionism induced by America's spiritual tradition, soon was obliged to fight against a revolutionary unionism which, like itself, was an offshoot of the socialism of the seventies. At first, the American Federation of Labor was far from hostile to socialism as a philosophy. Its attitude was rather one of mild contempt for what it considered to be wholly impracticable under American conditions, however necessary or efficacious under other conditions. When, about 1890, the socialists declared their policy of "boring from within," that is, of capturing the Federation for socialism by means of propaganda in Federation ranks, this attitude remained practically unchanged. Only when, dissatisfied with the results of boring from within, the socialists, now led by a more determined leadership, attempted in 1895 to set up a rival to the Federation in the Socialist Trade and Labor Alliance, was there a sharp line drawn between socialist and anti-socialist in the Federation. The issue once having become a fighting issue, the leaders of the Federation experienced the need of a positive and well rounded-out social philosophy capable of meeting socialism all along the front instead of the former self-imposed super-pragmatism.

By this time, the Federation had become sufficiently removed in point of time from its foreign origin to turn to the social ideal derived from pioneer America as the philosophy which it hoped would successfully combat an aggressive and arrogant socialism. Thus it came about that the front against socialism was built out from the immediate and practical into the ultimate and spiritual; and that inferences drawn from a reading of Jefferson's Declaration, with its emphasis on individual liberty, were pressed into service against the seductive collectivist forecasts of Marx.

CHAPTER 14

WHY THERE IS NOT AN AMERICAN LABOR PARTY

The question of a political labor party hinges, in the last analysis, on the benefits which labor expects from government. If, under the constitution, government possesses considerable power to regulate industrial relations and improve labor conditions, political power is worth striving for. If, on the contrary, the power of the government is restricted by a rigid organic law, the matter is reversed. The latter is the situation in the United States. The American constitutions, both Federal and State, contain bills of rights which embody in fullness the eighteenth-century philosophy of economic individualism and governmental *laissez-faire*. The courts, Federal and State, are given the right to override any law enacted by Congress or the State legislatures which may be shown to conflict with constitutional rights.

In the exercise of this right, American judges have always inclined to be very conservative in allowing the legislature to invade the province of economic freedom. At present after many years of agitation by humanitarians and trade unionists, the cause of legislative protection of child and woman laborers seems to be won in principle. But this progress has been made because it has been shown conclusively that the protection of these most helpless groups of the wage-earning class clearly falls within the scope of public purpose and is therefore a lawful exercise of the state's police power within the meaning of the constitution. However, adult male labor offers a far different case. Moreover, should the unexpected happen and the courts become converted to a broader view, the legislative standards would be small compared with the standards already enforced by most of the trade unions. Consequently, so far as adult male workers are concerned (and they are of course the great bulk of organized labor), labor in America would scarcely be justified in diverting even a part of its energy from trade unionism to a relatively unprofitable seeking of redress through legislatures and courts.[1]

But this is no more than half the story. Granting even that political power may be worth having, its attainment is beset with difficulties and dangers more than sufficient to make responsible leaders pause. The causes reside once more in the form of government, also in the general nature of American politics, and in political history and tradition. To begin with, labor would have to fight not on one front, but on forty-nine different fronts.[2]

Congress and the States have power to legislate on labor matters; also, in each, power is divided between an executive and the two houses of the legislature. Decidedly, government in America was built not for strength

[1] This assumes that the legislative program of labor would deal primarily with the regulation of labor conditions in private employment analogous to the legislative program of the British trade unions until recent years. Should labor in America follow the newer program of labor in Britain and demand the taking over of industries by government with compensation, it is not certain that the courts would prove as serious a barrier as in the other case. However, the situation would remain unchanged so far as the difficulties discussed in the remainder of this chapter are concerned.

[2] For the control of the national government and of the forty-eight State governments.

but for weakness. The splitting up of sovereignty does not especially interfere with the purposes of a conservative party, but to a party of social and industrial reform it offers a disheartening obstacle. A labor party, to be effective, would be obliged to capture all the diffused bits of sovereignty at the same time. A partial gain is of little avail, since it is likely to be lost at the next election even simultaneously with a new gain. But we have assumed here that the labor party had reached the point where its trials are the trials of a party in power or nearing power. In reality, American labor parties are spared this sort of trouble by trials of an anterior order residing in the nature of American politics.

The American political party system antedates the formation of modern economic classes, especially the class alignment of labor and capital. Each of the old parties represents, at least in theory, the entire American community regardless of class. Party differences are considered differences of opinion or of judgment on matters of public policy, not differences of class interest. The wage earner in America, who never had to fight for his suffrage but received it as a free gift from the Jeffersonian and Jacksonian democratic movements and who did not therefore develop the political class consciousness which was stamped into the workers in Europe by the feeling of revolt against an upper ruling class, is prone to adopt the same view of politics. Class parties in America have always been effectively countered by the old established parties with the charge that they tend to incite class against class.

But the old parties had on numerous occasions, as we saw, an even more effective weapon. No sooner did a labor party gain a foothold, than the old party politician, the "friend of labor," did appear and start a rival attraction by a more or less verbal adherence to one or more planks of the rising party. Had he been, as in Europe, a branded spokesman of a particular economic class or interest, it would not have been difficult to ward him off. But here in America, he said that he too was a workingman and was heart and soul for the workingman. Moreover, the workingman was just as much attached to an old party label as any average American. In a way he considered it an assertion of his social equality with any other group of Americans that he could afford to take the same "disinterested" and tradition-bound view of political struggles as the rest. This is why labor parties generally encountered such disheartening receptions at the hands of workingmen; also why it was difficult to "deliver the labor vote" to any party. This, on the whole, describes the condition of affairs today as it does the situations in the past.

In the end, should the workingman be pried loose from his traditional party affiliation by a labor event of transcendent importance for the time being, should he be stirred to political revolt by an oppressive court decision, or the use of troops to break a strike; then, at the next election, when the excitement has had time to subside, he will usually return to his political normality. Moreover, should labor discontent attain depth, it may be safely assumed that either one or the other of the old parties or a faction therein will seek to divert its driving force into its own particular party channel. Should the labor party still persist, the old party politicians, whose bailiwick it will have particularly invaded, will take care to encourage, by means not always ethical but nearly always effective, strife in its ranks. Should that fail, the old parties will in the end "fuse" against the upstart rival. If they are able to stay "fused" during enough elections and also win them, the fidelity of the adherent of the third party is certain to be put to a hard and unsuccessful test. To the outsider these conclusions may appear novel, but labor in America learned these lessons through a long experience, which began when the first workingmen's parties were attempted in 1828-1832. The limited potentialities of labor legislation together with the apparent hopelessness of labor party politics compelled the American labor movement to develop a sort of non-partisan political action with limited objectives thoroughly characteristic of American conditions. Labor needs protection from interference by the courts in the exercise of its economic weapons, the strike and the boycott, upon which it is obviously obliged to place especial reliance. In other words, though labor may refuse to be drawn into the vortex of politics for the sake of positive attainments, or, that is to say, labor legislation, it is compelled to do so for the sake of a *negative* gain —a judicial *laissez-faire*. That labor does by pursuing a policy of "reward your friends" and "punish your enemies" in the sphere of politics. The method itself is an old one in the labor movement; we saw it practiced by George Henry Evans and the land reformers of the forties as well as by Steward and the advocates of the eight-hour day by law in the sixties. The American Federation of Labor merely puts it to use in connection with a new objective, namely, freedom from court interference. Although the labor vote is largely "undeliverable," still where the parties are more or less evenly matched in strength, that portion of the labor vote which is politically conscious of its economic interests may swing the election to whichever side it turns. Under certain conditions [1] labor has been known even to attain through such indirection in excess of what it might have won had it come to share in power as a labor party.

The controversy around labor in politics brings up in the last analysis the whole problem of leadership in labor organizations, or to be specific, the rôle of the intellectual in the movement. In America his rôle has been remarkably restricted. For a half century or more the educated classes had no connection with the labor movement, for in the forties and fifties, when the Brook Farm enthusiasts and their associates took up with fervor the social question, they were really alone in the field, since the protracted trade depression had laid all labor organization low. It was in the eighties, with the turmoil of the Knights of Labor and the Anarchist bomb in Chicago, that the "intellectuals" first awakened to the existence of a labor problem. To this awakening no single person contributed more than the economist Professor Richard T. Ely, then of Johns Hopkins University. His pioneer work on the *Labor Movement in America* published in 1886, and the works of his many capable students gave the labor movement a permanent place in the public mind, besides presenting the cause of labor with scientific precision and with a judicious balance. Among the other pioneers were preachers like Washington Gladden and Lyman Abbott, who conceived their duty as that of mediators between the business class and the wage earning class, exhorting the former to deal with their employes according to the Golden Rule and the latter to moderation in their demands. Together with the economists they helped to break down the prejudice

[1] Such as a state of war; see above, 235-236.

against labor unionism in so far as the latter was non-revolutionary. And though their influence was large, they understood that their maximum usefulness would be realized by remaining sympathetic outsiders and not by seeking to control the course of the labor movement.

In recent years a new type of intellectual has come to the front. A product of a more generalized mental environment than his predecessor, he is more daring in his retrospects and his prospects. He is just as ready to advance an "economic interpretation of the constitution" as to advocate a collectivistic panacea for the existing industrial and social ills. Nor did this new intellectual come at an inopportune time for getting a hearing. Confidence in social conservatism has been undermined by an exposure in the press and through legislative investigations of the disreputable doings of some of the staunchest conservatives. At such a juncture "progressivism" and a "new liberalism" were bound to come into their own in the general opinion of the country.

But the labor movement resisted. American labor, both during the periods of neglect and of moderate championing by the older generation of intellectuals, has developed a leadership wholly its own. This leadership, of which Samuel Gompers is the most notable example, has given years and years to building up a united fighting *morale* in the army of labor. And because the *morale* of an army, as these leaders thought, is strong only when it is united upon one common attainable purpose, the intellectual with his new and unfamiliar issues has been given the cold shoulder by precisely the trade unionists in whom he had anticipated to find most eager disciples. The intellectual might go from success to success in conquering the minds of the middle classes; the labor movement largely remains closed to him.

To make matters worse the intellectual has brought with him a psychology which is particularly out of fit with the American labor situation. We noted that the American labor movement became shunted from the political arena into the economic one by virtue of fundamental conditions of American political institutions and political life. However, it is precisely in political activity where the intellectual is most at home. The clear-cut logic and symmetry of political platforms based on general theories, the broad vistas which it may be made to encompass, and lastly the opportunity for eloquent self-expression offered by parliamentary debates, all taken together exert a powerful attraction for the intellectualized mind. Contrast with this the prosaic humdrum work of a trade union leader, the incessant wrangling over "small" details and "petty" grievances, and the case becomes exceedingly clear. The mind of the typical intellectual is too generalized to be lured by any such alternative. He is out of patience with mere amelioration, even though it may mean much in terms of human happiness to the worker and his family.

When in 1906, in consequence of the heaping up of legal disabilities upon the trade unions, American labor leaders turned to politics to seek a restraining hand upon the courts,[1] the intellectuals foresaw a political labor party in the not distant future. They predicted that one step would inevitably lead to another, that from a policy of bartering with the old parties for anti-injunction planks in their platforms, labor would turn to a political ... of its own. The intellectual critic continues to

above, 203-204.

view the political action of the American Federation of Labor as the first steps of an invalid learning to walk; and hopes that before long he will learn to walk with a firmer step, without feeling tempted to lean upon the only too willing shoulders of old-party politicians. On the contrary, the Federation leaders, as we know, regard their political work as a necessary evil, due to an unfortunate turn of affairs, which forces them from time to time to step out of their own trade union province in order that their natural enemy, the employing class, might get no aid and comfort from an outside ally.

Of late a *rapprochement* between the intellectual and trade unionist has begun to take place. However, it is not founded on the relationship of leader and led, but only on a business relationship, or that of giver and receiver of paid technical advice. The rôle of the trained economist in handling statistics and preparing "cases" for trade unionists before boards of arbitration is coming to be more and more appreciated. The railway men's organizations were first to put the intellectual to this use, the miners and others followed. From this it is still a far cry to the rôle of such intellectuals as Sidney and Beatrice Webb, G. D. H. Cole and the Fabian Research group in England, who have really permeated the British labor movement with their views on labor policy. However, there is also a place for the American intellectual as an ally of trade unionism, not only as its paid servant. The American labor movement has committed a grave and costly error because it has not made use of the services of writers, journalists, lecturers, and speakers to popularize its cause with the general public. Some of its recent defeats, notably the steel strike of 1919, were partly due to the neglect to provide a sufficient organization of labor publicity to counteract the anti-union publicity by the employers.

CHAPTER 15

THE DICTATORSHIP OF THE PROLETARIAT AND TRADE UNIONISM

The rise of a political and economic dictatorship by the wage-earning class in revolutionary Russia in 1917 has focussed public opinion on the labor question as no other event ever did. But one will scarcely say that it has tended to clarity of thought. On the one hand, the conservative feels confirmed in his old suspicions that there is something inherently revolutionary in any labor movement. The extreme radical, on the other hand, is as uncritically hopeful for a Bolshevist upheaval in America as the conservative or reactionary is uncritically fearful. Both forget that an effective social revolution is not the product of mere chance and "mob psychology," nor even of propaganda however assiduous, but always of a new preponderance of power as between contending economic classes.

To students of the social sciences, it is self-evident that the prolonged rule of the proletariat in Russia in defiance of nearly the whole world must be regarded as a product of Russian life, past and present. In fact, the continued Bolshevist rule seems to be an index of the relative fighting strength of the several classes in Russian society—the industrial proletariat, the landed and industrial propertied class, and the peasantry.

It is an irony of fate that the same revolution which purports to enact into life the Marxian social program should belie the truth of Marx's materialistic interpretation of history and demonstrate that history is shaped by both economic and non-economic forces. Marx, as is well known, taught that history is a struggle between classes, in which the landed aristocracy, the capitalist class, and the wage earning class are raised successively to rulership as, with the progress of society's technical equipment, first one and then another class can operate it with the maximum efficiency. Marx assumed that when the time has arrived for a given economic class to take the helm, that class will be found in full possession of all the psychological attributes of a ruling class, namely, an indomitable will to power, no less than the more vulgar desire for the emoluments that come with power. Apparently, Marx took for granted that economic evolution is inevitably accompanied by a corresponding development of an effective will to power in the class destined to rule. Yet, whatever may be the case in the countries of the West, in Russia the ruling classes, the gentry and the capitalists, clearly failed in the psychological test at the critical time. This failure is amply attested by the manner in which they submitted practically without a fight after the Bolshevist coup *d'état*.

To get at the secret of this apparent feebleness and want of spunk in Russia's ruling class one must study a peculiarity of her history, namely, the complete dominance of Russia's development by organized government. Where the historian of the Western countries must take account of several independent forces, each standing for the Russian historian may well afford self on the high peak of government and, t of vantage, survey the hills and vales of hich it so thoroughly dominated.

Apolitism runs like a red thread through the pages of Russian history. Even the upper layer of the old noble class, the "Boyars," were but a shadow of the Western contemporary medieval landed aristocracy. When the several principalities became united with the Czardom of Muscovy many centuries ago, the Boyar was in fact no more than a steward of the Czar's estate and a leader of a posse defending his property; the most he dared to do was surreptitiously to obstruct the carrying out of the Czar's intentions; he dared not try to impose the will of his class upon the crown. The other classes were even more apolitical. So little did the several classes aspire to domination that they missed many golden opportunities to seize and hold a share of the political power. In the seventeenth century, when the government was exceptionally weak after what is known as the "period of troubles," it convoked periodical "assemblies of the land" to help administer the country. But, as a matter of fact, these assemblies considered themselves ill used because they were asked to take part in government and not once did they aspire to an independent position in the Russian body politic. Another and perhaps even more striking instance we find a century and a half later. Catherine the Great voluntarily turned over the local administration to the nobles and to that end decreed that the nobility organize themselves into provincial associations. But so little did the nobility care for political power and active class prerogative that, in spite of the broadest possible charters, the associations of nobles were never more than social organizations in the conventional sense of the word.

Even less did the commercial class aspire to independence. In the West of Europe mercantilism answered in an equal measure the needs of an expanding state and of a vigorous middle class, the latter being no less ardent in the pursuit of gain than the former in the pursuit of conquest. In Russia, on the other hand, when Peter the Great wanted manufacturing, he had to introduce it by government action. Hence, Russian mercantilism was predominantly a state mercantilism. Even where Peter succeeded in enlisting private initiative by subsidies, instead of building up a class of independent manufacturers, he merely created industrial parasites and bureaucrats without initiative of their own, who forever kept looking to the government.

Coming to more recent times, we find that the modern Russian factory system likewise owes its origin to governmental initiative, namely, to the government's railway-building policy. The government built the railways for strategic and fiscal reasons but incidentally created a unified internal market which made mass-production of articles of common consumption profitable for the first time. But, even after Russian capitalism was thus enabled to stand on its own feet, it did not unlearn the habit of leaning on the government for advancement rather than relying on its own efforts. On its part the autocratic government was loath to let industry alone. The government generously dispensed to the capitalists tariff protection and bounties in the form of profitable orders, but insisted on keeping industry under its thumb. And though they might chafe, still the capitalists never neglected to make the best of the situation. For instance, when the sugar producers found themselves running into a hole from cut-throat competition, they appealed to the Minister of Finances, who immediately created a government-enforced "trust" and assured them huge dividends.

Since business success was assured by keeping on the proper footing with a generous government rather than by relying on one's own vigor, it stands to reason that, generally speaking, the capitalists and especially the larger capitalists, could develop only into a class of industrial courtiers. And when at last the autocracy fell, the courtiers were not to be turned overnight into stubborn champions of the rights of their class amid the turmoil of a revolution. To be sure, Russia had entered the capitalistic stage as her Marxians had predicted, but nevertheless her capitalists were found to be lacking the indomitable will to power which makes a ruling class.

The weakness of the capitalists in the fight on behalf of private property may be explained in part by their want of allies in the other classes in the community. The Russian peasant, reared in the atmosphere of communal land ownership, was far from being a fanatical defender of private property. No Thiers could have rallied a Russian peasant army for the suppression of a communistic industrial wage-earning class by an appeal to their property instinct. To make matters worse for the capitalists, the peasant's strongest craving was for more land, all the land, without compensation! This the capitalists, being capitalists, were unable to grant. Yet it was the only sort of currency which the peasant would accept in payment for his political support. In November, 1917, when the Bolsheviki seized the government, one of their first acts was to satisfy the peasant's land hunger by turning over to his use all the land. The "proletariat" had then a free hand so far as the most numerous class in Russia was concerned.

Just as the capitalist class reached the threshold of the revolution psychologically below par, so the wage-

earning class in developing the will to rule outran all
expectations and beat the Marxian time-schedule. Among
the important contributing factors was the unity of the
industrial laboring class, a unity broken by no rifts between highly paid skilled groups and an inferior unskilled
class, or between a well-organized labor aristocracy and
an unorganized helot class. The economic and social
oppression under the old régime had seen to it that no
group of laborers should possess a stake in the existing
order or desire to separate from the rest. Moreover, for
several decades, and especially since the memorable days
of the revolution of 1905, the laboring class has been
filled by socialistic agitators and propagandists with
ideas of the great historical rôle of the proletariat. The
writer remembers how in 1905 even newspapers of the
moderately liberal stamp used to speak of the "heroic
proletariat marching in the van of Russia's progress."
No wonder then that, when the revolution came, the industrial wage earners had developed such self-confidence
as a class that they were tempted to disregard the dictum
of their intellectual mentors that this was merely to be a
bourgeois revolution—with the social revolution still re-
mote. Instead they listened to the slogan "All power
to the Soviets."

The idea of the "dictatorship of the proletariat"
reached maturity in the course of the abortive revolution
of 1905-1906. After a victory for the people in October,
1905, the bourgeoisie grew frightened over the aggressiveness of the wage-earning class and sought safety in an
understanding with the autocracy. An order by the
Soviet of Petrograd workmen in November, 1905, de-
creeing the eight-hour day in all factories sufficed to make
the capitalists forego their historical rôle of champions

of popular liberty against autocracy. If the bourgeoisie itself will not fight for a democracy, reasoned the revolutionary socialists, why have such a democracy at all? Have we not seen the democratic form of government lend itself to ill-concealed plutocracy in Europe and America? Why run at all the risk of corruption of the post-revolutionary government at the hands of the capitalists? Why first admit the capitalists into the inner circle and then spend time and effort in preventing them from coming to the top? Therefore, they declined parliamentarism with thanks and would accept nothing less than a government by the representative organ of the workers—the Soviets.

If we are right in laying the emphasis on the relative fighting will and fighting strength of the classes struggling for power rather than on the doctrines which they preach and the methods, fair or foul, which they practice, then the American end of the problem, too, appears in a new light. No longer is it in the main a matter of taking sides for or against the desirability of a Bolshevist rule or a dictatorship by the proletariat, but a matter of ascertaining the relative strength and probable behavior of the classes in a given society. It is as futile to "see red" in America because of Bolshevism in Russia as to yearn for Bolshevism's advent in the United States. Either view misses the all-important point that so far as social structure is concerned America is the antipodes of Russia, where the capitalists have shown little fighting spirit, where the tillers of the soil are only first awakening to a conscious desire for private property and are willing to forego their natural share in government for a gift of land, and where the industrial proletariat is the only class ready and unafraid to fight. Bolshevism is unthinkable in America, because, even if by some imaginable accident the government were overthrown and a labor dictatorship declared, it could never "stay put." No one who knows the American business class will even dream that it would under any circumstances surrender to a revolution perpetrated by a minority, or that it would wait for foreign intervention before starting hostilities. A Bolshevist *coup d'état* in America would mean a civil war to the bitter end, and a war in which the numerous class of farmers would join the capitalists in the defense of the institution of private property.[1]

But it is not only because the preponderance of social power in the United States is so decisively with private property that America is proof against a social upheaval like the Russian one. Another and perhaps as important a guarantee of her social stability is found in her four million organized trade unionists. For, however unjustly they may feel to have been treated by the employers or the government; however slow they may find the realization of their ideals of collective bargaining in industry; their stakes in the existing order, both spiritual and material, are too big to reconcile them to revolution. The

---

[1] Though writers and public speakers of either extreme have often overlooked the fundamental consideration of where the preponderance of social power lies in their prognostications of revolutions, this has not escaped the leaders of the American labor movement. The vehemence with which the leaders of the American Federation of Labor have denounced Sovietism and Bolshevism, and which has of late been brought to a high pitch by a fear lest a shift to radicalism should break up the organization, is doubtless sincere. But one cannot help feeling that in part at least it aimed to reassure the great American middle class on the score of labor's intentions. The great majority of organized labor realize that, though at times they may risk engaging in unpopular strikes, it will never do to permit their enemies to tar them with the pitch of subversionism in the eyes of the great American majority—a majority which remains wedded to the régime of private property and individual enterprise despite the many recognized shortcomings of the institution.

truth is that the revolutionary labor movement in America looms up much bigger than it actually is. Though in many strikes since the famous textile strike in Lawrence, Massachusetts, in 1911, the leadership was revolutionary, it does not follow that the rank and file was animated by the same purpose. Given an inarticulate mass of grievously exploited workers speaking many foreign tongues and despised alike by the politician, the policeman, and the native American labor organizer; given a group of energetic revolutionary agitators who make the cause of these workers their own and become their spokesmen and leaders; and a situation will clearly arise where thousands of workmen will be apparently marshalled under the flag of revolution while in reality it is the desire for a higher wage and not for a realization of the syndicalist program that reconciles them to starving their wives and children and to shedding their blood on picket duty. If they follow a Haywood or an Ettor, it is precisely because they have been ignored by a Golden or a Gompers.

Withal, then, trade unionism, despite an occasional revolutionary facet and despite a revolutionary clamor especially on its fringes, is a conservative social force. Trade unionism seems to have the same moderating effect upon society as a wide diffusion of private property. In fact the gains of trade unionism are to the worker on a par with private property to its owner. The owner regards his property as a protective dyke between himself and a ruthless biological struggle for existence; his property means liberty and opportunity to escape dictation by another man, an employer or "boss," or at least a chance to bide his time until a satisfactory alternative has presented itself for his choice. The French peasants in 1871 who flocked to the army of the government of Versailles to suppress the Commune of Paris (the first attempt in history of a proletarian dictatorship), did so because they felt that were the workingmen to triumph and abolish private property, they, the peasants, would lose a support in their daily struggle for life for the preservation of which it was worth endangering life itself. And having acquired relative protection in their private property, small though it might be, they were unwilling to permit something which were it to succeed would lose them their all.

Now with some exceptions every human being is a "protectionist," provided he does possess anything at all which protects him and which is therefore worth being protected by him in turn. The trade unionist, too, is just such a protectionist. When his trade union has had the time and opportunity to win for him decent wages and living conditions, a reasonable security of the job, and at least a partial voice in shop management, he will, on the relatively high and progressive level of material welfare which capitalism has called into being, be chary to raze the existing economic system to the ground on the chance of building up a better one in its place. A reshuffling of the cards, which a revolution means, might conceivably yield him a better card, but then again it might make the entire stack worthless by destroying the stakes for which the game is played. But the revolution might not even succeed in the first round; then the ensuing reaction would probably destroy the trade union and with it would go the chance of a recovery of the original ground, modest though that may have been. In practice, therefore, the trade union movements in nearly all nations [1] have served as brakes upon the respective national socialist movements; and, from the standpoint of society interested in its own preservation against catastrophic change, have played and are playing a rôle of society's policemen and watch-dogs over the more revolutionary groups in the wage-earning class. These are largely the unorganized and ill-favored groups rendered reckless because, having little to lose from a revolution, whatever the outcome might be, they fear none.

In America, too, there is a revolutionary class which, unlike the striking textile workers in 1911-1913, owes its origin neither to chance nor to neglect by trade union leaders. This is the movement of native American or Americanized workers in the outlying districts of the West or South—the typical I. W. W., the migratory workers, the industrial rebels, and the actors in many labor riots and lumber-field strikes. This type of worker has truly broken with America's spiritual past. He has become a revolutionist either because his personal character and habits unfit him for success under the exacting capitalistic system; or because, starting out with the ambitions and rosy expectations of the early pioneer, he found his hopes thwarted by a capitalistic preëmptor of the bounty of nature, who dooms to a wage-earner's position all who came too late. In either case he is animated by a genuine passion for revolution, a passion which admits no compromise. Yet his numbers are too few to threaten the existing order.

In conclusion, American trade unionism, no matter whether the American Federation of Labor keeps its old leaders or replaces them by "progressives" or socialists, seems in a fair way to continue its conservative function

[1] Notably in Germany since the end of the World War.

—so long as no overpowering open-shop movement or "trustification" will break up the trade unions or render them sterile. The hope of American Bolshevism will, therefore, continue to rest with the will of employers to rule as autocrats.

BIBLIOGRAPHY

The first seven chapters of the present work are based on the *History of Labour in the United States* by John R. Commons and Associates,[1] published in 1918 in two volumes by the Macmillan Company, New York. The major portion of the latter was in turn based on *A Documentary History of the American Industrial Society,* edited by Professor Commons and published in 1910 in ten volumes by Clark and Company, Cleveland. In preparing chapters 8 to 11, dealing with the period since 1897, which is not covered in the *History of Labour,* the author used largely the same sort of material as that in the preparation of the above named works; namely, original sources such as proceedings of trade union conventions, labor and employer papers, government reports, etc. There are, however, many excellent special histories relating to the recent period in the labor movement, especially histories of unionism in individual trades or industries, to which the author wishes to refer the reader for more ample accounts of the several phases of the subject, which he himself was of necessity obliged to treat but briefly. The following is a selected list of such works together with some others relating to earlier periods:

BARNETT, GEORGE E., *The Printers—A Study in American Trade Unionism,* American Economic Association, 1909.

BING, ALEXANDER M., *War-Time Strikes and their Adjustment,* Dutton and Co., 1921.

BONNETT, CLARENCE E., *Employers' Associations in the United States,* Macmillan, 1922.

BRISSENDEN, PAUL F., *The I. W. W.—A Study in American Syndicalism,* Columbia University, 1920.

BROOKS, JOHN G., *American Syndicalism: The I. W. W.,* Macmillan, 1913.

BUDISH AND SOULE, *The New Unionism in the Clothing Industry,* Harcourt, 1920.

[1] See Author's Preface.

CARLTON, FRANK T., *Economic Influences upon Educational Progress in the United States, 1820-1850,* University of Wisconsin, 1908.

DEIBLER, FREDERICK S., *The Amalgamated Wood Workers' International Union of America,* University of Wisconsin, 1912.

FITCH, JOHN L., *The Steel Workers,* Russell Sage Foundation, 1911.

HOAGLAND, HENRY E., *Wage Bargaining on the Vessels of the Great Lakes,* University of Illinois, 1915.

———— *Collective Bargaining in the Lithographic Industry,* Columbia University, 1917.

INTERCHURCH WORLD MOVEMENT, Commission of Inquiry, Report on the Steel Strike of 1919, Harcourt, 1920.

LAIDLER, HARRY, *Socialism in Thought and Action,* Macmillan, 1920.

ROBBINS, EDWIN C., *Railway Conductors—A Study in Organized Labor,* Columbia University, 1914.

SCHLÜTER, HERMAN, *The Brewing Industry and the Brewery Workmen's Movement in America,* International Union of Brewery Workmen, 1910.

SUFFERN, ARTHUR E., *Conciliation and Arbitration in the Coal Mining Industry in America,* Mifflin, 1915.

SYDENSTRICKER, EDGAR, *Collective Bargaining in the Anthracite Coal Industry,* Bulletin No. 191 of the United States Bureau of Labor Statistics, 1916.

WOLMAN, LEO, *The Boycott in American Trade Unions,* Johns Hopkins University, 1916.

Labor Encyclopedias:

AMERICAN FEDERATION OF LABOR, *History, Encyclopedia, Reference Book,* American Federation of Labor, 1919.

BROWNE, WALDO R., *What's What in the Labor Movement,* Huebsch, 1921.

INDEX

A

Adair Case, 202.

Adamson Law, 232.

Agrarianism, "equal division," 13; homestead movement, 35.

Amalgamated Clothing Workers' Union of America, 220, 247, 255.

American Anti-Boycott League, 195.

American Federation of Labor, departments, 223; eight-hour movement, 1890, 131; international labor movement, 242; politics, 139, 203; origin of program, 77; Reconstruction, 242; shorter hours by law, 199; socialism, 140; structure, 119, 122; Trade Union International, 261; unskilled, 116, 216; use of government, 202; World War, 233; see Federation of Organized Trades and Labor Unions of the United States and Canada.

American Labor Union, 214.

"American Plan," 252.

American Railway Union, 137.

Anarchists, Chicago, 79.

Anthracite Coal Strike Commission, 176.

Arbitration, see Collective Bargaining; see Railway Men.

B

Banks, complaints against, 11, 28.

Bargaining Theory of Labor Movement, 266.

Barnett, George E., 164.

Bascom, John, 72.

Benevolent Societies, 7.

Berger, Victor, 212.

Black International, 79.

Blacklist, laws of, 154.

Bolshevism, in Russia, 295; in America, 301.

Boycott, in the eighties, 85; law of, 155, 258; the Theiss, 101.

Brisbane, Albert, 29.

British Trade Union Congress, 111.

British Unions, 139.

Brook Farm, 29.

Bryan, William J., 141, 205.

Buck's Stove and Range Company Case, 202.

Building Strikes, 255.

Business Cycles, effects on coöperative movement, 277; effects on labor movement, 276.

C

Carey, Mathew, 20.

Carnegie Steel Company, 133, 196.

Carpenters, first strike, 3; strike in 1825, 8; national eight-hour strike, 132.

Central Competitive Field, see Miners.

Check-off, 169 *note,* 178, 179.

Chinese, agitation against, 62.

Cigar Makers' International Union, 68, 76, 78, 117.

Citizens' Alliances, 195.

City Central Labor Bodies, first on record, 9; in the thirties, 20; in the sixties, 43.

Clayton Act, 226, 257.

Cleveland, Grover, 135, 139.

Closed Shop, early, 6; in court, 151.